**WRITER**
*as*
**CRITIC**

# IN FLUX

For Michael

Best wishes,

Roy Miki

# TRANSNATIONAL SHIFTS IN ASIAN CANADIAN WRITING

WRITER AS CRITIC SERIES XII

*essays by*

# Roy Miki

INFLUX

NeWest Press

**NEWEST PRESS**

#201, 8540 – 109 Street
Edmonton, AB T6G 1E6
telephone: 780.432.9427
www.newestpress.com

*No bison were harmed
in the making of this book.*

Library and Archives Canada Cataloguing in Publication
Miki, Roy, 1942–
In flux : transnational shifts in Asian Canadian writing / Roy Miki ; edited by Smaro Kamboureli.

(Writer as critic ; 12)
Includes bibliographical references and index.
ISBN 978-1-897126-93-6

1. Canadian literature (English) — Asian Canadian authors — History and criticism. 1. Kamboureli, Smaro 11. Title. 111. Series: Writer as critic ; 12

PS8089.5.A8M55 2011     C810.9'895     C2011-901967-1

NeWest Press acknowledges the support of the Canada Council for the Arts, the Alberta Foundation for the Arts, and the Edmonton Arts Council for our publishing program. We acknowledge the financial support of the Government of Canada through the Canada Book Fund for our publishing activities. NeWest Press also thanks Transcanada Institute for its various kinds of contribution to the publication of this book.

printed and bound in Canada   1 2 3 4 5 13 12 11

FOR ROBIN BLASER

(1925 – 2009)

FOR ROBERT KROETSCH

(1927 – 2011)

*Preface*

In his introduction to *Asian Canadian Studies*, a special issue of *Canadian Literature*, Guy Beauregard announces that "Asian Canadian cultural criticism has entered an exciting and profoundly generative phase" (11). I agree with Beauregard and look forward to this phase, hoping that its practitioners continue the effort to address a racist past out of which Asian Canadian as a formation emerged, while simultaneously producing critical spaces for its creative acts and transformations. I am encouraged by a desire evident in the issue to keep the term Asian Canadian open to change and to resist attempts to foreclose what Chris Lee, one of the contributors, calls its "instability of identity," a quality that has been "extraordinarily generative insofar as it is the catalyst for a flourishing body of work by critics, activists, and artists" (32). If we follow on

Lee's assessment, then critical work on Asian Canadian writing needs to be conscious of Asian Canadian as a contingent formation with a double-edged effect: conditioned by forces — historical, social, and cultural — that constrain the terms through which it takes on appearances, it is also dependent on the agency of writers and cultural critics to translate those conditions into textual sites of change, transformation, and critical awareness. The complex interplay of context and intent has meant Asian Canadian has been understood, sometimes in contradictory ways, not only as symptomatic of Canada's racialized history, an extension, that is, of the alien/Asian in its national body, but also as a provisional framework that makes visible the cultural practices of those designated under its name. On the one hand, then, Asian Canadian has borne a legacy of racism and othering that is marked by such state policies as exclusion (for Chinese Canadians) and internment (for Japanese Canadians) but, on the other, it has become the face of literary and cultural possibilities with the power to critique as well as overcome the past. In the practice of writing, these two facets of Asian Canadian have been interwoven, sometimes across purposes and sometimes in complementary ways. This tension between the conditions of subject formation and the performance of its embodied life has pressured the work of literary and cultural criticism to address questions of terminology, positioning, and critical efficacy. For this reason, in the essays making up this collection, I have tried to be equally attentive to the literary ingenuity of Asian Canadian writers and the social and cultural contexts in which their work has been received, commented upon, and institutionalized in courses and academic publications.

My preoccupation with Asian Canadian as a formation goes back to the 1970s, a time when assumptions around cultural nationalism held much greater sway over writers and critics. When I was growing up in the postwar years, long before Asian Canadian as a literary space was a viable possibility, the Asian as an alien figure, the manifestation of the dreaded influx of "yellow peril" into Canadian life, was immediate and largely unquestioned in Canada's cultural institutions. Much of this early history was part of the memory spaces that I drew on while composing the essays in *Broken Entries: Race Subjectivity Writing*, an attempt to articulate the lingering effects of racialization, its history, and its shifting contexts for minority writers. But even as I wrote these essays in the 1990s, the Canadian nation-state that had abused Asian Canadians for many decades was undergoing change as the forces of globalization and the commodity culture that fuelled its capitalist machinery made its borders much more porous than they had previously been. Once the nation-bounded terms of Asian Canadian unravelled, old legacies and struggles were reshaped by the influx of new possibilities, including the possibility for Asian Canadian writing and its readers to go beyond national enclaves—in short, to go transnational—in order to open connections and exchanges with various Asian regions from the vantage of Canadian shores.

Given the fraught conditions of Asian Canadian writing as it negotiates the weight of cultural constraints, in the essays collected here Asian Canadian functions as a limit term that lacks a secure referential base but rather is constituted through the literary and critical acts that are performed under its name, my own included. This is perhaps another way of saying that the critical speculations presented in these essays are limited by the literary conditions that have shaped my writing and reading practices. These are conditions that are aligned with Canadian literature as a body of writing against which Asian Canadian writing has been understood, as well as the influence of East Asian writers in Canada, specifically Japanese Canadian and Chinese Canadian, whose works have most visibly embodied what Asian Canadian has signified in my critical work. No doubt, and thankfully so, as new work and criticism are produced, Asian Canadian as a formation may substantially expand on the range of its signifiers to include writing issuing from interrelated cultural fields, such as South Asian Canadian writing, which has been read initially through the lens of Commonwealth literature and more recently through the critical framework of postcolonial literatures. If, to adapt Beauregard's comment, both writing and criticism on and by Asian Canadian writers has "entered . . . a profoundly generative phase," then we are likely to see more radical shifts than the ones that are discussed in these essays. While I look forward with great anticipation to these shifts, I remain hopeful that the critical complexities of writing and reading that have held my attention in these essays — and which I see as a collective concern in Asian Canadian writing — will continue to resonate with future readers.

*Acknowledgements*

Even though the essays making up *In Flux* have been revised for publication, some more substantially than others, they still retain vital connections with earlier versions that were presented at conferences and symposia. In at least two instances, content from shorter presentations has been blended into an essay, especially when its inclusion made for a more comprehensive discussion. Despite the revisions, I want to recognize the occasions that generated initial versions of the essays, not only to provide a sense of their intellectual and temporal circumstances, but also to emphasize the importance of such communities of scholars and writers for my own work as a teacher, researcher, and writer. I remain forever grateful for being given so many opportunities to explore critical concepts and possibilities in a generous spirit of collaboration and exchange.

Portions of "The Difference that Difference Makes: Nation Formation, Asian Canadian, and the Unravelling Case of Roy K. Kiyooka" were presented at a conference, Social Integration and National Identity in Multi-Cultural Societies, held at Kyoto University, July 7, 2006. An earlier version of the section on Kiyooka was first presented at a conference on his life and work, sponsored by the Belkin Gallery (University of British Columbia) and Emily Carr University of Art + Design, in Vancouver, October 2, 1999. "Altered States: Global Currents, the Spectral Nation, and the Production of Asian Canadian" was presented as a keynote address for Renegotiating Identities, the 2nd Asia-Pacific Conference in Canadian Studies and the Biennial Conference of the Association for Canadian Studies in Australia and New Zealand, at the University of Wollongong, July 1, 2000. "Turning In, Turning Out: The Shifting Formations of 'Japanese Canadian' from Uprooting to Redress" was presented as a keynote address for Changing Japanese Identities in Multicultural Canada, a conference sponsored by the Centre for Asia-Pacific Initiatives, at the University of Victoria, August 23, 2002. A version of "Can Asian Adian?: Reading Some Signs of Asian Canadian," then titled "Minority Writers and New Reading Practices," was presented as a keynote address at a conference sponsored by the English Teachers Association, in Taipei, November 12, 2004. "'Inside the Black Egg': Cultural Practice, Citizenship, and Belonging in a Globalizing Canadian Nation" was presented at a workshop on Cultural Citizenship sponsored by the John F. Kennedy Institute, at the Free University of Berlin, June 19, 2003. "The Poetics of the Hyphen: Fred

Wah, Or the Ethics of Reading Asian Canadian Writing"
was presented at a conference, Virtually American? Denationalizing North American Studies, at the University of
Siegen, October 6–7, 2005. "Are You Restless Too? Not to
Worry, So Is Rita Wong: Towards a Poetics of the Appre-
hensive" was presented as a keynote address for a graduate
student conference, Natural and National Crises: The Shift-
ing Sands of the Literary, at the University of Montreal,
May 12, 2006. "Rewiring Critical Affects: Reading Asian
Canadian in the Transnational Sites of Kerri Sakamoto's
*One Hundred Million Hearts*" was presented at a conference,
New Borders in American Studies?, at the University of
Siegen, October 14, 2008. Finally, "Doing Justice to CanLit
Studies: Belief as/in Methodology as/in Form" was presented
as a keynote for a conference, TransCanada 3: Literature,
Institutions, Citizenship, at Mount Alison University, July
18, 2009.

The critical and cultural work that I have had
the pleasure to undertake over the past several decades,
and especially during the period from the late 1990s to
the present, the period during which the essays collected
here were composed, would have been impossible without
the goodwill and friendship of many people. Such work
never exists in a social vacuum and depends heavily on the
support and hard work of many dedicated researchers and
writers. I have been very fortunate to have been part of a
vibrant network of friends and colleagues who have shared
their work with me through ongoing conversations, collaborative projects, and publications. I am also extremely
grateful for the invitations offered to me to present my

thoughts at conferences inside and outside of Canada. For friendship and conversation over the long haul, my thanks to my older friends Fred Wah, Pauline Butling, George Bowering, Smaro Kamboureli, Michael Barnholden, Baco Ohama, David Fujino, and Grace Eiko Thomson, and to my younger friends, Glen Lowry, Ashok Mathur, Kirsten Emiko McAllister, Monika kin Gagnon, and Scott McFarlane. My thanks as well to companion writers and artists, Larissa Lai, Rita Wong, Cindy Mochizuki, Shirley Bear, Jeff Derksen, Louis Cabri, David Chariandy, Sophie McCall, Hiromi Goto, and Ayumi Mathur. For the opportunity to share my work outside of Canada, I want to thank Gerry Turcotte in Australia; Guy Beauregard and Andy Leung in Taiwan; Ayako Sato, the late Yoko Fujimoto, Yeonghae Jung, and Takaomi Eda in Japan; and Mita Banerjee and Katja Sarkowsky in Germany. A special note of thanks to the late Greg Placonouris for sharing with me his research on Roy Kiyooka.

For guidance, support, and superb editorial advice, I am especially indebted to Smaro Kamboureli. I have appreciated her critical feedback and her careful attention to detail in all phases of the editorial process. Her response to an earlier manuscript led to revisions that helped shape the book as a whole. Thanks as well to the anonymous readers who made useful comments in reviewing the manuscript for NeWest Press.

Finally, I thank my life partner Slavia for lively everyday conversations on the matters that matter. In all the most crucial ways, she continues to make all things possible for me.

## ACKNOWLEDGEMENT OF PREVIOUS PUBLICATIONS

"Altered States: Global Currents, the Spectral Nation, and the Production of 'Asian Canadian'." *Journal of Canadian Studies* 35.3 (Fall 2000).

"Can Asian Adian?: Reading the Scenes of 'Asian Canadian'." *In-Equations: can asia pacific*, eds. Sook Kong and Glen Lowry. *West Coast Line* 34.3, No. 33 (Winter 2001).

"Unravelling Roy Kiyooka: A Re-Assessment Amidst Shifting Boundaries." *All Amazed: For Roy Kiyooka*, eds. John O'Brian, Naomi Sawada, and Scott Watson. Vancouver: Arsenal Pulp Press, Morris and Helen Belkin Art Gallery, Collapse, 2002.

"Turning In, Turning Out: The Shifting Formations of 'Japanese Canadian' from Uprooting to Redress." *Changing Japanese Identities in Multicultural Canada*, eds. Joseph F. Kess, Hiroko Noro, Midge M. Ayukawa, and Helen Landsdowne. Victoria, BC: Centre for Asia-Pacific Initiatives, 2003. Also published in *Situating 'Race' and Racisms in Space, Time, and Theory: Critical Essays for Activists and Scholars*, eds. Jo-Anne Lee and John Lutz. Montreal and Kingston, ON: McGill-Queen's University Press, 2005.

"'Inside the Black Egg': Cultural Practice, Citizenship, and Belonging in a Globalizing Canadian Nation." *Mosaic* 38.3 (September 2005).

"The Difference that Difference Makes: Literature, Nation, and 'Asian Canadian' Cultural Production in Canada." Japanese translation: *Tabunka-shugi Shakai no Fukushi Kokka (The Welfare State in Multi-Cultural Society)*, ed. Toshimitsu Shinkawa. Kyoto: Minerva Shobo, 2008.

"The Poetics of the Hyphen: Fred Wah, Or the Ethics of Reading 'Asian Canadian' Writing." *Virtually American? Denationalizing North American Studies*, ed. Mita Banerjee. Heidelberg, Germany: Winter, 2009.

"i never saw the 'yellow peril' in myself"

**ROY K. KIYOOKA**, *Pacific Windows* (170)

*The Difference that Difference Makes*
NATION FORMATION, ASIAN CANADIAN,
AND THE UNRAVELLING CASE OF ROY K. KIYOOKA

## DIFFERENCE AND NATION FORMATION

The question of literature and nation is deeply woven into the history of Canadian culture and the institutions that have represented its values and assumptions. The relationship of literature to the nation has always been governed by the shifting forces of the dominant social, economic, and political formations that have shaped the everyday cultural lives of its citizens. Although these formations have themselves been determined by elements of uncertainty, they have, to varying degrees, also been managed by state initiatives intent on forging a particular kind of nation, one structured through hierarchically designated identities. For this reason, the nation has itself been a malleable formation, its social and discursive boundaries shifting in accordance with the changing contexts of both internal and external conditions. The constant element in nation making—a process always under construction—has been the production and management of that elusive phenomenon called *difference*, the politics of which has been instrumental in the construction of the Canadian nation out of the violence of its colonial history.

In this cultural history, two prominent tensions have scripted the difference that the politics of difference has made. There has been the tension between the centripetal forces of state actions to manage a diverse population by engineering a coherent Canadianness and the centrifugal forces that have limited the state's sovereignty, initially its colonial ties to the British empire but eventually its mediation of the omnivorous reach of US power. This dynamic has motivated various nation-based cultural efforts, including the production of Canadian literature and its institutions, that have attempted to locate a Canadianness that is consonant with the historical narrative of a progressive movement from so-called colony to nation. Alongside this tension has been another that is inherent in the notion of Canadianness, a tension between the centripetal forces of dominant groups, initially of Anglo-Saxon and later of European origins, maintaining state power to further their values and assumptions, and the centrifugal forces of the others who were categorized as minorities and who were expected either to assimilate or accommodate themselves to the will of the majority. In the first tension, Canadian nationalists would envision their country as in a beleaguered condition, whereas in the second, these same nationalists would be seen as occupying a power base that protected their cultural and social privileges through exclusionary policies and actions.

During the postwar years, the state took on a decidedly interventionist role, approaching cultural production, including literary works that valorized connections between place and identity—what would become CanLit—as a means of forging a more coherent citizenry. According to the cultural nationalists of the time, the nation's boundaries had to be thickened to produce an enclosed space, supposedly to resist imperial ambitions from the south and the colonial attraction of the old world, as well as to create a Canadian national imaginary. Readers and critics became preoccupied with large national tropes (wilderness, landscape, nature) and sweeping national narratives (escape from the garrison, contact with nature), and valorized those authors (E.J. Pratt, Margaret Laurence, Pierre Berton, Margaret Atwood) who best exemplified the cultural occupation of the territory called Canada. The Massey Report of 1951, which advocated place-based culture as a means of vitalizing the nation-state, would lead to the establishment of the Canada Council in 1957, an institution that developed an elaborate system of grants to individuals and organizations to achieve this goal.

Significantly, these state initiatives were undertaken in the wake of the Citizenship Act passed in 1947, an act that inaugurated the "Canadian citizen" as a new identity to supplant the "British subject," the term used to signify legal belonging to Canada. The move from subject to citizen generated an optimism that Canada had achieved the status of a legitimate nation, one that was respectful of citizenship rights, and so could proceed to develop its own cultural autonomy. It was in this historical context that Asian Canadians renegotiated their relations with the Canadian state. Their disenfranchisement throughout the twentieth century was clearly a violation of the United Nations' "Universal Declaration of Human Rights," a declaration signed in 1948 that Canada supported. With the added pressure of intense lobbying by Chinese Canadians, Japanese Canadians, and Indo-Canadians, the federal government finally moved to lift the ban on voting. Chinese Canadians and Indo-Canadians received the franchise in 1947, and Japanese Canadians followed in 1949, the two-year delay resulting from the continued abrogation of their rights.

Aside from the presence of Asian Canadians, whose numbers were controlled by immigration policy, the postwar years brought a large influx of immigrants from various European regions, and here again social engineering on the part of the state was mobilized to mediate their difference from the WASP (white Anglo-Saxon Protestant) ruling group. With French Canadians mostly confined to one province, the state adopted the strategy of assimilation as a method of incorporating the new Canadians into an Anglo-conformist model of social and cultural identity. In English Canada the assimilation process was aided by what Daniel Coleman has described as a constructed Britishness, an identity formation that enabled the reconceptualization of "formerly hostile groups of Anglo-Saxons and Celts that populated the British Isles into a coalitional identity that gave them access to the offices and spoils of empire" ("From Canadian Trance" 33). This "coalitional identity," transplanted in Canadian colonial spaces, promoted a British culture in the new place.

According to Coleman, this invented Britishness was evident in the song "The Maple Leaf Forever," written by Alexander Muir in 1867, on the occasion of Canada's confederation. As its first stanza announces,

> In Days of yore,
> From Britain's shore
> Wolfe the dauntless hero came
> And planted firm Britannia's flag
> On Canada's fair domain.
> Here may it wave,
> Our boast, our pride
> And joined in love together,
> The thistle, shamrock, rose entwined,
> The Maple Leaf Forever.

In the postwar years, it was the unofficial anthem for English Canadians before "O Canada" was officially adopted as the national anthem on July 1, 1980. The reference to "thistle, shamrock, rose," the floral emblems on Canada's coat of arms, signified the amalgamation of the three groups — the Scots, Irish, and English, respectively — that were represented as British in colonial Canada.

Although Anglo-dominant perspectives were normative in the immediate postwar years, not surprisingly, enforced assimilation could only be a temporary stopgap measure. The challenges to Britishness intensified in the 1960s with the emergence of a new kind of identity politics, perhaps encouraged by the civil rights movements of the late 1950s and 1960s, movements that encouraged individuals to see themselves as members of various historically wronged groups. In Canada there was, on the one side, the cultural and political empowerment of the Quebeçois as an emergent nation and, on the other, the new critical mass of groups, such as Ukrainian Canadians and Italian Canadians, who sought recognition as distinct ethnicities. It was in this context of destabilization that several policies were set in place to manage the shifting politics of difference:

- In 1965, the federal government, weathering a furor of debate and resistance from staunch Anglo-Canadians, announced a new Canadian flag, with the image of a single maple leaf, which replaced Britain's Union Jack as the official flag.

- The government's 1965 Royal Commission on Bilingualism and Biculturalism (the B&B Commission) scripted an official policy of bilingualism that also designated the English and the French as the two founding groups.

- The final section of the B&B Commission's report, resembling an afterthought, made reference to the contributions of the "Other Ethnic Groups," a category that lumped together all non-English and non-French groups who were officially declared to have ethnic identities each with a culture of their own.

- The B&B Commission excluded reference to indigenous collectives, a sign that they were not deemed to be part of the national mainstream. Instead, in

1969 the government issued a White Paper declaring its intent to disband the Indian Act altogether, in effect abandoning indigenous collectives altogether. The plan was shelved in the face of vigorous opposition from leaders of First Nations (a political term of identity that emerged at that time) groups who held the government accountable for its policies of cultural deracination and its betrayal of treaty rights and who formed the Assembly of First Nations to achieve their objectives.

– In 1967, Canadian citizens, aided by healthy grants from the federal government, celebrated the centennial of the nation amidst an unprecedented outpouring of nationalist sentiments.

– In 1969, the federal government instituted regulations in its Immigration Act to remove explicit references to preference based on race categories and adopted the so-called points system as a means of determining eligibility.

– Then, in 1971, Prime Minister Trudeau issued the White Paper on Multiculturalism outlining an official multicultural policy.

This flurry of state-initiated policies in the 1960s is symptomatic of the dynamics of difference at the time. Their appearance hinged on the narrative of a crisis of nationhood. In this crisis, the nation was seen to be caught in a moment of transition from an (old) colonial to a (new) national identity. Yet the coherence of this narrative depended on the dangers posed to the nation by the restlessness and discontent of its incorporated others. The state's manoeuvres to mould its citizens on more common grounds to encourage a stronger sense of unity can then be read as an extension of its containment and management policies. Rationalized as necessary to reinvent the representational frameworks of the changing demographics of the nation, these policies advanced strategies that allowed for a reconfiguration of the dominant relations of power. In this scenario, the pressing concern was the threat of a disruptive cultural nationalism from Quebec, a situation that posed a serious challenge to what was still an Anglo-dominant nation-state whose position depended on the cooperation and complicity of French Canadians. The official bilingualism policy would then be the glue to hold them together, while their dual founding status would help maintain the hierarchic structure of the historically constructed nation-state.

These efforts together enabled the continuation of a liberal democratic system with relatively strong centralist control, which was made possible through federal government policies that kept in check the politics of difference. Asian Canadian "difference" would take shape out of this politics, and by the 1980s writers such as Joy Kogawa, SKY Lee, and Fred Wah were being read as the faces of the new visibility accorded to Asian Canadian representations of experience and history. The relation between literature and nation, however, would be altered more critically during this decade as the Cold War ended and the forces of globalization gained momentum. It was then that culture conceived as instrumental in the creation of a nation for centralists was modified to include culture as yet another commodity in the world of economic globalization. Nations were no longer primarily collectives but were constituted through disparate groups whose alliances often ran beyond the nation, and the state in turn came to be seen not as a nation maker, but as a conduit for the flow of capital. As transnational corporations became more powerful than political leaders, and as the nation became more porous in its cultural and social boundaries—hence more transnational in the sense of being connected to countries of origin for its citizenry—former identities, especially those minoritized through racialization, Asian Canadian among them, were themselves transformed in the indeterminate spaces of new cultural allegiances and creative practices.

This transformation would resituate Asian Canadian in new cultural flows, as it shifted from the boundaries of the nation that had initially justified its appearance as a nation-based formation began to unravel in the face of transnational and broader global forces. Of course, from the perspective of its long history in the Canadian nation, Asian Canadian was never connected transparently to a stable reference point, and was, at the most, only a minor note in a nation that had always treated it as an alien presence to be reckoned with, a yellow peril that had to be monitored, contained, and managed through federal strategies and policies. Indeed, an argument could be raised, even by those associated with the term, that Asian Canadian lacks the substance required to make it a believable identity. As a descriptor, Asian represents an abnormally high level of abstraction, denoting vast geographical regions and political entities that homogenize to the extreme national groups with quite different histories, cultures, and languages. Moreover, as an abstraction invented in Western contexts, Asian has functioned as a stand-in for the other through which the British/European self has been constituted, and therefore as the direct effect of racialization. In Canadian history, Asian has been tied to the marked bodies of those who were classified as the external boundary for a whiteness privileged as the norm of its social, political, and cultural institutions. If such is the case, the use of Asian Canadian, a term that has been applied to Canadians with backgrounds in various Asian countries, could be considered as nothing more than the perpetuation of racialization. And yet, through its discursive appropriation by those who have been identified and who have also identified themselves, as Asian Canadian, a growing body of influential literature, described in critical discourse as Asian Canadian literature, has come to visibility in the past three decades.

Far from being simply the effect of multicultural tolerance, Asian Canadian signifies more complexly as a formation that embodies the contradictions that have been enacted in the politics of difference in Canada. Although collectives that fall under its name — such as Japanese, South Asian, and Chinese Canadians — may have been portrayed as aliens and strangers, as outsiders, in the long history of their struggles to attain the full rights of citizenship, they have imagined themselves as insiders to the nation, but insiders who have suffered the burden of externalization in a nation constructed out of a hierarchically organized system of designated identities. For this reason, the term Asian Canadian exposes the limits through which the politics of difference has been scripted. For instance, in the literary narratives through which Japanese Canadian and Chinese Canadian histories came to social visibility—Joy Kogawa's *Obasan* for the former and SKY Lee's *Disappearing Moon Cafe* for the latter—the Canadian nation is presented as a construct that is held together as a hierarchic system of power relations in which canonic groups enjoy privileges of class, gender, and ethnicity that are denied to those who are relegated to the status of minorities, and who are often racialized.

The edges of nation making come into sharp focus through the lens of the minorities that bear the signs of its exclusionary effects. Cultural theorist Homi Bhabha has noted that the "affective experience of social marginality— as it emerges in non-canonical cultural forms—transforms our critical strategies" because these forms enable us "to engage with culture as an uneven, incomplete production of meaning and value, often composed of incommensurable demands and practices, produced in the act of social survival" (172). Bhabha is speaking about the struggles for empowerment by marginalized groups—and Asian Canadians would fit this profile—that have had to fight to have their stories told and to open up cultural spaces for their creative work. However, these stories—of generational conflicts and miscegenation in *Disappearing Moon Cafe* and of internment and internalized racism in *Obasan*—are not merely subjective and supplemental. Although the impetus may have arisen out of the painful experience of subordination in a white-dominant nation, the cultural products of the experience, the texts that have been written, function to make the nation strange to itself so that its limits become apparent. In an essay that argues for the continuing importance of the "category of the nation" for what she calls "cultural citizenship," particularly in light of current forces of globalization, Donna Palmateer Pennee says that "[m]inoritized literatures remind us that nations are made, not born, and are thus open to refashioning" (78). To this extent, it becomes possible to read Asian Canadian literature out of a subjugated national past and into alternate transnational formations.

By the time the Liberal government of Pierre Elliott Trudeau announced its multicultural policy in 1971, the demographic make-up of the groups that would soon become the basis for Asian Canadian as a cultural possibility was starting to take shape. Between the centennial year and this date, in 1969, Japanese Canadian artist and writer Roy K. Kiyooka, a *nisei* who had been born into racialized conditions of exclusion and who had been branded Enemy Alien in the 1940s, was appointed by the Canadian government to represent his country at the 1970 Osaka World Fair by designing and constructing a sculpture for the Canadian pavilion. This pivotal moment in Kiyooka's life trajectory continues to provide a critical measure of the shift in fortunes of the term Asian Canadian from that time forward. In a Janus-like moment on the cusp of the 1970s, Kiyooka could look back to see the social and cultural distances he had travelled in the country of his birth to connect with a Japan he could only imagine, and at the same time begin to imagine the social and cultural spaces beyond the racialized nation that had shaped him.

When Kiyooka spoke of his minority positioning in the Canadian cultural scene that formed in the decades after the Second World War, he drew on the specificity of a snapshot term to pinpoint the boundary given to him — and by implication to others who occupied and continue to occupy similar zones of containment: "growing up in this country and being beholden to the white culture, its institutions, I have nonetheless grown up athwarted." Being "athwarted," he explained, means that "You are of it, and you are not, and you know that very clearly." Kiyooka traced his consciousness of this pivot between insiderness and outsiderness back to the "1950s in the years following the war." In those early Cold War years, "the taint of racism was still left" (qtd. in Miki, *Broken Entries* 71). Left, for Kiyooka and others of his generation, from the dispersed traumatic effects of the engineered racialization that is now called "Japanese Canadian internment," the incarceration and dispossession of Canadians who were categorized as "of the Japanese race" and stripped of their citizenship rights.

Kiyooka's subjectivity, in negotiating a nation-state that had constructed his identity as Enemy Alien, reflected the athwartedness of racialized artists and writers who worked on the progressive edges of the burgeoning cultural nationalist frameworks of the 1950s and early 1960s. On the one hand, the limits of the frameworks' internal contradictions — i.e., liberal and at the same time white dominant — would situate him within a nation-based trajectory as an avant-garde artist whose practices and personal connections all across the country enacted the effects of Canadian localisms; the exemplification of this participation is most lucid in the cultural journeying that drives the serial form of his *Transcanada Letters* (1975; 2005). On the other hand — or in the other land — as a Japanese Canadian racialized in the country of his birth, he wrestled with the localisms that haunted the images projected in his writing, the ghosts of a splayed family history, the disappearance of "mother tongue," and the incommensurabilities that visited his consciousness through the back (though more properly the lack) door of alterities in an unspoken "alien nation" that was both his own and not his own. "You are of it, and you are not, and you know that very clearly."

Kiyooka often playfully made references to himself as the "oriental" and his artists friends often referred to him in the same way. The discursive reality of his subjectivity pervaded all "nitty-grits," as he might say, of his public and personal enactments. This knotted condition, however, need not be construed as anomalous, i.e., as simply "marginal," but symptomatic of the largely unspoken and covered-over racialization that enables the construction of the "individual" in liberalism — for Kiyooka the dominant paradigm of nation-based Canadian cultural values in his formative years — and the subsequent depoliticization of the Eurocentric aesthetics of Canada as a place possessed through cultural production. The implications of this constitutive blindness in liberal frameworks fold into Wendy Brown's argument in *States of Injury*: "to the extent that political membership in the liberal state involves abstracting from one's social being, it involves abstracting not only from the contingent productions of one's life circumstances but from the *identificatory* processes constitutive of one's social construction and position" (56). As a racialized artist, Kiyooka was constrained by always-fraught relations with the social and institutional contexts of his creative acts. These acts may have been premised on a similar reification of place and localism as "the contingent productions of one's life circumstances" evident in the work of his (white) fellow artists, but simultaneously the substance of "the *identificatory* processes constitutive of [his] social construction and position" could not be represented as such within the nation-based aesthetics that shaped the terms of his own formation as an artist and writer. Kiyooka certainly did recognize the exclusionary divide, but without ever resorting to the maudlin and the reactionary — and it is important to remind ourselves that the counter-discourses of resistance and opposition to the racialized and ethnocentric exclusions of Canadian cultural politics were not yet available in the public domain. The immediacy of an aloneness in the midst of a proliferation of literary and artistic works amongst his mostly white peers provided an underlying sense that in his own positioning as a writer he was working from scratch, doing "everything the most difficult way imaginable because you had to explore the whole terrain before you got a purchase on it" (Miki, "Roy Kiyooka: An Interview" 61).

Kiyooka was born in Moose Jaw, Saskatchewan, in 1926 and grew up on the working-class, immigrant streets of central Calgary. Although far away from the BC coast in 1942, the Kiyooka family was targeted as Enemy Alien and uprooted, along with other Japanese Canadians. Forced out of Calgary, they moved to a small Ukrainian farming town, Opal, Alberta. The impact of the years of ostracization is effectively compressed in Kiyooka's own statement in a letter sent to the Japanese Canadian Redress Secretariat, the federal office established to administer the Japanese Canadian redress settlement in September 1988:

> In and through all the ideological strife we avidly attended via the local paper and the radio a small "i" felt as if a punitive fist kept clenching and unclenching behind my back but each time I turned to catch it flexing it would disappear into the unlit corners of our small log house. ("Dear Lucy Fumi" 125)

When Kiyooka regained some mobility, it was already 1946. By then a young man, he sought to fulfill his dream of becoming an artist by enrolling in Calgary's Institute of Technology and Art (now the Alberta College of Art). Despite, and perhaps in a direct challenge to the predominant whiteness of the contemporary art world, Kiyooka immersed himself thoroughly in a nascent art culture, absorbing by a kind of osmosis the language of artistic production as both a personal act of liberation from the legislative control of racialization and a social and cultural dialogue with the "nation" that had abrogated his freedom in the name of an identity tied to the possessive "of the Japanese race." Though a central figure in whatever artistic localisms he moved in — from the important Regina years of the late 1950s to the initial Vancouver years of the early

1960s, and through the Montreal years that led to the Expo '70 assignment, to Halifax, and back to Vancouver — he always remained that singular figure, "of" but "not of" the artistic and literary movements that would eventually be identified as the "nation"-based cultural mainstream.

Although Kiyooka sought to work at the radical edges of contemporary art and culture, he never forgot that he came to maturity in a largely white, Anglo-conformist Canada. In other words, he had been educated in the belly of the postwar push for a national Canadian culture. As his career developed in the 1950s, Kiyooka gravitated towards the progressive practices of US abstract impressionist artists, producing works that soon brought him national and international acclaim. But the injustices of the war years continued to haunt him, and finding his art limited as a medium for exploring his personal history, by the early 1960s he began addressing the effects of racialization in his writing. In the summer of 1963 Kiyooka traveled to Japan, where he finally met his sister Mariko, who had grown up in Japan and had been unable to join the family in Alberta because of the restrictions placed on Japanese Canadians. He returned home and published a series of poems based on his trip, his first book, *Kyoto Airs* (reprinted in *Pacific Windows*).

Poetry — and soon photography — offered Kiyooka the aesthetic and textual spaces in which he could draw on his history. However, in taking on the practice of writing, Kiyooka remained aware of his own dichotomous positioning as a racialized minority writer in what was for him, especially in his formative years, a largely Anglocentric nation. Even his English, a second language that had become his first in the loss of fluency in Japanese, had to be approached as both familiar and foreign. In a talk on "growing up yellow in a white world," Kiyooka admitted that "whatever my true colours, I am to all intents and purposes, a white anglo-saxon protestant, with a cleft tongue" ("We Asian North Americanos" 116–117). To show his difference, he adopted the word "inglish" (with a lower case "i"), rather than "English," to describe his slant on the language he performed in his texts.

It was in the fall of 1969 that Kiyooka was invited to design and construct a sculpture for the Canada pavilion at Expo '70 in Osaka. That contract, of a representative Canadian artist, was ironically a rare instance when his always-tentative and distant Japanese connection racialized Kiyooka into an appealing figure for Canada in Japan. This trip led to several shifts that would determine the subsequent direction of his work: being initiated into photography as an artistic practice, as performed in his long poem "Wheels" and his photo-text series *StoneDGloves*; turning away from painting, an art form through which he had built the reputation in Canadian art circles that had brought him to Expo '70; and perhaps most crucially, as evident in the textual drama of "Wheels," encountering the elements of alterity — his own "i" returning to haunt him — that would push him to compose those athwarted textual spaces which today harbour new geo-cultural possibilities.

Claiming a victim position should not be equated with the recognition of "trauma" as the constituting form of subjectivities in nation-state regimes that organize their citizenry through the projection of otherness onto those racialized as "alien," as Japanese Canadians were during the 1940s. Here, it is useful to draw on Stuart Hall's reminder, in his essay "The Local and the Global," that current globalization is tied, though not necessarily in a linear pattern, to an earlier globalization that was called imperialism and colonization—the legacies of which have all too often been disavowed in a settler colony such as Canada, where cultural formations have served the interests of nation formation, especially in the period Kiyooka came to maturity. In the valorization of geographical determinants, the concept of a native cultural identity—appropriating the language of First Nations' entitlements—hinged on the scripting of a land that, like a blank page, lay in waiting for its naming by settler colonists and their descendants, who had been transported across the global divide on a racialized ship called manifest destiny. Such a narrative proceeded on the basis of a discursive mapping through national, regional, and local geographies that yielded an entity called Canadian, which, as minoritized artists like Kiyooka well knew, was able to take on transparency because, first, it was invented on the basis of Canada as victim of both US and British imperialisms and, second, because it translated the codes of colonialism into an identity politics, i.e., the nation as a cultural sphere where its Anglo-European legacies were reinscribed in this ostensibly new place ("possession" was a word often heard).

The conjunction of victim positioning and cultural arrival served to allow for both the erasure and disavowal of the foreclosures that externalized the not-whites in the body politic, not only the First Nations collectives, but also the "others" who included those identified under the general discursive category of "Asian," or as "Japanese," or "Chinese." Externalization, however, as theorists of subject formation such as Bhabha (in *The Location of Culture*) and Judith Butler (in *Excitable Speech*) have argued, never ceases to be double edged and is therefore always open to destabilization and translation: the exclusion as "outsider" is also the insider as "minority," in Kiyooka's case, a racialized minority. In other words, the internalization of Kiyooka's athwarted positioning is not to be conceived as outside the nation's cultural forms but as a manifestation of containments and boundaries, so that minority subjectivities — while highly specific in their individuated signs — are also double edged: as exposures of the gaps, fissures, and contradictions that have to be contained in regimes of cultural dominance, but also as singularities that perform the figures of trauma at the limit of normative boundaries.

When Kiyooka was invited to represent Canada with a sculpture at the Canadian pavilion for Expo '70 in Osaka, his identification as Japanese in Canadian contexts, despite his birth in Canada, ironically made him an appropriate "Canadian" candidate for the national project. Here the gain was also a loss, because in occupying both ascribed identities — Japanese and Canadian — he was uncomfortably neither: not a bona fide Canadian in Canada and not a bona fide Japanese in Japan. Entering into this athwarted condition, quite amazingly, Kiyooka transformed his discomfort into a creative process. While designing his sculpture for the Canadian pavilion, he explored this subjective state through the interface between a series of photographs that he took, day by day, of the workmen's gloves he found discarded on the Expo site and a series of poems that he composed at the same time. The exhibition and book produced out of this process, *StoneDGloves*, do not try to resolve the tensions of being in-between identity boundaries but, instead, perform these tensions through the localized attention of Kiyooka's imagination. The gloves, turning to stone before his very eyes, take on the contours of the dislocated body of his own history. His subjectivity awakens to the weight of personal and collective trauma and, precisely because of that weight, it is attuned to its troubled movements across the more fixed borders of nation-states.

During this pivotal moment in his life as a writer and artist, Kiyooka also began the first draft of what became the text of "Wheels," a major poem that is included in *Pacific Windows: The Collected Poems of Roy K. Kiyooka* (1997).

In this serial poem, beneath the apparently soft touristic surface narrative of a jaunt around Honshu with his aging *issei* father, accompanied by a friend, guide, and interpreter, Syuzo, the *nisei* (i.e., Canadian-born) son/artist/ writer exhibits an underlying anxiety, un-articulated except through the generality of the silences in his relationship with his father. His Japanese-born father is projected as a figure who remains distant, not only from his son but even from the passing landscape of the country of his birth, as he consumes his Canadian whiskey, bottles of which are stashed in his suitcase. While transparent in physical terms — which is to say temporarily removed from the racialized codes operative in Canadian contexts — this Japanese Canadian narrator-artist, perhaps to circumvent the sense of estrangement from his father, mediates his own consciousness of the journey through the technology of the camera. The camera — "my faithful Canon" (*Pacific Windows* 137) — functions as both a frame (an art form) and a framing device (a means of constructing temporal and spatial order) — and of course it also proposes the limits of a touristic gaze, the ironic implications of which are never too far from the narrator-poet's consciousness.

It is the framing power of the camera (click click click and phenomena are "caught" by the technician-artist) that leads the poet into the atomic bomb museum at Hiroshima where horrifyingly deformed representations of the bomb's violence — a mangled bicycle, the shadow of a human figure imprinted on cement, a clock stopped at the precise moment — are on display. But through the lens (click click click), as he frames what has already been framed, he is suddenly caught in the aura of his own complicity in the aesthetic appropriation of images projecting intolerable suffering and trauma:

> o the bronze angel with a charred hole for a face
> o the lurid, lopsided, sake bottles
>
> (click)
>
> which hand
> pulled the trigger?
>
> which hand
> turned gangrenous? (168)

Outside the museum, he looks out from the "pedestrian overpath in front of Hiroshima Station" (170) and realizes that the reconstructed city has apparently covered over what had been deformed — the symptoms of the trauma also apparently covered over by a renovated urban space. In a letter to his mother back in Edmonton, however, the distances collapse as the Hiroshima images invoke a complex of memories that inscribe the traumatic epicentre of his own racialization in Canada:

> i remember "JAPS SURRENDER!"
> i remember all the flagrant incarceration/s
> i remember playing dead Indian
> i remember the RCMP finger-printing me:
> i was 15 and lofting hay that cold winter day
> what did i know about treason?
> i learned to speak a good textbook English
> i seldom spoke anything else.
> i never saw the 'yellow peril' in myself
> (Mackenzie King did) (170)

The moment of recognition in "Wheels" sutures a doubling back and forward process. In displaying the traumatized "i" as a figure both embedded in historical specificity and a projection of a constitutive lack in a racialized psyche, the text then performs the contours of the very conditions of the in-betweenness that exposes "jap" (and by association Asian, too) as the externality that helps found a national whiteness, signified by Mackenzie King's visual capacity, taken to one extremity of administrative violence in the ritualized mass expulsion of Japanese Canadians from their homes. At the same time, "jap" (and, again, by association Asian) also points to an interiority, and hence a memory, that is inescapably bound into the effects of trauma. The trauma as figured forth in its historicity, but read at a more general level, is symptomatic of the minoritized subject who is produced through externalization as the perennial alien—for instance, as the Asian in Canadian who is both of and not of a nation formation. Never a presence but at many times treated as "an inferior but useful other" (Simmons 30). This is why the moment of framing that frames the framer—the minoritized artist exposed as a marked subject within the nets of his own textualizing—explodes the transparency of power relations that privilege the norms of a cultural nationalism constituted through the lack required of its figures of externalization.

What remains compelling in reconsidering the trajectories of Kiyooka's artistic life is the resilience of his imagination and his determination to circumvent the language of victimization, even though the temptation to rail against the social conditions of his birth into the lexicon of Enemy Alien must have often been nearby, not too far around the next bend. "I don't want to go on moanin' the old 'yellow peril' blues the rest of my days. Gawd save us all from that fate" ("We Asian North Americanos" 117). Even so, the underlying uneasiness and the declarative mode suggest that the yellow peril blues had played some riffs in his work. The trauma of racialization, always kept at a distance in Kiyooka's postmodernist poetics of open form, nevertheless produces the very tension that enables his works, particularly his texts and photographs, to open a productive Janus-like space: linked to the past as a minority writer who underwent the era of cultural nationalism but pointing to a future that may be witness to radical cultural transformations—transformations in which Asian Canadian formations may no longer be elsewhere but here, wherever that localism may be forged (pun intended).

For me, Kiyooka's work offers a measure of the transformations that the cultural politics of difference has undergone in the past six decades. As a prolific writer and artist during the Cold War era, he understood the in-between zones of the nation that marked him as a racialized minority. But instead of retreating, Kiyooka addressed the conditions of his minority status, recognizing the cultural inequalities that are more familiar to us in the era of globalization. In turn, the cultural nationalism with which he had to contend has become more visible as an idealized form of a state liberalism that covered over its exclusionary practices. It would fail to achieve its objectives, and even the multiculturalism that was a supplement to its efforts to unify the nation would not be enough to withstand the globalization process of the late 1980s. But then again, and Kiyooka's major work *Transcanada Letters* is prescient in this regard, even in the late 1960s and 1970s, Canadian cultural processes were already the mirror of inter- and intra-national forces—forces that cultural nationalists at the time read as destructive. When Kiyooka composed *Transcanada Letters*, his wild critical speculations, his innovative use of genre, and his frenzied spatial movements — between Canada and Japan and across the geographic extent of Canada

—appeared eccentric to mainstream readers of Canadian literature. Published by Talonbooks, a small literary press in Vancouver, *Transcanada Letters* was a big, thick book that was strikingly designed—in other words, a bold, even audacious publication by an internationally known artist. In a series of highly crafted letters, the writer of the text composes a vast canvas of a Canadian nation that is riddled with political conflicts, social and cultural contestations, and diverse aesthetic forms—in short, a living time capsule of ongoing cultural processes. He recognizes his distance from the cultural nationalists whose roots were still tied to Anglo-dominant historical frameworks. For instance, in a letter to Phyllis Webb, a friend and fellow poet, he says of Margaret Atwood's *Survival*, a popular text for Canadian literary nationalists:

> Yes i have read Peg's SURVIVAL tho not re-
> read it yet. its got to be one of the deep probes
> into Canuck-Psyche via mainline W.A.S.P. eyes.
> I mean Peg does belong to the companions of Canadian
> Shield Seers who via literature probe the litter
> /compost of our i-denti-ties. But her is it thesis
> is too pat for yours truly who does not if
> he has had thoughts abt it at all think of himself as
> an anima/ victim despite the hazards of the 49th
> Peril and Yankee mendacities.(*Transcanada Letters* 2005, 289)

*Transcanada Letters*, although largely unrecognized except among a small group of Kiyooka readers, had remained an oddity in Canadian literature until, in an uncanny sense, the social and cultural effects of globalization caught up to its preoccupations. For this reason, it was appropriate that this text would recently be republished through the editorial efforts of Smaro Kamboureli, who also edited its sequel, *Pacific Rim Letters*, a work in process at the time of Kiyooka's death in 1994. In his late work, Kiyooka was highly critical of the increasing threat that the commodity culture of transnational corporations brought to the integrity of the locally situated imagination. For him, creative practices remained a critical means of negotiating the uncertain and uneven conditions of economic globalization, particularly in its commodification of culture.

## THE TERRAIN OPENED BY ROY KIYOOKA

The critical question that has dogged these speculations has to do with the ethics of reading through the signs of trauma — in which "through" carries the spatial implication of resisting the critical manoeuvres to read the signs back into the nation's forms merely for recuperative or redemptive purposes. Such a move, accommodational in its positioning, would foreclose an "elsewhere" through which the history of "Asian" identification can be unravelled in a cultural space of indeterminacies — perhaps a premonition of new localisms as viewed through Kiyooka's "pacific windows," the title he chose for his collected poems. Asian Canadian can begin to signify, in the heterogeneity that it implies, a provisional body of texts whose locations are in flux but pointing towards future geocultural configurations. Kiyooka's own isolated position in Canadian national culture can then be aligned with postcolonial writers in other national contexts, who often worked alone to resist the forms of dominant language conventions and, against the odds, carved out a hybrid lingo that was "in" the language of the white majority but was not "of" the values embedded in it. Kiyooka enacted forms of resistance, but without the coalitional framework of a network of like-minded artists and writers, and this gives his work a quality of interiority always verging towards the void of speechlessness. Even as this edge pressed in on his language, however, Kiyooka refused the path of assimilation and instead imagined a future of readers through whom his language might accumulate new social and cultural values.

What was a constraint, the condition of being athwarted, may have been linked to Kiyooka's isolation as the often lone "jap" minority figure in any given cultural network that he inhabited, but it also provided him with the leverage to hold to the specificities of his *own* — in terms of family history, overt racialization, and the complications of his ties to an imagined Japan — despite the lack of critical recognition in the very cultural formations that he helped to create. There is, for instance, that remarkable moment in Fumiko Kiyooka's film *The Return*, when Kiyooka looks into his daughter's camera and addresses his exclusion from a national exhibit of the Regina painters with whom he had worked and taught so closely over a crucial period of his artistic life. Rather than reading himself into their space, Kiyooka re-articulates the racialized boundaries marking the social spheres of art production — perhaps even suggesting why he set painting aside after Expo '70 in favour of writing and photography:

In hindsight, I could say, given the kind of politics that gets spoken today, that I was surrounded by exemplary people of the white-Anglo-Saxon-Protestant society — and I was defined by them. My ambitions became like theirs. Yes they did. I had no other models, you might say.

And later in the film, but during the same interview, he continues:

The thing I want to say is that, as I've gotten older, I remember them all with a certain kind of fondness without exception, but it is a pure nostalgianess in a certain sense. They play no part in my immediate life. They take up no space at all in my thoughts, because, as I've gotten older, I realize that, as much as I want to excel in terms of their values, that isn't what I want to be. That's what I've come to realize, so my own curiosities and everything are just taking me somewhere else that has nothing to do with what we were.

Asian Canadian, as a cultural formation, started to take on more material possibilities in the last years of Kiyooka's life, a period when he intensified dialogues with an imagined Japan and an imagined Asia that had for so long troubled his Japanese Canadian-Canuck-inflected imagination. One textual instance brings home Kiyooka's consciousness of this cultural topography near the end of his life. In 1993, while typing into his computer and revising many of the texts that are collected in *Pacific Windows*, Kiyooka added some lines to "of seasonal pleasures and small hindrances," a serial poem written in the fall and winter of 1973–1974. The lines follow a section reflecting on the violence of the Japanese Canadian internment, an event attributed to the "WASP supremacy of / the Mackenzie King era." What is new serves to transform the 1972 alienation into a negotiation, in effect renewing that past even as he re-routed its trajectory—a word magician to the end:

> 'Viva la Two Solitudes' . . . I
> thought thinking of myself under a third no less conspicuous
> pacific pilgrim's solitude (*Pacific Windows* 100–101)

*Altered States*

GLOBAL CURRENTS, THE SPECTRAL NATION,
AND THE PRODUCTION OF ASIAN CANADIAN

PROLOGUE: ARRIVALS AND DEPARTURES

*"I see some lights," said Jonathan. "They're coming."*

*The "coming" is a story told by Steve Chao, a reporter for Vancouver Television. His eyewitness account of the moment of encountering appears in an alternate magazine of Asian Canadian locations,* Rice Paper, *curiously distant from the other more powerful news outlets. "The Backlash Against Chinese Migrants: One Reporter's Perspective" positions the I of the writer/witness as a signifier in the unfolding drama, a fold in the textual performance of the contemporary crisis of an arrival of the other as one's own.*

*The "aliens" are on their way, and Chao is summoned by his superior to act as reporter/translator — he speaks "their" language — after all, he is Chinese, or Asian, and they have crossed the oceanic divide. But he is also one of four Canadians who have waited "under a pier in the dead of night" in a skimpy aluminum* boat — "*two cameramen, a cook, and myself.*" *Sighting the ship, they move out to sea, and then Chao recalls, a mere twelve hours prior he had been in Vancouver "covering a protest," an event that becomes strange to itself, just as his own Chinese Canadian cultural identity begins to oscillate in his memory.*

*He had always wanted to be a voice for Chinese Canadians, "fiercely proud of where I came from," but he does not say whether the "where" is a cultural matrix, a hyphenated community within the nation, or a country of origin. The ambiguity, however, is constitutive and unfolds in and through the estrangement that descends on him as he finds himself drawn into and then immersed in the "Fujian migrant" crisis — a crisis of global proportions that would destabilize his own imagined history as a Chinese Canadian.*

*From Ottawa, where he was getting ready to go backpacking, when he accepted an offer from Vancouver Television to help explain Chinese Canadians to viewers, to the seas off Campbell River to cover the "arrival," and then to China: September 1999, he is given the task of investigating the local determinants that produced the migrants. There he collects knowledge of the parasitic underside of global capitalism — what's not told in the Nike ads with the suave and smiling Michael Jordan. As Masao Miyoshi writes, "In Indonesia, [Nike contractors] pay young girls $1.35 for sewing shoes all day. Overtime is often mandatory. There are no union protections. A pair of Nike shoes sells in the United States for between $45 and $80 but costs only $5.60 to produce. Michael Jordan's reported $20 million fee for promoting the brand was more than Nike's entire payroll of these young workers in its six factories in 1992" ("Sites of Resistance" 61). The necessity of exploitable labour to run the new economy of transnational corporations on the hunt for any means to proliferate capital produces the conditions for the* emergence of "snakeheads," or smugglers. These are the brokers who deliver up labouring bodies to sites of mass production. They feed on the class fantasies of the poor and desperate, who are willing to indenture themselves for the fleeting opportunity to move into the future time of corporate capitalism's mediated representations of plenitude. "Snakeheads," Chao learns, "charge anywhere between $35,000 to $38,000 US for the journey." Since few can afford that exorbitant amount, they are forced into years of slave labour in restaurants and sweatshops, and "women are forced to sacrifice their bodies in massage parlours and brothels." A prime destination is New York, where "it's estimated there are more than a half a million Fujinese." The snakeheads have extensive global connections and flourish on the culture of commodification that requires large pools of labouring bodies.

Chao also discovers that some Chinese Canadians are connected to the snakeheads in this global traffic of bodies. But this was not as traumatic as the defensiveness — the lack of empathy — demonstrated by many Chinese Canadians. "'Send them back to where they came from' has been the typical sentiment," he writes, confirmed by a poll "that showed more than 80 per cent supported the government's lock up of migrants and a 'get-tough' policy."

The backlash against the Fujian migrants, a group he came to see as an extension of his own, exploded the trajectory of his own identity formation, so that the article concludes, "I wanted to be the voice for the Chinese community in Canada. Now, I'm not so sure I want to anymore."

It may be easy to dismiss Chao's reporter's perspective as merely personal — but then the personal itself, to draw from Michel de Certeau, "is a locus in which an incoherent (and often contradictory) plurality of . . . relational determinations interact" (xi).

*His entry into the efficacy of global currents in making the nation strange to itself, even transforming its once-model minority community into the voice of xenophobia, brings the crisis of time into all the rivulets of our social and cultural relations. Steve Chao, then, is one of "us" in his estrangement — an estrangement bringing back home the awareness that racialization can no longer be read as out there — it never was — and that the arrival of the global/local throws all subject positions and all values into altered states. "Meanwhile," to appropriate a linguistic prop of fictional time, the re-articulation of the nation not only becomes possible, but is also necessitated in the moment of arrival.*

*So let's return to the movement out at sea. The camera lights go on, and as Chao's gaze is directed at the "listing" ship with its hull eaten away by rust, he confronts the appearance of "the ghostly faces of more than 150 weak and frightened men and women [who] stared hauntingly at us. Many looked gaunt, clothes hanging off them as if draped on clothes racks. It was evident they had endured a hellish voyage." What to say?*

*I asked in Mandarin where they were from.*
*One woman replied, "Zhong guo." China.*

*Arrivals as departures. Where are you we us from?*

*   *   *

We live in a globalized world where imperialist and national structures, differences between the tangible and the intangible, the monumental and the everyday, and even the very notion of humanity are no longer the same as our characterizations of them twenty years ago.

NÉSTOR GARCÍA CANCLINI,
"The State of War and the State of Hybridization" (38)

## A CRISIS IN TIME

Do we not now live in our various national enclaves, or seem to, on the cusp of a present evanescing even as it supposedly materializes before our very eyes? Is there not now a race for knowledge that can forestall the inevitable unravelling of social and cultural formations and that makes us yearn for the stability of "identities" to close the gaps? Do we not sense that even as we produce a proliferation of commodities we are accomplices in transactions with their seductive discourses that make us yearn for a future language of brands and marks to subsume the nation? How can we — or can we? — resist or otherwise negotiate the undercurrents to the crisscrossing of borders in the modus operandi of a now-dominant globalization process that makes us aware (and wary) of the prominence accorded the figurative and literal passports that delimit our movements?

Such speculative questions suggest that the now-familiar adoption of the prefix *post* to point towards new temporal conditions, as in the postmodern, post-national, and postcolonial, is less a sign of progress and more a sign of a crisis of time — with the arrival of globalization as a term that portrays as well as produces a move away from the modern, the national, and the colonial as an extension of the linear and progressive (hence empty) time of imperial and colonial expansion. In Canada, for instance, the notion of the modern as a movement beyond the colonial functioned to produce the time of the nation that subsumed the time of colonial invasion, and therefore the time of the aboriginal presence that was appropriated. Anne McClintock's critique of the term postcolonialism in "The Angel of Progress" still rings true. Seeing it as simultaneously an effect of colonialism and the sign of a crisis, she writes, "the almost ritualistic ubiquity of 'post-' words in current culture (post-colonialism, post-modernism, post-structuralism, post-cold war, post-marxism, post-apartheid, post-Soviet, post-Ford, post-feminism, post-national, post-historic, even post-contemporary) signals, I believe, a widespread, epochal crisis in the idea of linear, historical 'progress'" (292). In Canadian terms, the crisis in the time of the nation is manifest as a decreasing capacity to conjure the present, hence what we inhabit, as presence. The recourse to *post* when no other term appears appropriate gestures towards the beyond or the future as fraught with uncertainty and the anxiety of irresolution.

The crisis brings in its wake the unease of "a world without meaning," to borrow a phrase from the title of Zaki Laidi's study of the impact of globalization. Laidi argues that the Cold War era was the last one to play out the legacy of a European-produced enlightenment, with its universalizing discourses of meaning that naturalized assumptions about progress, rationality, and collectivity.

Paradoxically, the imagined end of the Cold War was to be the moment of fulfillment, the moment when the forces of liberalism would bring about a new global order. But when one of the most monumental material symbols of the era, the Berlin Wall, was dismantled in November 1989, there was no triumph of liberation. Life simply went on, in more disarray than ever, and the lack of allegorical completion brought onto the stage a social and cultural emptiness — a temporal vacancy.

The vertigo effects of the emptiness — into which commodity culture is filtered — takes on the aura of an altered state, a condition that embodies the instability of a kind of double-or-nothing end: the end of the boundaries governing Cold War nation time and also the end of the nation-based social and historical identities that had been mediated, scripted, or otherwise mapped as the measure of the dominant. These ends produce the effect of the temporal as a dislocation. It is in this nexus of incompatible projections that the normalized coordinates of space and time — geography and history — appear dislodged from the linear assumptions of progress and are cast into an unfolding but nebulous and seemingly boundless global future that is paradoxically more and more the limit against which the present — and hence the past — performs variations on a vanishing act. Future time, in the operative language of global capitalism, always beckons with the rainbow fantasy of a pot of golden commodities that vanquishes time.

As removed as English studies may seem to be from the mass culture of commodification, it nevertheless occupies a zone of intersections within institutional domains where knowledge production is invested. No longer conceived as its own end — the arc is now from the lab to the marketplace — knowledge as such has also taken on the identity of commodities, accommodating itself to the logic of capitalization. No one is immune from this rush towards an "end" that must forever await the advent of technologies to produce new and newer formations. In the "practice of everyday life," to draw from de Certeau, our subjectivities become a variation of the un-settled, a variation of transient formations that are increasingly sutured into the time of global capitalism's networks of contingencies whose infrastructures remain beyond apprehension. And as the consumers who are so necessary to capital's expansionary processes, we are washed in the proliferation of images that present the dissemination of newly forming subjects in global scenarios, of bodies undergoing forced movements and expulsions as refugees in flight from homelands, and of migrants whose displacements and passages across borders have become central narratives of our time. From the position on the raft, the shore seems forever out of reach.

As we learned in the opening story of Steve Chao, a local manifestation of the altered state of Canadian social consciousness involved the "sudden arrival" of unidentified but Asian-identified figures in rundown ships, some of them emerging in the nation's space from the confines of cargo containers. Dubbed, first, as the "boat people" — a phrase linking them discursively to the Vietnamese refugees who arrived in the late 1970s — and later simply as "migrants," these figures entering the Canadian mediascape in the summer of 1999 were instantly enmeshed in representations that occluded their visibility as contiguous with a global capitalist economy in which bodies — often Asian-identified bodies — are reduced to labour machines. In the logic of capital, in other words, their arrival was already conjured across the oceanic divide to serve corporate agendas — agendas that bring economic and ideological benefits to Canadians. The reaction of the media and some vocal Canadians, including some Chinese Canadians, who accused the would-be refugees of the impropriety of queue jumping, disguised the more violent desire to demonize the figures and to expel them from the territorial and symbolic boundaries of the Canadian nation. Already exhausted from the long and terrifying ordeal of travelling across an ocean, "a voyage during which two people from the second ship died" (Direct Action Against Refugee Exploitation 10),[1] these figures turned out to be economically deprived individuals from the Fujian region of China who desperately wanted to find a safe haven in what they imagined as a bountiful Canadian nation.

But what was the identity of the nation that was being defended? What substance in its precious and reified border justified the line drawn between alien and normal? When those who called for expulsion — in the familiar "send them back where they came from!" or "Go Home," to cite one newspaper headline — and who found no difficulty in disregarding the refugee policy set up to counter such xenophobia, in what manner did they imagine the national inside that needed to be shielded from the aliens knocking at their door?

The processes of economic globalization are producing contradictory and unpredictable effects in nation-state formations including those of Canada. Here, for instance, the social and cultural mechanisms that stabilized national identity around a centre have been compromised and even undermined by global forces that Jan Penrose has described as "supra-state economic networks and systems" and "multi-state organizations" (29) that promote the removal of barriers and that arrest the ability of nation-states to control their own affairs—in Canada, the Free Trade Agreement (FTA) and the North American Free Trade Agreement (NAFTA), both of which paved the way for transnational corporations to challenge state powers.[2] At the same time, or in the same flows, the nation becomes a conduit for the influx of global capital, trading off its controls for a share of the market pie, hence its complicity with the corporate agendas that give rise to the flow of migrant bodies while simultaneously shoring up its territorial borders to prevent those bodies — all too often racialized — from becoming citizens.

The speculation, then, is that the discrepancies generated by — and indeed sustained for the sake of — global capitalism bring with them the losses and gains that propel the normalizing language of its market economy. The loss of state control over structures of social cohesion is not simply a determinism, though it may be named as such by corporate interests and by politicians who mime these interests; rather, it offers the often-enormous financial gains made possible through the strategic deployment of political mechanisms that facilitate the entrance of multinational corporations (mostly US corporations in Canadian contexts)[3] into its national spaces. The compromised role of nation-states in capital expansion results in a dissolving language of cultural nationalism, which, in its unravelling process, makes the nation — as if suddenly — strange to itself. Social life takes on a spectral quality, an altered state, as national borders are perceived as being open to threat by alien forces that can no longer be normalized through its historically constituted codes of racialization and differential relations of subject positioning.

In this altered state, the future begins to loom as a vacant elsewhere, and social, cultural, and political formations are no longer reliable measures of meaning, but become more uncertain and unpredictable. It is into such a void that the fantastic images of capitalist commodity culture bring in their wake a host of material and intellectual commodities that have the power to mediate the loss of meaning and to generate and placate the desire of their consumers. Who needs the identity of the nation's time, their voices say, when there are commodities about to be born with the potential to remake the very boundaries of the human? We read in the local newspaper, the *Vancouver Sun*, that Jeremy Rifken (author of *The Biotech Century*) believes we can look forward to biotechnological wizardry to increase the intelligence of newborns. The merging of the discourses of biology and consumer capitalism looks towards future generations of so-called designer babies in which national allegiances with ties of lineage, ethnicity, and citizenship will survive only in archives: "In the future the parent becomes an architect and each child becomes the ultimate shopping experience" (Urquhart, "US Scientists 'Close' to Identifying Genius Genes"). The ultimate fantasy in this biotechnological venture perhaps resides in the not-so-bizarre image of the deceased body held in a cryonic suspension, awaiting the moment of its arrival on wholly other shores in a post-ethnic, post-historical, post-contemporary, post-future, post-whatever time — but only if the forces of capitalism are obeyed. So is this, then, the rub? Who can know who is drugged or who is on the placebo? And what may be your preference?

Against this soporific temptation of the atemporal, the migrancy of altered states, in a transformative iteration, turns and re-turns the affects of what Bhabha calls the "unhomely" (445) that marks the arrival of the postcolonial. The unhomely is the event of a disjuncture, a crisis in spatialized time, between here and there, near and far, one's own and one's alien, internal and external; the I doubled up, subject and object, in the alterior spaces between shifting formations. When the influx of globalization makes the nation strange to itself, the present takes on the face of the uncanny and what was (now previously) in place is set adrift — to encounter the spectres of estrangement, loss, nostalgia, and liminality.

From a position of critique, the effects of destabilization make visible the borders of nation-based formations, bringing into relief the constructedness of the norms in a process of "articulation" (Stuart Hall's term) through which the coherence of historical narratives are enabled. As Hall explains in an interview with Lawrence Grossberg, "the so-called 'unity' of a discourse [and by extension a formation] is really the articulation of different, distinct elements which can be re-articulated in different ways because they have no necessary 'belongingness'." Articulation has to do with a "connection" or "linkage" made "under certain historical conditions" in a formation that is "not necessary, determined, absolute and essential for all time" (Grossberg 141), but provisional and always subject to change.

Hall's notion of articulation helps to expose Canadian nation-formation and the identity discourses it produces as not "natural,"[4] that is, as givens that both precede and supersede its individuated subjects, but an articulation of historical trajectories through which its subjects were marked and translated — in certain ways — from the signs of colonial invasion and territorialization into the abstract language of citizenship. Hall's "theory of articulation asks how an ideology discovers its subject rather than how the subject thinks the necessary and inevitable thoughts which belong to it" (Grossberg 142). The question of how — by what kind and manner of discourses — the Canadian nation-state has been articulated in the twentieth century thus contains within it the prospect of a re-articulation that can negotiate the ambivalent ends of its current altered state.

There is some advantage, then, in imagining that the global currents making the Canadian nation strange to itself expose its interior as an articulation linked to the colonial moment of invasion and the subsequent forging of a national unity. As the post-Cold War national formations unravel, so does the nation's unity that has been shaped, on the one hand, by ethnocentric and racialized social and cultural hierarchies and, on the other, by state mechanisms that would ensure the ascendancy of ruling groups whose colonial backgrounds would constitute the norms of the new nation. The translation process has been complex and always adjusting to shifting conditions, but it has worked most effectively through the discursive apparatus of identity-making (which is to say, difference-making), most evident, for instance, in such state discourses as the Indian Act, which produced what Marcia Crosby has aptly identified as the "imaginary Indian"[5] and the complex weave of immigration and citizenship regulations that produced a nation in which privilege and positioning were determined through the normalization of the differences through race, gender, ethnicity, and class. In this historical formation, the minoritization of women, non-whites, and gays and lesbians in the history of citizenship has worked to occlude the racialized privileges accorded to white, male, heterosexual norms, thus placing the burden on them to erase, remake, or otherwise elide their differences in order to gain access to its spaces — in effect, to camouflage themselves as transparent to these norms. Or, to see it from a more tactical perspective, they have had to don what Stacy Takacs describes as a "prosthetic" (596) identity that disguises their marked status as minorities, in this sense undergoing an assimilation process through which they have been able to occupy dominant positions through mimicry (and learning ways to inhabit contradictory subjectivities) or, in more compliant terms, have accepted positions prescribed for them.

While the state has worked to naturalize the differences that constitute its minority subjects, it has been at the point of entrance — the point of arrival at the borders of the nation-state — that the most intense beams of racialization have shone. The question of marking legitimate from illegitimate bodies is not a recent phenomenon, but a preoccupation that has played itself out in its immigration regulations. As several cultural historians[6] have noted, the discourses of immigration — of who gets in and who does not fit — come alive as the site of a social engineering process in the service of the dominant groups. "Nation-building," then, "is a dual process, entailing the management of populations and the creation of national identity" (Mackey 23). Nothing has been more indispensable for shaping the racialized body of Canada's identity than the legalization of policies that would support the eugenic agenda of the dominant Anglo-centric group at the turn of the nineteenth century. The territories that were secured by invasion, colonization, and the authority of the British North America Act (1867) that created Canada as a state could not be properly occupied without the formation of a collective identity, a nation that would protect the "white settler societies" (the English and the French) from the influx of otherness.

The construction of a nation-state, Penrose reminds us, "frequently bears a remarkable likeness to the self-image and aspirations of those who have power to forge it" (27). The dominant group or groups, as in the case of the English and French colonialisms in Canada, will act in their own best interests and, in conditions of challenge to their control, will devise accommodations (think here of the discourse of multiculturalism)[7] in order to maintain their founding status. In describing the "vision of [English] Canada which emerges from its history of nation-building," Penrose sets out the now-familiar determining profile, crucial for constituting the normative discourse of the Canadian imaginary: "The hegemonic ideal prescribed that, in customs, Canadians would be British; they would speak the English language (though some French had to be tolerated, temporarily at least); they would hold to the Christian faith (preferably Protestant); and, incontrovertibly, they would be white" (27).[8]

At the outset of the century the "color-line," announced by US writer W.E.B. DuBois in *The Souls of Black Folk* as "the problem of the Twentieth Century" (v), had to be drawn in shaping the Canadian nation-state. And it was accomplished by discursive means through the valorization of the desirable subjects over those who were racialized as the "undesirable," a category that made its first appearance in the 1906 Immigration Act, was reinforced in its 1909 version, and then implemented as state policy in the decades ahead. These acts were articulated during another moment of crisis in nation making, in another period of capitalist expansion (c. 1896–1914) when the Canadian economy, stimulated by an unprecedented growth of a more diverse population of immigrants, entered into a global market hungry for Canadian natural resources. With cheap labour in high demand, Canadian capitalists welcomed an exploitable pool of Asian bodies to provide the labour for nation building—the thousands of Chinese railway workers among them. While their bodies crossed over state borders, their subject status was monitored through policies that named them as outside the nation then in formation, as the "undesirables,"[9] who threatened the purity of a "white Canada forever" (to cite Peter Ward's study of anti-Asian racism in the history of British Columbia).

These externalized "undesirables" within would translate over time into Asian Canadians who would not receive the franchise until the late 1940s. Even then, and more likely to placate his predominantly white constituencies, Prime Minister Mackenzie King could dip into the inkwell of racialized immigration policy to reassure his fellow Canadians that his government had subdued the monstrous menace of "yellow peril":

> The policy of the Government is to foster the growth of the population of Canada by the encouragement of immigration. The government will seek . . . to ensure the careful selection and permanent settlement of such numbers of immigrants as can advantageously be absorbed in our national economy . . . I wish to make it quite clear that Canada is perfectly within her rights in selecting the persons whom we regard as *desirable* [emphasis added] future citizens. It is not a "fundamental human right" of any alien to enter Canada. It is a privilege. It is a matter of domestic policy . . . The people of Canada do not wish, as a result of mass immigration, to make a fundamental alteration in the character of our population. Any considerable Oriental immigration would . . . be certain to give rise to social and economic problems . . .
> (House of Commons, May 1, 1947;
> qtd. in Kelley and Trebilcock 312)

For the Asian migrants who arrived at the borders of this colonial-cum-national-cum-state articulation in the transitional years between the late nineteenth and early twentieth century, the language of racialization would produce them as the "strangers within our gates," to invoke the title of J.S. Woodsworth's 1909 book that addressed the coming of Asians into Canada. Woodsworth's book came on the heels of the infamous 1907 riot in Vancouver's Chinatown and Japantown, a riot that was instigated by the Asiatic Exclusion League, a broad coalition of influential white-identified organizations that sought to expel or otherwise exclude Asian immigrants. These "strangers" would also face a complex of now-well-known legislated terms to curtail and expunge Asian presence in the developing Canadian nation. There was the head tax levied on Chinese immigrants, which started at $10 in 1884, rose to $50 in 1885, to $100 in 1900, and to an exorbitant $500 in 1903. When even these measures did not stop immigration, the federal government in 1923 passed the Chinese Immigration Act (aka the Exclusion Act), an act that banned those identified as Chinese from Canadian territories, in effect until 1947. There was also the so-called Gentleman's Agreement, made with Japan by Minister of Labour Rodolphe Lemieux in 1907, which limited emigration to 400 people per year and drastically cut the flow of Japanese into Canada. Then came the Continuous Journey policy, which required that Asians could enter Canada only through a continuous route directly from their ascribed country of origin, even if they did not reside there. With the absence of regular steamship lines coming directly from India, this policy, in addition to successively higher landing fees, severely reduced the numbers of Indians entering Canada. As Kelley and Trebilcock write, "The number of East Indian immigrants fell from 2,623 in 1908 to 6 the following year. It rose to 10 persons in 1910, and fell again the next year to 5. Between 1908 and 1915, slightly more than 100 East Indians were admitted to Canada" (149).

Those already within the nation, moreover, had to contend with a barrage of policies and laws of disenfranchisement, such as the notorious Provincial Elections Act of BC, which stipulated: "No Chinaman, Japanese or Indian shall have his name placed on the Register of Voters for any Electoral District, or be entitled to vote in any election." By preventing those signified as "Japs," "Chinese," and "Hindoos" from placing their names on the voters' list, this legislation in effect barred them from participation in the democratic process until 1947 for South Asians and Chinese Canadians and 1949 for Japanese Canadians. As a rule, restrictive policies that affected capital expansion (e.g., outright exclusion of Asians, which was proposed many times by the BC legislature) were denied by the federal government and those that affected identity formation (e.g., gaining the right to vote) and therefore the right to belong to the nation were upheld. The cultural legacy of this history, of course, reaches into our own time.[10]

On the other hand, when the norms of a "hegemonic ideal" undergo a sea change, as they have in the large-scale demographic shifts of Asian Canadians since the late 1960s, the white founding settler identities — despite retaining their institutionalized powers through entrenched historical precedents — lose the substance of their authority in the heterogeneity of the contemporary. The nation has already moved elsewhere, and in its displacement there are signs of an "alien-nation," a formation that Takacs says marks "both the sense of psychic alienation experienced by the majority population when faced with the prospect that they will no longer compose a majority by the year 2050, and the sense that the root cause of this alienation is, literally, the presence of aliens (both legal and illegal) within the nation" (612).

Are those strange glances from across the lane the isolated optics of individual estrangements, or can the social be reconceived as a web of incommensurate subjectivities prompted to navigate the elsewhere in the alien-nation? Can this be the premonition of an alter-nation beyond the hierarchic frames of difference making — of social positionings modelled on migratory intersections rather than centralist settlement?

## RE-SITUATING ASIAN CANADIAN AS A CRITICAL FORMATION

The re-articulation of the past to account for the emergence of alterior narratives of the nation opens the possibility that Asian Canadian, as one site of visibility, can be read into the moment of alteration. As a formation linked to the nation and simultaneously in excess of its borders, it is marked by the "processes of globalization, and their impacts," which "cannot be fully understood without reference to attendant processes of fragmentation" (Penrose 45). It is these processes of fragmentation that initially instill a sense of estrangement in nation-based contexts, as those who have been subjectivated—Judith Butler's paradoxical term, from Michel Foucault, which "denotes both the becoming of the subject and the process of subjection" (*Psychic Life of Power* 83)—disarticulate themselves from their variously compromised positions to produce the vertigo effect of the same as suddenly "alien." This condition then becomes a crisis that could stimulate xenophobic responses of defensiveness, scapegoating, and othering, recalling the formative phase of nation-state construction, but at the same time—and this is the direction I hope critical thought can pursue—be read as a field of transitions in which, and through which, attentive vocabularies of resistance can begin to create alternate forms of collectivity.

From this critical location, the very contradictions inherent in Asian Canadian begin to suggest its social and cultural value in the crisis of the *post*, the crisis of what might be understood as the nation's constructed time. This is the time that unfolds in its narrative of progress from its colonial moment to its maturation as a modern liberal nation. Asian Canadian, when dislodged from the foreclosure of such a narrative, becomes a revolving sign that re-articulates and thus exposes discourses of both globalization (i.e., towards Asian markets and economies) and a reactionary nationalism (i.e., as a "yellow peril" that is asianizing white Canada). It then becomes both a localized subject—of research, cultural production, interrogation—but also a double-edged site: where relations of dominance can be remobilized (more of the same), *or* where critiques of the nation can posit future methodologies of resistance and collective formations.

Thought of in a provisional manner, globalization as such need not be conceived as a monolithic force. While its economic power to level local cultural specificities and to reduce everything to a standardized mass culture should never be underestimated, it also has its limits. The subjects of global mass mediation, while formed by the influx of so-called information technologies, are never passive recipients but always engaged in re-inscriptions, some of which reproduce normative assumptions but some of which challenge and undermine these assumptions through the production of cultural contradictions and even deformations that elicit unpredictable performances. There is, despite the hollowed out language of determinism, always the potential for new collectivities to form in response to dominant representational systems. According to Roland Axtmann, for instance, "The social groups and collectives that are the recipients of the 'global message' interpret, or bestow meaning upon, these messages on the basis of their own specific experience and memories as they grew out of their own particular histories and cultures; they creatively modify 'messages' and cultural products in light of their own local needs and requirements" (37).

What I want to propose, then, is that the fragmentation of formerly (more or less) coherent public spheres can provide the motivation for practices of critique, counter moves, and alliances. These practices have the capacity to enable a rethinking of *nation* as a complex of heterogeneous global/local formations, not constituted solely as enclaves of identification but more generatively produced by or through negotiations across and within temporalities and boundaries.

The time of the nation needs to be reconceived as non-synchronous—in contradistinction to the linear and totalizing time of imperialism and colonization—so that texts, and especially racialized texts, can have the mobility to open cultural transactions that encourage the re-articulation of a more radical democratic system of values. This would be a move beyond a hierarchy of "differences from" a normative centre to a more limited field of indeterminacies where social subjects assume responsibility for the production of meanings tied to the range of positions they occupy—positions that are themselves the local sites that set limits on what can or cannot be enunciated.

### READING BEYOND? THE LOCAL AND THE POSTCOLONIAL

The contemporary interest in Asian Canadian texts may be, in part, the consequence of an ethnocentric nationalism achieving obsolescence, in stages, during the period from the early 1970s to the late 1980s. The phenomenon, if it can be characterized as such, hinges on a contradiction that is both aside from and tied to the affects initiated by these texts in more localized contexts, arriving perhaps as representational compensation for absences in dominant cultural institutions. Their presence has been conceived in the critical narrative of an emergent minority literature, a narrative that has covered over the externalization of Asian Canadians in the overall construction of the modern Canadian nation-state from the late nineteenth century to the present.

What is important to recognize, however, is that the so-called minority spaces that would come to visibility during the 1970s and 1980s simultaneously produced and were produced by a largely unstructured network of racialized writers and artists who initially identified themselves through the marks of hyphenation — for instance, Japanese Canadian and Chinese Canadian. These marks, in turn, would call for an acknowledgement of linkages, not through some prior cultural homogeneity, but in the warp and weave of the nation's formation—a condition that attests to the burden of representation in such a term as Asian Canadian. While such naming establishes limits that can be used in coercive practices, it can also function as the horizon towards which cultural processes can project the situated imagination of writers and artists. It is in the material expression of their imagination — in literary texts, for instance — that the internal seams of the nation's contradictions, ambivalences, inequities, traumas, and conflicted loyalties find themselves localized as inscriptions that run counter to dominant Canadian literary formations. And they do so no longer as other, but as cultural signs that can be approached as a localism that exceeds the nation, even as they inscribe its internally constituted differentiations.

In its specificities, this localism would then both re-member and inscribe the legacy of racialization and externalization wherein the traumatic comes to embody the effects of the inner violence used to establish and maintain the state's centrality, the very violence that has been covered over to give a benign face to the nation's liberal values. This conceptualization of the contradictory social and cultural zones in which the term Asian has circulated does not diminish in any way the subjective instances of cultural resistance, community activism, and creative agency that have been enacted by individuals and collectivities formed under its signs; instead, it proposes that the term operates as an interface in its always shifting and shifty negotiations with the term *Canadian*. However imagined, the existence of Asian in Canadian has always been a disturbance — a disarticulation that had to be managed originally as the "Asiatic," as the "Oriental," and subsequently as a sign of the multicultural, as the "Visible Minority," in order to sustain the figure of the citizen as the end of assimilation — rather than a subject position vested with privileged differences based on racialization (white), ethnicity (Anglo/European), sexual orientation (hetero), and gender (male).

The tension between inscription and excess in Asian Canadian cultural production is aligned to unpredictable and potentially volatile public spheres of social and institutional interventions, ranging from compliance to complicity to resistance to defiance — which is to say, risk is always an omnipresent critical variable. There is, for instance, the internal temptation of a nation strange to itself — and I include its institutions — to retreat into a defensive posture, unleashing the politics of backlash and blame. Or there might be an attempt to overcome estrangement through reversions to remodelled colonial tactics of appropriation, containment, and management, translating what is alterior into an extension of its "own" on the liberal assumption of a minority desire to be incorporated or, worse, to become a site of desire in and for dominant cultural formations. As colourized versions of CanLit, then, texts such as Joy Kogawa's *Obasan* (1981), SKY Lee's *Disappearing Moon Cafe*

(1990), Hiromi Goto's *Chorus of Mushrooms* (1994), Larissa Lai's *When Fox Is a Thousand* (1995), Fred Wah's *Diamond Grill* (1996), Ashok Mathur's *Once Upon an Elephant* (1998), and Kerri Sakamoto's *The Electrical Field* (1998) can be read into —rather than as critiques of—a nation articulated through racialized cultural codes. Moreover, such a reading into a national formation that is all but spent implicates the more ambivalent desire of a salvage operation: a reconstituted —even "improved"—Canadian can be retrieved through minority subjects who are supposedly connected to vital cultural networks with the resources to rejuvenate a nation that, by implication, has made them possible. Such a reification process, in turn, could inflict a form of critical and institutional branding that replays the function of the brand name in commodity capitalism—the curious inversion of a branding through a re-racialization process. We are here returned to the site of the transaction—i.e., of readers and texts—and the already-instrumental role of the discourse of commodification in corporate modes of production.

Consider, for instance, the escalation of the brand name into the status of creator in mass culture (largely US-controlled, of course). The Gap brand is only one of a complex of commodities incarnated through an aesthetics that was previously the domain of art culture, and thus, in a free trade mode, it elides the boundary between the economic and the creative. The brand name announces the rebirth of the author function, producing a line of post-modern commodities in which form is the content. The consumer, not unlike a reader, inhabits a style, deriving pleasure in performing the product, literally wearing it on the body. The power of this cult of commodification is so pervasive that cultural producers — of the biological sort — are themselves re-presented in its discourses as authors who strive to become brand names — packaged identities that accrue cultural and economic capital according to the market logic of mass consumption and distribution. This is why the practice of creative enactments, especially those once thought to be counter-narratives of national exclusions (i.e., those exemplified in the 1980s through the institutionalization of Kogawa's *Obasan*), cannot be repeated with the same effects. In the new commodification of identities, authorial signs are much more malleable and thus open to appropriation and invention, so that the so-called repressed of the era of nation-state stability may emerge in the new faces of born-again difference in the liberal culture of capitalism.

Thus, if we were to speculate that the heightened visibility of Asian Canadian texts is part of a compensatory response to the collapse of once-normalized nation-based cultural representations, a potentially troubling question is the extent to which this process interacts with, or otherwise conditions, the desires of writers who set out to produce creative texts. Or, approached from another angle, when the nation turns spectral, the figure of the Asian Canadian in that nation is then dislodged from its minoritized state. But what would/does a post-Asian Canadian look like? How would/does it write? As it encounters the global currents that unravel its former nation-based identity, can it be immune from the realm of the spectral? Is there that moment when the transformation of Asian Canadian releases the ghosts in the system that only existed as nominations? Who, in this instance, was then the Asian in Canadian? How are we to read the future in the past?

In any case, the baseline of global capitalism, informing as well its discourse of liberalism and individualism, is the maximization of profit—no surprises there. Its reductive powers have meant that the market economy has come to be more the common denominator than ever before, leaving less provisionality for cultural works that undermine, or even refuse, the model of consumption that underwrites its anticipations. The textual productions that circulate as Asian Canadian cannot in themselves withstand the aesthetic and social expectations of market constraints — constraints whose reach extends to the currently fashionable commodification of difference as pleasure, the exotic consumed as versions of cultural enhancement. The resistance to modes of reading as ingestion alone has to be articulated through critical interventions that continually negotiate and navigate the locations of production, addressing, in highly site-specific fields of attention, the nexus of power relations out of which differential subject positions are formed. Even though a term such as postcolonial has been contested as inadequate to deal with the consequences of colonial violence[11]—and I am mindful of the charge that it may itself be read as an effect of "global capitalism" (Dirlik 517)—its advantage, specifically in this moment of altered states, may reside in its undecidability. The mobility of its articulations and re-articulations may then offer a critical potential to expose and unravel homogeneities — of culture, identities, discourses—which cover over global/local indeterminacies in the production of aesthetic forms. The arrival of what I have suggested is the elsewhere of the spectral nation is not to be understood only as a periodization, i.e., as a *post* that argues a liberation from the colonial, but more as a lateral move that undercuts and refuses the binaries (centre/margin, self/other, white/visible, we/they) of the now-obsolescent nation formations. What comes to appearance in this lateral move are the more specific and singular inflections of the local as a mobile configuration of global/local relations. Not as a territory possessed and named as property—but the local as simultaneously the site and cite of enunciation. The subjects of the local then come to formation, as texts do, "out of a specific history, out of a specific set of power relationships" (Hall, "Local and the Global" 185). For cultural creators such as writers and artists, the local may then be considered the nexus of historical, social, cultural, and economic variables that situate the boundaries of subjectivity, but which are always appearing in the signs of relationships — including provisional collectivities—that are underwitten by the power dynamics of what comes to be taken as normative in given public spheres.

While a postcolonial frame may itself be both a symptom and product of the crisis in the nation's time, and this is my suggestion, it may also function as a transitional point of transference. In this instance, as terminology itself undergoes severe semantic indeterminacies, it offers at the very least a discursive screen to project and thus reflect on the fragmentation of subject positions and the figures of alterity that continue to haunt the social and cultural parameters of nation-based representations. For Hall the "concept *may* help us . . . to describe or characterise the shift in global relations" and "help us (though here its value is more gestural) to identify what are the new relations and dispositions of power which are emerging in the new conjuncture" ("When Was 'The Post-Colonial?'" 246).

I would like to imagine, then, that the social intersections of the global/local in our midst, even as they dissolve old terminologies in a relentless process of obsolescence, also harbour the ingredients for the emergence of critical reading practices to address and account for the complicities of subject positionings that both produce and are produced in relations of power. This always open-ended and site-specific dynamic cannot be sustained without the nuanced ethics of critical discourses — the very ethics that is at issue in the reading practices we bring to cultural texts. These texts, and especially those issuing from Asian Canadian and other comparable locations, provide the occasions for reading processes that bring into play a complex of subject positions, often contradictory and conflicted but also in correspondence, which call for ongoing negotiation and reflexivity. Against the teleology of consumerist intake, such a critical reading practice would out-take the discursive positions that make meaning possible; in effect, it would break the gaze of subject-object relations and allow cultural texts to become signs of contestation, incommensurability, and singularity. An ethics of reading would seek to perform those social spaces that refuse the exertion of power over subjects and instead speculate on what we might call the postcolonial imaginary of an alternate nation beyond the spectral. But more than this, these texts also offer the possibility of an aesthetics that can locate the reading act in the present — a present that Bhabha writes "is not a transcendental passage but a moment of 'transit', a form of temporality that is open to disjunction and discontinuity and that sees the process of history engaged, rather like art, in a negotiation of the framing and naming of social reality — not what lies inside or outside reality, but where to draw (or inscribe) the 'meaningful' line between them" (448). If we can call this line the moment of the postcolonial, then the term can be read as an acknowledgement of the non-totalizable temporalities coexisting in the nation. It would then provide a hinge for critical vocabularies to generate those readers who are themselves the evidence of alternate histories.

Everything on earth has its moment of testimony:

its valorous presence as a witness to mutability.

**ROY K. KIYOOKA**, *Pacific Rim Letters* (305)

*Turning In, Turning Out*
THE SHIFTING FORMATIONS OF JAPANESE
CANADIAN FROM UPROOTING TO REDRESS

Gazing into the crystal ball of shifting formations has never been a straightforward procedure, and
the prospect of tracking something so seemingly isolate
as Japanese Canadian (JC) from uprooting to redress is no
exception. Indeed, as its familiar national boundaries —
real and symbolic — dissolve to give way to skepticism and
uncertainty, the prospect becomes more daunting and even
anxiety producing. In naming a group of Canadian subjects,
the term has been historically attached to those who have
identified themselves *and* have been identified through its
circulation, most dramatically so because of their internment
during the 1940s at the hands of the federal government. But
even so it has remained open to unpredictable transformations. I began to discover something of this potential for
change in reflecting on the mutability of a constructed I

who performs the critical function of the gaze. Isn't there, I or he asked himself, the risk of a tautological folly, as one who is already presented as a JC, a curious creature of history and imagination, gazes at JC as a shifting formation?

To begin with, this qualifying question is not meant to be an excuse for what may turn out to be folly, but an acknowledgement that attempts to address JC from a subject positioning tied to personal investments may tempt the conceptual closures that it sets out to open. This identity formation, of course, has preoccupied this I for decades in all of the most immediate ways imaginable, from the personal and familial to the social and historical. Nonetheless, even if JC has been a given, or what I have been given, for more years than memory can safely retrieve, it has never remained static; rather, it has consistently been experienced as contingent and mobile, producing in its mediated relationships a network of signifying effects — effects that have been dynamic, sometimes turbulent, sometimes imprisoning, sometimes liberating, and sometimes dumbfounding.

But here is a dilemma that this question poses: how to speculate on the historical production of JC, its context-specific configurations, variations, and significances, without falling back on a point of reference, some origin that it stands for? I didn't want in any way to diminish all the complicated lives lived in all their minute particularities over many decades under its name. At the same time I wanted to avoid some unquestioned assumptions — aware that doing so entailed accepting other assumptions. In other words, however normalized the designation appears to be, the reach of the representational boundaries of JC should never be taken for granted. For me, it is the very unpredictability of its movements that calls for critical reflection, especially in relation to the ways it has been inhabited, shaped, and resisted by those social subjects who have fallen under its spell (pun intended). This self-reflexive exercise, it seems to me, has taken on some urgency at this moment when its twentieth-century formations, forged as they were in the crucible of racialization under the aegis of the Canadian state, appear so much less tangible in the blurred border zones of transnational and global flows. Reflection on the shifting formation of JC now turns towards the arrival of yet-to-be-articulated transformations, a process that necessarily implicates the historical limits of this I's formation. (Turning in, turning out, so a voice whispers.)

## AN ASAKUSA TURN

Given the current porosity of the borderline between Japanese and Canadian under the influence of transnational processes, I want to return to a moment, an anecdotal one, when these two formations found themselves, not negotiating, but clashing with each other in a much younger consciousness.

It was the summer of 1970. It was the year of Expo '70 in Osaka. I was sauntering along a street in Asakusa, in Tokyo. I was drawn to the insistent rhythm of a barker's voice. A tightly knit crowd had cohered around him. Entering that circle, my imagination suddenly shuttled back and forth from the voice to the site of the Royal American Show in my Winnipeg childhood. There, at least for a "normal" kid, the barkers were mesmerizing for the uncanny ability they had to perform a stream of constant talk. I fantasized that, one day, I too might be able to perform so fluidly in the English language. But it wasn't only the voice that attracted me; it was also its discursive calling into appearance the object of its gaze — the so-called freak show.

Here were men and women doing wondrous feats, such as swallowing a sword or breathing fire, but alongside them were others whose bodies were the spectacle, the objects displayed for their divergences from the normative gaze: the fattest or tallest person in the world, the bearded woman, twins whose bodies were joined, the limbless body. In the crowd at Asakusa, among the normative bodies there, my own invisibility took on some uncanny effects. Without thought, I found myself slipping into the barker's world: anticipating the gaze, enticed by the sample others — so familiar from childhood memory yet so alien in Japanese bodies — displayed on a makeshift stage beside him.

Those bodies, acting as what memory theorist Daniel Schacter has called a "retrieval cue" (70), struck a deep chord of an estrangement located in my body's memory. It was the ease with which, sixteen months after moving to Tokyo, I could enter the language and "pass" in a critical space that began to warp in my imagination. Against the Japanese-identified body that made the kid growing up in Winnipeg visible, I was transparent in the Asakusa crowd; but instead of feeling relaxed by the ability to comprehend — after all, I had been studying Japanese — the act of slipping into the barker's voice made me conscious of my own displacement in the crowd. The translation process that allowed the barker's voice to be folded into the remembered childhood moment disrupted my consciousness of the scene, exposing what might be described (in Roland Bleiker's provocative terms in *Popular Dissent, Human Agency and Global Politics*) as a "discursive void, the space where . . . multiple and overlapping discourses clash, where silent and sometimes not so silent arguments are exchanged, where boundaries are drawn and redrawn" (189). As the barker's voice trailed on, there I was, on a warm and pleasant Saturday afternoon, utterly immersed in the memory of a racialized, hence "freakish" as well, body that haunted my childhood in Winnipeg.

In what was then a largely unconscious move to redraw boundaries, I decided to return to Canada, convinced that the I in the crowd at Asakusa would never be Japanese, whatever that term might have meant at the time. Read as a conventional autobiographic moment, this revelation was an individual crisis of identity that led the subject to alter the course of his life. But for a JC, one born into the aftermath of uprooting and cultural deracination, the same moment initiated a turn away from Japan as a point of origin and towards Canada as the site of future critical work.

The social and cultural spaces of the nation that I re-entered were themselves undergoing a turn—coincidence or not, who can tell?

Strangely, my own realization that "Japanese" could not provide an origin for subjectivities produced in the historical contexts of the Canadian nation-state was countered by an emergent identity politics. It was based on efforts to make visible previously covered-over histories and to appropriate the narrative of the nation to construct ethnic variations on the dominant narrative of settlement and nation-building. With all the attendant ironies, and in a climate in which the state generated a language of multiculturalism to contain, or otherwise mediate, the growing internal challenges to Anglo-dominant liberal discourses, even JCs, a relatively small group who had had no real public voice since the 1940s, found themselves awakening to transformed social spaces. As if the process were alchemical, lo and behold, the modifier Japanese, once anathema to transcending the gate of assimilation, was accruing cultural value as an ethnicity that should be recognized and preserved.

One telling sign of the shifting valence of JC came in the form of capital support for a project—the only national one—that had been languishing for years. Back in the late 1950s, Ken Adachi had been awarded the contract from the National Japanese Canadian Citizens' Association (NJCCA), which became the National Association of Japanese Canadians (NAJC) in 1980, to write the official history of JCs. Here it was, some fifteen years later, and the book had yet to reach a state of publication, though the manuscript had apparently been completed. In one of its first projects, the newly created Multicultural Directorate planned to commission a series of ethnic histories. Hearing about Adachi's manuscript, the Directorate approached the NJCCA to offer direct financial support for publication. What better way to inaugurate the multicultural series than with the history of JCs, a model minority in the government's eyes? *The Enemy That Never Was* was subsequently published in 1976 by McClelland and Stewart "in association with Supply and Services."[1] The timing could not be more fitting. The following year would be the celebration of the Japanese Canadian Centennial, an event that received substantial government assistance and through which Japanese Canadian was reinvented as a hyphenated or multicultural identity—in other words, as a sign of arrival in the narrative of the nation. To understand how this reinvention worked, it is necessary to recall that the concept of a centennial was very much a product of the times. The nation's centennial had been celebrated a decade before, and the narrative construction of the so-called settlement era was in vogue. The idea for a "Japanese Canadian Centennial" came from Toyo Takata (1983), who, in researching his book *Nikkei Legacy: The Story of Japanese Canadians from Settlement to Today*, determined that the first settler was Manzo Nagano, who, based on historical evidence, "arrived in Canada in Spring 1877, as this country's first Japanese settler" (9). Thus the ascribed year of origin was not simply arbitrary but invented to align the history of JCs with the history of the Canadian nation. By celebrating a centennial, the racialized JC subject could move from the position of "Enemy Alien" to "friendly Canadianized alien."

The adoption of the narrative of the nation[2]—a narrative that, in fact, constituted the formation of the Canadian nation out of the violence of colonial invasion and territorialization — was a dramatic turn for the JCs whose memories were still tied closely to the trauma of mass uprooting and dispossession of the 1940s. The irony (which I will return to) was that the turn would be enacted through the discursive frameworks of nation building — frameworks that had once excluded JCs as Japanese or "Asiatic" and therefore deemed "undesirable" or "unsuitable" in the language of the Immigration Act.

Worth mentioning here are three projects that emerged in the 1970s and subsequently took on critical importance during the redress movement of the 1980s:

> (1) In the mid-1970s, Ann Sunahara, benefitting from the influence of well-known *nisei* Tom Shoyama, then deputy minister of finance, was the first researcher to access the federal government files on the mass uprooting. Her research would uncover material evidence to show what JCs knew but could not prove, namely that the mass uprooting was not a military necessity but a political move made possible through the intense racialization of JCs. The results of her work were circulating in the late 1970s; her book would be published in 1981 with the telling title, *The Politics of Racism: The Uprooting of Japanese Canadians During the Second World War.*

> (2) Around the same time that Sunahara was carrying out her research in Ottawa, in the same city Joy Kogawa had herself uncovered the archive of *nisei* writer and community activist Muriel Kitagawa, whose voice, particularly in the letters she wrote

to her brother Wes Fujiwara in Toronto amidst the turmoil of the uprooting, would infuse the writing of *Obasan*. Kogawa's novel would be published first by Lester and Orpen Dennys in 1981, and then in its more familiar Penguin edition in 1983. It was immediately acclaimed as a novel that brought JC internment to a contemporary Canadian generation that was apparently receptive to a tale of injustice in the nation. The front cover blurb of the Penguin edition announced it as "A moving novel of a time and a suffering we have tried to forget."

(3) Simultaneous with Sunahara and Kogawa's writing, a small group of community activists in Vancouver, myself included — mostly *sansei* and young *nisei*, collaborating with young *shin-issei* (that is, recent immigrants from Japan) — constituted themselves as the Japanese Canadian Centennial Project (JCCP) and decided, as a collective voice, to write and produce the official history project for the 1977 centennial celebrations, *A Dream of Riches: Japanese Canadians 1877–1977* (1978). This photo-history, with commentaries in English, French, and Japanese, would open in Ottawa and subsequently tour several JC centres. A core of this group later formed the JCCP Redress Committee and brought the issue of redress to the public's attention.

In short, during the 1970s the production of identity was at a high pitch. As if overnight, it was not only acceptable but even good to be JC. The tenacity of those so named to read themselves into the nation's narration demonstrated their incredible resourcefulness in negotiating with a formation that had previously written them out. Yet despite this recognition, JC would remain implicated in the racialized history out of which it has arisen. Unable, finally, to stand alone as "Canadian" or as "Japanese," this identity formation, even in its positive incarnation, could not extricate itself from the history that it embodied. This critical perspective did not arrive after, in a belated fashion, but was concurrent with anti-colonial critiques of the Canadian nation-state emerging on the critical edges of identity politics in the 1970s. The conjunction of race and the nation, in this framework, allowed for — and allows for here — a reconsideration of the negative production of JC, the memory of which, no doubt for many, tempered and made much more resonant the sense of pride that surfaced in the 1970s.

## NEGOTIATING CANADIAN RACIALIZATION

We need to constantly remind ourselves of the scene of arrival for the Japanese *issei* who were the first to cross the territorial border of the twentieth-century Canadian nation-state in the making. From the moment they entered its racialized borders, they had to engage in a process of negotiations with a powerful network of social, political, and cultural formations already premised on their alien status. Though they carried in their cultural and psychological baggage a complicated network of their own subjective identifications and references, the real and symbolic territories the *issei* came into were laced with legal and ideological determinants that interpreted their bodies according to the prevalent orientalism, especially virulent on the BC coast, the specific geographical site of their arrival. Positioned as a minority according to the colonializing codes of nation-making at the time, they had to contend with a barrage of constraints, legal or otherwise, that conspired to restrict their entry and, once admitted, to contain and manage them as the perpetual alien — equivalent to the "stranger" who is seen as a contaminant that threatens a fantasized racial purity and necessitates regulatory mechanisms to protect and police its borders.

In *Strange Encounters*, a study of the figure of the stranger in the theoretical approaches to nation formation — approaches compatible with Canadian conditions — Sara Ahmed proposes that those demarked as strangers inhabit an "abject" body. This body occupies an exteriorizing zone that functions to solidify and authenticate the dominant subjects whose bodies, largely produced as white, male, and heterosexual, signify the constituted norm. What remains important, though, is to recognize that the exclusionary effects of abjection "involve prior acts of incorporation" (52), so that the figure of the "outsider" is the obverse of an "insider" who has been named as the different — colloquially a social freak — against which the same assumes its normalized or goes-without-saying position. In this social and political configuration, the very possibility of home, or at-home-ness, comes to be governed by internal borders that allow certain subjects to take ownership of the geocultural spaces of the nation, but not the others who remain strangers. This, then, accounts for the pervasive thematic of the unhomely in Japanese Canadian as well as Asian Canadian cultural work, an affect familiar to those who, racialized as strangers, have appeared in the nation as spectral, aberrant, even at times monstrous. But their status as outsiders, as Ahmed carefully reminds us, has been bound into a social and political system that produces them as such in the interests of its national agendas: "The strange body can only become a material 'thing' that touches the body-at-home, or a figure that can be faced in the street, through a radical forgetting of the histories of labour and production that allow such a body to appear in the present" (53–4).

## UNDERGOING MASS UPROOTING

The violent implications of naming hit home for JCs with a vengeance in the most traumatic turn of events that would subsequently underwrite their subjectivities: their mass uprooting and dispossession, carried out under the Canadian state's War Measures Act and enabled through the shifty and deceptive power of the state-produced language of racialization that permitted the gross violation of rights in a supposedly liberal democratic regime. Of course, JCs, such as *nisei* writer Muriel Kitagawa, were not at all fooled by the effects of the legislation that converted her, a citizen by birth, into the "Jap," the "Enemy Alien." As she wrote to her brother Wes Fujiwara, on March 4, 1942, the day she found out that even those born in Canada would be subject to mass expulsion from their homes, "Oh we are fair prey for the wolves in democratic clothing" (91). Then, again, in a letter written two days later: "Lord, if this was Germany you can expect such things as the normal way, but this is

Canada, a Democracy! And the Nisei, repudiated by the only land they know, no redress anywhere" (93).

What a difference discourse can make. In Naomi's reported words of Aunt Emily in Kogawa's *Obasan* on the abjection of JCs: "None of us, she said, escaped the naming. We were defined and identified by the way we were seen. A newspaper in B.C. headlined, 'They are a stench in the nostrils of the people of Canada.' We were therefore relegated to the cesspools . . . There was a tidy mind somewhere" (118). The process of symbolic identification as a "stench" in the nation that had to be corralled, contained, and dispelled was preceded by a literal process of registration the year before, when all JCs were fingerprinted, "duly registered in compliance with the provisions of Order-in-Council PC 117," and required to carry a registration card with their photograph and "specimen of signature."[3] The stage, then, had already been set for the federal government to mobilize the language of racialization to transform the JC subject from "citizen" to "Enemy Alien." First, there was the more routine Order-in-Council PC 365 (January 16, 1942) to remove male enemy aliens (of all national backgrounds, including Japanese nationals) from the coast for security purposes. This regulation paved the way for Order-in-Council PC 1486 (February 24, 1942), under the signature of Minister of Justice Louis St. Laurent, in which the discourse of race took the place of nationality.

Between those two dates, only a month apart, the federal government had decided, against the advice of the RCMP and the military, as Sunahara documents, to carry out the mass removal of all JCs. In the notice directed to them, they are henceforth to be named and identified and therefore discursively contained through the prepositional phrase "of the Japanese race." That simple epithet would prove to be the most powerful weapon in the government's arsenal to skirt the very liberal discourse of rights they were supposedly defending in their war efforts. The unspoken racializing syllogism that functioned to fix Japanese Canadians in the ministerial directive followed a sleight-of-hand logic: (a) Japanese nationals are enemy aliens; (b) enemy aliens are "of the Japanese race"; (c) Japanese Canadians are "of the Japanese race"; (d) Japanese Canadians are therefore enemy aliens.

While some progressive efforts were made by idealistic *nisei* in the 1930s to eliminate the barriers to the franchise, all of these were erased by the seemingly monolithic language that produced them in the crucible of the mass displacement as the face "of the Japanese race" in Canada, a script so powerful it would be internalized by those who were subjected to its relentless application. Consider, for instance, the consequences for the members of the Nisei Mass Evacuation Group who protested the family break-up policy of the BC Security Commission that, they rightfully argued, served no purpose, especially because JCs had agreed to cooperate with the government's supposed security measures. In other words, they were not the enemy. They were Canadians, as they said forcefully in their cogent letter to the BC Security Commission rejecting the break-up of families:

> When we say "no" at this point, we request you to remember that we are British subjects by birth, that we are no less loyal to Canada than any other Canadian, that we

have done nothing to deserve the break-up of our families,
that we are law-abiding Canadian citizens, and that we
are willing to accept suspension of our civil rights. (qtd.
in Miki and Kobayashi 37)

The request was flatly turned down, and when they continued to mount their protest movement, they were taken into
custody by the RCMP, placed in the Immigration Hall, and
sent to barbed wire prisoner-of-war camps, first at Petawawa
and then at Angler, both in Ontario. Many languished in
a discursive limbo, erroneously re-scripted as prisoners of
war under the jurisdiction of the military.

The reduction of a once-highly differentiated collective to a one-dimensional category — "of the Japanese race"
— would be followed by another re-inscription as the war
drew to a close. Once the language of security threat was
no longer tenable, other means were needed to disallow JCs
from returning to the BC coast. After all, in the logic of
racialization in Prime Minister Mackenzie King's address to
the House of Commons on August 4, 1944, it was their very
visibility as a group that accounted for the racism directed
against them. Therefore, for their own good — in a move that
replayed the protective custody myth used to uproot them
— the prime minister announced to all MPs, none of whom
challenged him: "The sound policy and the best policy for the
Japanese Canadians themselves is to distribute their numbers
as widely as possible throughout the country where they will
not create feelings of racial hostility" (qtd. in Adachi 433).

The policy Mackenzie King had in mind would, in
fact, be two-pronged, and it would reach the still-confined JCs

in the form of two notices posted, or otherwise distributed, side by side. I'm referring, of course, to the infamous notices with two new terms that would once again determine the futures of the subjects under their jurisdiction. These were "repatriation" (to Japan) or "dispersal" ("east of the Rockies," i.e., out of BC). The subjects were offered a choice that was no choice; in other words, the federal scriptwriters had devised yet another language trap. First off, there was no option to remain in BC. Then again, the vast majority of those who were asked to consider repatriation had Canada as their patria, so they could not by definition be repatriated. The brutal reality was that they were being asked to consider their own deportation or exile from the country of their birth. Finally, the connotations of dispersal were ominous and threatening, implying both that repatriation would signify loyalty to Japan and that rejection of dispersal would signify disloyalty to Canada. Consider the language used in this notice:

> Japanese Canadians who want to remain in Canada should now re-establish themselves East of the Rockies as the best evidence of their intentions to cooperate with the Government policy of dispersal.

> Failure to accept employment east of the Rockies may be regarded at a later date as lack of co-operation with the Canadian Government in carrying out its policy of dispersal.

> Those who do not take advantage of present opportunities for employment and settlement outside British Columbia at this time, while employment opportunities are favour-

able, will find conditions of employment and settlement considerably more difficult at a later date and may seriously prejudice their own future by delay. (From Notice: To All Persons of Japanese Racial Origin Now Resident in British Columbia, reproduced in Miki and Kobayashi 48)

The repatriation and dispersal policies caused untold grief and anxiety, often tearing apart friendships and families, forced as JCs were to demonstrate their loyalty to a country that had violated their rights, dispossessed them, and cast them as enemies of the state. In the end, as the records show, some 4,000 were shipped to war-torn Japan. "The main casualties," Ken Adachi writes, "were the Canadian-born, who comprised over half of the repatriates, 33% of whom were dependent children under 16 years of age" (318).

By the time the war ended, the JC presence on the west coast had been erased, and the robust collective that was uprooted en masse in 1942 had become a tattered remnant of the complex fabric of the identity formations — of, for instance, geographic location, employment, class, religion, political stance, and region (or *ken*) of origin in Japan — that once constituted their social and cultural relations. Now undifferentiated in the raced language of federal policies as merely persons "of the Japanese race," they found themselves reduced to a fixed identity, at least in the language through which their movements were policed and monitored.

With the war's end, the more explicit discourse of racialization mobilized by the government was no longer as transparent as before. In his speech in the House of Commons, Mackenzie King was conscious of avoiding any accusations of racism by distancing his policy from the "hateful doctrine of racialism which is the basis of the Nazi system everywhere" (qtd. in Adachi 433). What is also striking in the rhetoric of his articulation of the so-called "Japanese problem" is his use of the identity formation "Japanese Canadian." In Mackenzie King's language, the persons "of the Japanese race" who had been uprooted and dispossessed were now more benignly designated as "Japanese Canadians." The shift in terms is certainly neither an accident nor a reflection of enlightenment on Mackenzie King's part. Instead, it conformed to the intent of the government's dispersal program. The addition of "Canadian" in this instance may have softened overt racism, but it manifested a strategy of Canadianization that amounted to forced assimilation. Now you see them, now you don't.

## GROWING UP IN THE POSTWAR YEARS

The public effect of Mackenzie King's infamous 1944 speech in the House of Commons was to construct the figure of a JC subject who, once incorporated into the postwar nation, was expected to be not seen, and certainly not heard as a collective of individuals, citizens even, who had been betrayed by the very democratic system that should have protected them. The absorption of the supposedly rehabilitated Japanese into Japanese Canadian functioned—in a forgetting process that liberalism itself fosters—to cover over the violence of the mass uprooting. But for the JCs who emerged from the war years and turned into a model minority, often more Canadian than other Canadians, the legacy of the trauma would linger on, sometimes in self-imposed silences and other times in whispered exchanges among friends, relatives, and in the enclave of family narratives.

It was not so much a simple repression of memory but more what I would call a disarticulated history of loss and displacement that marked the 1950s and early 1960s, even in the face of upward social mobility. It was a history whose unresolved tensions would filter through the margins of my own formative years in Winnipeg. Remember the mantra of the times: education, education, and more education. Enter the professions. Gain proficiency in English. Don't speak Japanese. And, of course, don't think of yourself as Japanese. But as a kid growing up in a white-identified city, it was difficult not to be tagged with a connection to Japanese, especially when in childhood I was usually the only identifiable "Jap" in sight. Remember all those war movies when the demonic Japanese get it in the end? Well, those scenes were played out on the neighbourhood streets, too. Internal resistances to that childhood interpellation process came much later, and would eventually open the speculation that perhaps the secret to identity could be found in that other place — that place where my grandparents came from. Little did I know then that other *sansei*, as we began to identify ourselves more collectively, were also aroused by a curiosity about our so-called roots. Hence the search for origins in Japan, a search that dead-ended, for me, that day in Asakusa. In returning to Canada, in an act that uncannily remembered my own grandparents' entry, I got involved in a process of negotiating the nation that marked the 1970s for JCs and others whose histories had not been voiced in the dominant narratives of Canadian history.

In recalling the effect of my return to Canada, I thought of Butler's statement in *Excitable Speech* on the disjuncture that distances social naming from personal naming. "The time of discourse," she says, "is not the time of the subject" (31). The subject who left in search of "Japanese" and came back in search of "Canadian" re-entered a social and cultural space in which the Japanese of Japanese Canadian was undergoing a complex reinvention process of its own. No longer necessarily attached to the abjection of the stranger, it appeared to have flipped over to become a sign of a multicultural discourse in an expanding liberalism. Yet the obvious fact that JC subjects could not stand alone as Canadians, that the modification of Japanese was still necessary, belied a continuing racialization in a nation that was itself adjusting to centrifugal forces altering its hegemonic structures.

Nevertheless, from this turn in the shifting fortunes of JC we can draw at least one salutary conclusion. The agency exercised by JCs in the 1970s, and then taken in unprecedented directions through the redress movement in the 1980s, shows that processes of racialization are never simply one-way and imposed, but are dynamic and folded into specific limits. The contingencies that made the power of racism indeterminate could then become the nexus of a subject-oriented discourse of identity making, resistance, and opposition. The complication, of course, is that this nexus of social agency is also contingent on the zone of interaction between "them" and the nation in which they have already been named or identified.

The stage was set for a much more compelling question: if we can read ourselves into the narrative of the nation, as evident, for instance, in the production of *A Dream of Riches*, then should not this nation acknowledge *Democracy Betrayed*? I am here referring to the title of the redress brief issued by the NAJC in November 1984, an event that marked the entrance of the redress movement into national public spheres.

## SEEKING SOCIAL JUSTICE AND REDRESS

The logic of the shift from identity making in the 1970s to social justice in the 1980s in one sense appears inevitable from the subjective perspective of JCs. The process of reclaiming history could only expose the blank spaces—the unspoken lack—left in the persistent memories of the wartime trauma. Without an official acknowledgement that they had been the victims of a "democracy betrayed" by a systemic capitulation to racialized policies, they would continue to live under the shadow of the category "Enemy Alien."

The language of redress located its impetus in a deep-seated grievance that called out for resolution, most urgently because of the age of those affected. Redress as a discourse took on a tangible existence, functioning as a medium through which JC as an identity formation could be aligned with social justice, anti-racism, participatory democracy, and human rights, all issues that became central to the social and cultural activism of the 1980s. In the wider social contexts, at times distant from the inside turmoil and confusion that infiltrated the nooks and crannies of local JC communities, those who were formerly uprooted and dispossessed began to make visible the contradictions of the liberal democratic assumptions that were built into the language of the Canadian state. How then to account for the legacy of racism and injustice in its own backyard? Think now of the intense politics surrounding the patriation of the Canadian constitution; the constitutional hearings that attracted considerable press coverage, and to which JCs were invited to present the story of their mass uprooting; the passage of the Charter of Rights and Freedoms, a document that, so Canadians had been told, would prevent any minority group from being abused in the ways JCs had been in the 1940s; and the fanfare surrounding the publication of the all-party *Equality Now!* report on recommendations to enable so-called visible minorities to overcome racist barriers in Canada, including one supporting redress for JCs (see Canada). These were only a handful of the signposts for the contexts in which the redress movement found itself incorporated into the national politics of the time.

In considering the relationship between the redress movement and the shifting formation of JC, I want to fast forward to the redress settlement of September 22, 1988. I recall how struck I was by a question posed to Art Miki, the president of the NAJC, at the press conference following the official signing. Miki was asked about accepting the agreement: "Do you think you're being used at all for political purposes, and does that bother you?" When my brother hesitated to answer, I sensed that he was momentarily a bit dumbfounded, as I was, at what seemed pretty obvious, but perhaps we were missing something. We thought it was quite clear that redress was undertaken as a social justice movement whose goal was political, despite the diverse subjectivities of the JCs involved. More, in negotiating the agreement with the federal government, the NAJC had engaged in a political exchange. The questions of "being used" and "bother," on the other hand, could be explained through a misalignment: between the political discourse out of which the reporter's question arose and the time of the traumatic uprooting and dispossession out of which the redressed subjects had come to represent themselves.

It seemed to me that the reporter, in a systemic rather than conscious mode, was speaking from a social discourse that identified the JCs named in the agreement as the model minority who were being "used" by the political system. But hadn't JCs, through the NAJC, in effect used the political system to negotiate a redress agreement? Since the press conference did not allow for follow-up reflections, the ramifications of the question disappeared as quickly as it took for another question to be asked. What the moment exposed, however, was what Katherine Verdery has referred to as the "nation as a construct, whose meaning is never stable but shifts with the changing balance of social forces" (230). As such, the nation is necessarily plural in the field of meanings it generates—in that case for the reporter, and for my brother as the voice of JCs—and so takes on different formations depending on subject positioning and relations of privilege and disadvantage to their dominant representations. To take this one step further, we can then posit that the nation performing the acknowledgement of the injustices endured by JCs was not the same as the nation that was officially redeemed by the actions of the prime minister in the House of Commons, even though the event itself, the redress settlement, constituted itself as a resolutionary act that produced a new substance, in this case a nation that sought to renew itself through the reification of its citizenship.

Against the global politics that has come to dominate the post-redress era, it may be possible to read the settlement back into the underlying crisis of the nation, circa 1988, as a sign of an attempt to re-invoke a postwar identity formation that had lost its efficacious hold on the body politic. At the time of the settlement, in September 1988, the most heated social and political issue was the Free Trade Agreement (FTA) followed by the North American Free Trade Agreement (NAFTA). While the moment of redress may appear to bear no relationship to these signs of the end of the Cold War era — the Berlin Wall would come down a year later to provide a more global sign — their conjunction marked a turn in the Canadian nation away from cultural nationalism towards the market agendas of transnational corporations with their neoliberal values that encouraged self-serving individualism and unfettered consumerism. In the more restricted sphere of JC subjectivity, the moment of the redress settlement in the House of Commons, as ephemeral as it was, was bound to the history of attempts to negotiate with the Canadian nation, most unsuccessfully in the 1940s, but extending back in a chain of moments — back, for instance, to October 19, 1900, when Tomey Homma applied to have his name placed on the voters' list because, as a naturalized Canadian, he was not the "Japanese" identified in Section 8 of the Provincial Elections Act (Adachi 53).

He was refused. Homma's follow-up court challenge was endorsed by the provincial and federal courts, but then was flatly denied, in England, by the House of Lords. Had he won, it remains fascinating to speculate, the course of JC history could have taken very different turns in the decades ahead. The mass uprooting might have been averted, or at least challenged through the same legal machinery that justified the abrogation of rights. For JCs, then, redress signified the culmination of nearly a century of struggle for recognition and citizenship rights. At the same time, redress as an event was already entering into further negotiations with changing cultural conditions under the influence of transnational forces. Even while JCs were conceived as citizens who were wronged and whose redress would redeem the racist past of the nation, they also came to exemplify the enlightened nature of Canadian multiculturalism, and this benign cultural face of the nation could be used to engage the emerging transnational language of economic globalization.

## GOING POST-REDRESS

The transformations of JC that I have tracked so far demonstrate that identity formations are always being interrupted by alterior spaces and times, forcing further negotiations that transform former states. These formations, in other words, are always provisional—the effect of an ensemble of practices that shape our subjectivities. Systems of power and the relations that those systems produce are not external to our subject formations but constitute the flows and processes through which we both act and are acted upon.

This point was brought home to me in viewing Linda Ohama's film *Obaachan's Garden* (2001). One point of urgency in the film is the search in Japan by filmmaker Ohama, her daughter, and her mother for the lost daughters of Ohama's grandmother, Asayo Murakami — lost to her before Asayo arrived in Canada in the mid-1920s. This fact is kept secret as Ohama begins filming what she thought would be a more or less conventional documentary biography. But midway through, Asayo, then over 100 years old, reveals that she had been married before, had lost her two young daughters to a domineering mother-in-law who had also broken up her marriage, and had come to Canada to escape Japan. The film follows the search through records in Japan and the magical meeting with one of the daughters (the other had died a few years earlier), nearly eighty, who thought her mother had died long ago. The film features the mother and daughter meeting after some seventy-five years of separation, as if in a dream landscape but actually in the reconstructed garden of Asayo's restored home in Steveston, BC, where she and her family lived before they were uprooted during the Second World War.

By uncovering this secret or concealed history of a woman who came to Canada as a "picture bride" — women married on agreement to Japanese men in Canada, usually after the exchange of photos — the film both widens the lens of history and brings its transnational conditions to bear on the most minute aspects of daily existence. All through her life and marriage, giving birth to many children, undergoing the ordeal of incarceration, and rebuilding her family after the war, Asayo had carried a photo of her two girls.

She had held in her imagination a dream that one day she would be reunited with them, and her dream had come full circle with the remaining daughter.

What I found so compelling was that Ohama's film itself had become, through the unexpected disclosure of Asayo's secret, an effect of a shift from a nation-based identity to one that is conditioned by the spaces of transnational networks that re-connect JCs to Japan. As Asayo releases her secret, in that very gesture, the identity formation of JCs, which had been formed linearly through its negotiations with the Canadian nation-state, was altered by the more malleable and spatially more encompassing signs of Japan in their history. We might say that the film performs an opening that releases JCs from the need to be constantly vigilant in declaring themselves Canadian and not Japanese. This had been one of the elements of their social survival during the postwar years, when, as a racialized minority, they had to maintain an expected model minority role as loyal subjects of Canada.

The transnational scope of Ohama's film, then, points towards what we might call a post-redress time. The branding as "Enemy Alien," as the alien "Jap" figure contained through racialization, struck to the core of JCs, and it was this haunted identity formation—the unredressed citizen of injustice — that was released from its historical confinement in the moment of the redress settlement of September 22, 1988. But paradoxically, and here the complexity for JCs comes home to roost, this unprecedented shift from an unredressed state to a redressed state came to constitute a resolution that simultaneously, and inevitably, announced the passing of that identity. Turning in, turning out.

"I looked up at the signs."

**HIROMI GOTO,** *Chorus of Mushrooms* (90)

*Can Asian Adian?*
READING SOME SIGNS OF ASIAN CANADIAN

Much of the critically aware creative writing by Asian Canadian writers for the past two decades has raised an important critical question concerning the study and teaching of literary texts: how do we, as readers and teachers, address and deal with the multiple and often contradictory subject positions that govern the boundaries of our reading and consequently complicate our understanding of the textual practices of these writers? This question is especially relevant in a country such as Canada, where the social processes of racialization have been so instrumental in producing the cultural effects of its preoccupation with its national identity.

To begin to consider some answers, I want to focus on critical reading practices called for in the name of Asian Canadian literature. It has now become much more common than ever before for teachers and scholars alike to view Asian Canadian writing as a relatively new field of Canadian literature. While this critical interest is a welcome change, it also demands more critical awareness on the part of readers. Given the racialized conditions that Asian Canadian writers historically have faced, and continue to face, we need to develop critically informed reading practices to address the scene of reading as a social site that is bound up in dominant assumptions of Canadian cultural institutions. These are reading practices that are reflexive in being attuned, on the one hand, to Asian Canadian as an identity construct and, on the other, to the textual strategies employed by writers whose subjectivities are inseparable from the social, cultural, and historical specifics out of which, and often against which, they have been formed.

In proposing the development of reflexive reading practices for studying Asian Canadian literary works, I also want to emphasize that its acceptance in established institutional frameworks, such as in university courses and academic journals, is less an innocent instance of knowledge production and more an incorporative act that constitutes itself through the boundaries of representations made legitimate by disciplinary regulations and norms. To cite Butler in *Excitable Speech*, considering the I in her sentence, in this case, as an institution: "The question is not what it is I will be able to say, but what will constitute the domain of the sayable within which I begin to speak at all" (133). If the arrival of Asian Canadian as a legitimate field of academic study works to establish "the domain of the sayable," then it also functions as a process through which an entity such as Asian Canadian takes on a social and cultural identity and accrues value as a discursive category, in other words, as a sphere of public knowledge. The danger resides in the conclusion that such an identity has a stable point of reference and is not the outcome of the constitutive process and thus a representation that is always subject to change and negotiation. When the boundaries of institutional incorporation are covered over, or otherwise elided in our reading practices, Asian Canadian literature may simply become an object of knowledge — and what may then be rendered unsayable as enabling such knowledge are the social, cultural, and historical contingencies that uphold and sustain the privilege of representational priorities. What happens to Asian Canadian writing — its material conditions of production — as it crosses the threshold of established institutional frameworks is, for this reason, an issue that both provokes tension and allows for critical reflection.

In non-academic cultural communities, Asian Canadian has circulated as a more or less benign term since the late 1980s. It has been adopted as a term of choice intermittently by community activists involved in forging alliances across more ethnic-specific identities, such as Chinese Canadian and Japanese Canadian. A further descriptive normalization has come with the new visibility of writers and artists who have allied themselves, or have been identified as aligned, with cultures, histories, and geographies that are Asian, reinforced perhaps by the powerful institutional effects of Asian American studies. But as a discursive formation its components, Asian and Canadian, are far from stable, and even less so in these times of rapid social and economic transformations brought on by the shifting demographics of transnational flows, especially in Canada where the so-called Asianization of social and cultural spaces is producing new forms of cultural anxiety and racialized conflicts.[1] Because of these conditions, it is important to question what the institutional boundaries of Asian Canadian contain, or to what extent the future of Asian Canadian as a cultural formation may depend on its negotiations with dominant representational regimes, or in what ways its enunciation as a creative practice may elicit certain textual preoccupations from writers and artists. In other words, it may be critically productive to read Asian Canadian as a kind of "signifier without the signified" (Zizek 99), and to approach its uncertain status as the effect of continuing conflicts in the social sites of those who identify themselves or are identified as Asian Canadians.

## VEGETABLE POLITICS IN CHORUS OF MUSHROOMS

Here I want to invoke the first of three textual instances of Asian Canadian as a performance of social and discursive codes and transactions. The scene is a mainstream Canadian site in Hiromi Goto's novel *Chorus of Mushrooms*, a Safeway supermarket in an urban milieu. Enter a silent Asian woman circulating as a figure of *difference*; she pauses in a circumscribed area where the marginal is commodified, in what the writer-narrator-shopper calls "the ethnicChinesericenoodleTofupattieexotic vegetable section" (90). While her body falls in sync with codes of visuality that display a Canadianized language of racialization, the conjunction produces the Asian body as produce — as an other sign in the constitution of Anglo-European/white norms. The playful elision of spaces between words performs the textually visible equivalent of an indiscriminate fusing of culturally specific particularities into a distilled abstraction. Here, in familiar fashion, only certain select objects (noodles, tofu, and the "other" vegetables) come to stand in for, i.e., represent, the Asian as standardized, or as otherwise identified through signs of commodification.

In this social site, the writer-narrator quietly goes about the tactile business of shopping for images that bring her pleasure. Still, Safeway is not all that *safe* for bodies marked as *difference* as they make their way through. The coincidence of the narrator's body in this already-determined space ignites a social exchange — the drama of a racialized encounter:

> "What is that, exactly? I've always wondered."
>
> I looked up from my reverie and a face peered down on me. A kindly face. An interested face.
>
> "It's an eggplant."
>
> "Oh really!" Surprisewonderjoy. "How wonderful! This is what *our* eggplants look like. They're so different!" She held up a round almost-black solid eggplant. Bitter skin and all." (90)

The "kindly face" scans the signs posted for Chinese-named vegetables, and then the interaction resumes:

"What are they called in *your* language?"

I looked up at the signs.

"I don't speak Chinese," I said.

"Oh, I'm sorry." (90)

The sign, "Japanese eggplants $2.09/lb," is right above the eggplants. The narrator points this out in exasperation, as she "smacked" the eggplant in her hand "smartly against the sign." Then she struggles to retrieve her earlier reverie. But the moment has already dissipated. "Leave me in peace," she thinks without speaking. "Let a woman choose her vegetables in peace. Vegetable politics" (91).

This brief scene from *Chorus of Mushrooms* encapsulates the moments of misrecognition all too familiar to those associated with an Asian-identified body in Canada. Enacted through the everyday language of dominant social spaces, the narrative exposes a complex of critical issues that the term Asian Canadian brings into circulation. In breaking the reverie of the narrator, the voice performs an interpellation process that presumes the power of the majority—embodied in Safeway as a representational social field based on "western" (read: "white") food as the norm—to claim rights of entry into whatever comes into its referential frame. "What is that, exactly? I've always wondered." The mock anthropological ritual that Goto's text presents replays a socially scripted language ("our norms" versus "your difference") in which minoritized subjects are saddled with the burden of representation. In such a linguistic territory, the Asian signs are visualized as belonging to Canada, as represented by the "interested" and "kindly" face.

On the other hand, the reaction, "I'm sorry," when the narrator says she doesn't "speak Chinese," opens the small but telling space of a mis-communication that discloses the gaps that are covered over. The disturbance, in turn, activates her to defy, to resist, and to claim a language of articulation, all of which is apparent in the textual construction of the scene itself. "Sorry for what?" the narrator asks, but only to herself, her silent thought bubble, in this instance negotiating the confrontation that vocalization would surely provoke. But feeling sorry "for" maintains the hierarchic relation and allows for the linguistic transaction to dissipate without further interruptions, except, of course, for the reader who may be positioned at variable points on the social continuum that extends between the narrator's subjectivity and the social voice of the questioner.

"Vegetable politics" is another way of pointing towards "race politics," or "ethnic politics," or "cultural politics," all phrases that fold back into a national and colonial history in which the Asian body has been formulated through a dense web of administrative and legal mechanisms. The Asian inside Canada, which is to say, the fabricated Asian, has functioned less as a descriptive term and more as the sign of the not-white — the formative lack — against which the white settler body has been valorized as a centralizing figure. This Asian has undergone an externalization process, or an orientalization, through which it is either seen as a perilous face in a "yellow peril" discourse or the benign face of a model minority that has undergone assimilation.

Such racialized formations, however, are never static, even when the divisions they spawn, such as minority versus majority, are taken as givens through social assumptions. They maintain their efficacy through the constant shoring up of their boundaries, and thus can be understood as vested frameworks that accrue power through the demarcation of otherwise incommensurable relations. The formations themselves are founded on the codes of visibility through which social value and legitimacy are articulated. Those imagined as a divergence from the normal—in the administrative terminology devised by the Canadian state, those marked as "visible minorities"—are intimately familiar with the pervasive unspoken codes of what amounts to a social unconsciousness that covers over the racialization that scripts "visible minorities" as the enabling term for the normalization of whiteness. In the social zones that are themselves extensions of this unconsciousness, those whose bodies circulate in a transparency of goes-without-saying relations find themselves, except through intentional modes of critical intervention, in the situation of not seeing the signs of everyday racialization. In Canadian contexts, much of the coherence of dominant cultural and social formations has been enabled by a malleable liberal discourse of individualism bolstered by a common-sense empiricism in which the not-seen need not be addressed and the unsayable has no legitimacy—even when the national media and official state legislation, such as the Canadian Multiculturalism Act of 1988, acknowledge that racism is alive and well in our midst. What is censored is the critical awareness that the acknowledgement and the concealment constitute two sides of the same social coin.

If the processes of racialization are, in this sense, aligned with power sources that script social hierarchies and privileges in the invisible ink of liberal individualism, it is then in moments of confrontation, reaction, crisis, and defensiveness — which is to say, in moments of intervention — that the effects of transparency can get exposed. Cultural work takes on creative value in the face of such moments, and not surprisingly, much of the intellectual energy of racialized writers and artists has been expended in negotiating the production of cultural representations. New readers, too, have been formed in this preoccupation and their critical attention has given the impression that the social acceptance of so-called emergent voices confirms a progressive move beyond racialization. But even here, or especially here, some crucial critical questions arise to haunt the institutional scenes of reading Asian Canadian literature. When, for instance, Asian Canadian writers and artists are assumed to speak the internal spaces of subjugated or otherwise-subordinated histories and subjectivities, how does the listening take place? What methodological or pedagogical limits mark the boundaries of knowledge production? How and where do the critical readings get circulated? What is rendered inaudible? What is gained, what lost? How is the negotiation process represented? Such questions, and more, open up the problems of bringing to critical consciousness the tensions that structure the relations between the specificities of each singular textual formation and the social and cultural fields out of which (racialized) subjects have been named and have also come to articulation. How these tensions are mediated directly implicates the language of subjectivities and the institutional frames that constitute those subjectivities as objects of knowledge.

The writer whose name displays an Asian Canadian identity — call it Chinese Canadian — and who writes a narrative of coming into subjective formation necessarily comes into contact with social and cultural expectations governing the limits of representation and reception. The point of negotiation, nonetheless, can offer up an occasion to provoke uncertainty and indeterminacy. This is especially the case in a Canadian liberal nation that sutures difference in the language of multiculturalism wherein difference is mandated according to prescribed ethnic allegiances.

The second textual scene I want to invoke to examine this process of negotiation is a heightened moment of meaning-making in Denise Chong's *The Concubine's Children*, a text that has been read as representative of Chinese Canadian history and identity formation. Its narrator, Denise, and the central figure in her text, her mother Winnie, journey to their ancestral origin, the small Chinese village of her grandfather, the man who purchased her grandmother as his concubine-wife. The trip performs a pivotal function in Denise's narrative in bringing to closure the broader pattern of Canadianization that has concerned her, but even as it does so it exposes a critically revealing contradiction at the heart of Chong's text.

The narrator has already told her readers that she has adopted an "omniscient" perspective in shaping her mother Winnie's story in order to retain "objectivity." The implication of such loaded terms is that her text can be — or needs to be — read through the codes of documentary "realism," and that her readers can assume that its details and conclusions are based on verisimilitude and reliable historical facts (ix–xii). On the other hand, in her capacity as both writer and daughter, she necessarily assumes the role of her mother's translator, taking the raw material of Winnie's life story and shaping it into a coherent social and aesthetic representation. But then again, these presuppositions are belied by her vested interests: as the signified "author" of *The Concubine's Children*, in writing her mother's life she also assumes responsibility for the narrative unfolding of her own subject formation. These textual conditions, in which the author is simultaneously an omniscient narrator—both a voice for her mother and an autobiographer—would suggest that, despite the use of historical data and her professed objectivity, the book performs a subjectivity in negotiation with the legacy of a Canadian racialization that shaped her family history. The discourse of omniscience and realism, offered to its readers, is less a means of making this text of a so-called Chinese Canadian and/or Asian Canadian representation more credible vis-à-vis mainstream modes of reception and codes of multiculturalism, though of course it may do that, too. Rather, it enables the textual efficacy of a narrative framework that depends on the terms Chinese and Canadian being interchangeable points of reference that function through a sleight-of-hand relationship with each other.

Chinese, often used in the text when such a naming of identity seems unnecessary, especially when an insider perspective is already explicit, exceeds referential stability to signal an unnamed tension. On the one hand, as the ostensible identity that grounds the book, it can be claimed as the matrix of the narrator's grandparents, her mother, and by extension herself, too; on the other, the historical and cultural distances the term Chinese opens in Canadian contexts allows the narrator to claim a Canadianness against which Chineseness can be measured — and finally transcended.

As we now turn to the scene in question, what is initially striking is the anthropological overtone that enters the narrative, particularly in the construction of a life movement forward in the journey from Canada to a small village in China as a movement "back" in both space and time. The trip is represented as a return to the past of the travellers who, given their Canadian perceptual positioning, envision the landscape, the village, and the villagers in terms of a primitivism from which they were rescued by virtue of their Canadian status. For Winnie, according to the narrator, the potential bitterness of discovering that so much precious money earned in Canada was sent to the village to fulfill her father's familial obligations is redressed once she recognizes that she was saved from social and economic hardships by having grown up in Canada:

> For Mother, who had lived her childhood in a shadow of sacrifice for the Chinese side of the family, her parents' act of immigration to the new world and her mother's determination in pregnancy to chance the journey by sea had been her liberation, the best gift of all. (286)

As Canadians, the narrator and Winnie form their own community of two in the Chinese village where living conditions are rudimentary and where their own allegiance to normative Canadian standards has them soon "hankering for our western ways." During the meal, the narrator even comments: "Mother and I shared a glance of disapproval at the sight of the fly struggling to pull itself free from the eyeball of a fish, and at our relatives spitting bones and refuse onto the floor at their feet" (284).

Earlier in the narrative, and as preparation for the China trip, the status of Canadianness as a privileged identity formation is confirmed in the narrator's evocation of a childhood memory. When forced to confront the racialization of her identity as Chinese, her mother gives her a strategy to mediate its effects and affects:

> Taunts chased us to school: "Chinky, Chinky Chinaman, sitting on a fence, making a dollar out of fifteen cents." At recess, children threw stone-laden snowballs in our direction; after school they waited in ambush to knock us off our bicycles. Mother's advice to feign deafness worked, and she and Father made it clear to other parents that they wouldn't put up with abuse. Acceptance and friendship soon followed, and we ourselves soon forgot that we were any different from our white playmates. (240)

"Forgot" is the word, resonant with ruffled edges, that stands out in the passage. What would have happened had the narrator not forgotten? Would she then not have been able to enter the sphere of the sameness occupied by her "white playmates"? The suggestion is that the entry into sameness depends on the act of forgetting the discourse of "yellow peril"—"Chinky, Chinky Chinaman"—and that the gift of this forgetting is the acceptance and friendship that followed in its wake. But then again, what would constitute the discourse of this friendship, this acceptance?

For mainstream Canadian readers, the apparently separate discursive sites of Chinese and Canadian in *The Concubine's Children* enable reading practices that do not disrupt the assumptions already sanctioned by multicultural formations. The textual transparency the terms perform has the effect of offering to readers simultaneously an exotic instance of otherness in their midst (of Canada, in this sense) and a narrative that mollifies (or otherwise muffles) the very racialization of Asian Canadian that continues to mark the boundaries of what is central and what is marginal. They are, moreover, led along the path of reassurance that redress for the Chinese Canadians who were subjected to severe exclusionary practices, such as the head tax and the Chinese Exclusion Act, was the gift of becoming Canadian. The subjects then become a model minority who are interpellated by a state-endorsed multiculturalism and not the victims of a history that produced the category Chinese as an alien other. To cite one of the cover blurbs, "*The Concubine's Children* is, above all, a moving portrait of a people for whom the ethos of family and home was so deeply ingrained that entire lifetimes were sacrificed to it." Who are these unnamed "people" but those who are not of the same? The language of the blurb contradicts the import of the narrative. Even while Winnie and her daughter Denise stake their claim to Canadianness as salvational, the commodification of their stories depends upon their otherness as members of "a people," the sign for the Chineseness that gives the book its social and market value.

This contradiction in the reception of *The Concubine's*

*Children* suggests that the narrator who professes to pass as a bona fide Canadian cannot, in fact, erase the marks of a Chineseness that precedes Canadian, just as her book, the material product of her subject formation, relies for its value on the structures of difference that frame the field of reception in which it arrives in its readers' hands. The force of this contradiction is therefore constitutive, surfacing in crucial moments to remind more critically engaged readers that assimilation cannot wash away all the marks of trauma and estrangement. Posing in front of a "new dim sum house" in Chinatown, for instance, many years after the family's move away from that site so intimately associated with Chineseness, the narrator is reminded by her mother of the continuing presence of "a broken end of a water pipe jutting out from a building." It is the same pipe "she had run into when playing jump rope as a child" and from which she received a "scar" (258). The narrator comments: "I thought to myself: 'Somebody ought to have fixed that pipe by now'" (258). Yes, someone "ought to have," but who? Her seemingly simple comment — the voice of a civic complaint — is a stark reminder that the past has not disappeared, but like the "broken pipe" can still wound unsuspecting children at play. When the narrator adds that her mother's sight of the pipe "was the first time in years that Mother had made mention of her past," the image functions to stir up her memories of a past that contained her internalization of its social conditions. The triggering effect of the image, in other words, reveals a darker side to the narrative that is left unexplored. The immigration process may have supposedly saved Winnie, but it has nonetheless left its marks on her body.

The discursive field of Canadian-made racialization, as the dramatic moments in *Chorus of Mushrooms* and *The Concubine's Children* show, always comes into play in tension with (and against) the otherness it produces to constitute the positive terms of its colonizing and nation-making formation. Both the coherence and stability of this formation depend very much on a constantly reiterated elision, often expressed as disavowal, of the fissures that both contain and call forth resistant as well as accommodating minority subjects, including Asian Canadian writers. These are subjects whose subjectivities, in the minute details of historical and social flows, embody the racialization concealed in the language of a Canadian liberal democracy that prides itself on values such as respect for individuality and equality.

It is within and against the now-you-see-it-now-you-don't historical legacy of racialization processes that Asian Canadian writers, either by choice or not, have come to public voice. Their encounters with Canada as a nation-state built on the externalization of its non-white subjects — most severely and violently in the case of its colonization and appropriation of Native lands — have never been free of ambivalent negotiations with the internal and internalized figure of the alien-Asian inside its body politic. Any claiming of Asian Canadian as a cultural framework, for this reason, is always entangled in contradictions that cannot simply be resolved, but instead call for tactics of response that are site-specific, provisional, and necessarily open to change as conditions and terminologies shift. Each move towards cultural resistance and transformation has also risked accommodation and compromised representations.

If we can think that the borderlines between white-Canada and Asia-China are externalized in *The Concubine's Children*, and hence stabilized by the discourse of difference that measures bodies according to race and gender codes and permits assimilation for those model minorities who learn to "forget," then in Fred Wah's *Diamond Grill* they come home to roost in the hyphenated condition of the performing writer. But it is not the hyphen of the idealized multicultural subject who can be known as a modified citizen, a Chinese-Canadian or a Japanese-Canadian, for instance. The teleology here is that once an alien-Asian has assumed a so-called Canadian identity, even then, or even so, the transparency is, at the same time, foreclosed.

Some of the implications of this process are invoked in a critical scene. The author of *Diamond Grill*, who ascribes the genre of "biotext" (ix) to his text, a term that calls attention to a writing process in which the autobiographical is textualized, finds himself standing in a public space just across the street from the King Restaurant. For him, the restaurant is a domain of ambivalence, with hints of trauma, a site in which he imagines beforehand an encounter with a Chineseness that has interpellated his subjectivity. The interpellation process, though, has occurred in such a way that he sees himself as a stranger—a misfit, even. Why? Because his patronymic, Wah, signifies in excess of the codes rendering his body socially transparent, conferring on him a kind of extraordinary consciousness of passing. This effect, one of the pure products of racialization itself, comes into play when the power of the visual appearance of the body contradicts the language of a prescribed identity formation. The signifier *Wah* is referenced as Chinese, making it a name inheriting what the writer, in controlled anger and play, carnivalizes as

> an Amor de Cosmos Pariah, a Celestial, a John A. Macdonald mongrel, an Onderdonk question mark, a Royal Commission cuckoo, an Asiatic Exclusion League problem, a huckster, a leper, a depraved opium ghoul, a pest, a wanton Cyprian, a Chinkie-Chinkie Chinaman, a nignog, an Ishmaelite, a cooley, a yellow belly — just another hungry ghost, just another last spike. (59)

But in his own body — in the apparent absence of colour in his skin — he can slide into whiteness.

The writer's acute awareness of being able to oscillate between visibility and invisibility, depending on the site-specific elements of his experience, prompts him to pause before the entrance. In that pause he finds himself drawn into an uneasy ethical quandary: he is attracted by the desire to consume Chinese food, which valorizes his links with his dead father, a figure who haunts the text; yet he finds himself also resisting an underlying guilt that tells him he should be loyal to a racialized lineage. It is here, in this place that is no place but a performance, that the writer is able to ruminate on the historical forces that brought him to this moment of indecision. "Physically," he says, "I'm racially transpicious and I've come to prefer that mode" (136). The word that immediately sticks out is "transpicious": neither "conspicuous" nor "inconspicuous," but the prefix "trans" (a crucial linguistic pivot in Wah's poetics) with "spicuous" forms a term for passing, a phenomenon the writer ties to his childhood:

> I want to be there but don't want to be seen being there. By the time I'm ten I'm only white. Until 1949 the only Chinese in my life are relatives and old men. Very few Chinese kids my age. After '49, when the Canadian government rescinds its Chinese Exclusion Act, a wave of young Chinese immigrate to Canada. (136)

While growing up, the writer maintained his invisibility by aligning himself with whiteness, even playing against Chinese Canadian kids in sporting events — "my buddies at school call them Chinks" (136). But the line "By the time I'm ten I'm only white" refuses to settle down. How is the phrase "only white" to be read, especially in a social realm where whiteness signifies transparency, and where being non-white provokes the easy shift from signifier ("Chink") to signified (a racialized body)? The qualifier "only" implies a lack, exposing "white" as itself a state of incompletion, a state that is not enough for him. It is as if the more of whiteness has produced less for him, coming as it does at the expense of his familial ties and a lineage that comes through his father, Fred Wah Sr. But the "only" also exposes his subjective distance from that lineage because his body enables him to pass. Despite the patronymic, his capacity to see through whiteness and not be seen through whiteness stirs an anxiety in him that his desire for the cultural specificities of "Chinese" cannot appease. For this reason, he tells his readers, he has had to devise a defensive strategy for navigating his way through "Chinese cafes and China-towns":

> Camouflaged enough so they know I'm there but can't see me, can't get to me. It's not safe. I need a clear coast for a getaway. Invisible. I don't know who I am in this territory and maybe don't want to. Yet I love to wander into Toronto's Chinatown and eat tofu and vegetables at my favourite barbecue joint and then meander indolently through the crowds listening to the tones and watching the dark eyes, the black hair. (136)

To see and not be seen is the fantasy of kids and voyeurs (and perhaps of tourists, too), but in the social codes that formed Wah as white until ten and then later as Chinese, the condition of the camouflaged subject calls forth a rec-ognition of the boundary zones marking the ethical limits of his consciousness of passing.

King's Restaurant is now run by Lawrence, the son of Shu, who was the cook in Wah Sr.'s Diamond Grill, the restaurant that provides the title for Wah Jr.'s book. Over-coming his hesitations, Wah Jr. decides to face the scene of ambivalence awaiting him, attracted as he is by the pull of family relationships and his hunger. By crossing the street and entering King's he then passes between the two zones that his subject formation has internalized as the site of the "hyphen," the space in between whiteness and Chinese that he says "always seems to demand negotiation" (137). Inside, while nervously remaining an outsider to Chinese as a language, he undergoes the familiar and familial ritual of talking about an extended family (with cousins he does not even know anything about), and of course he consumes the food he craves. "But then," he acknowledges,

> after we've exchanged our mutual family news and I've eaten a wonderful dish of tofu and vegetables, back outside, on the street, all my ambivalence gets covered over, camouflaged by a safety net of class and colourlessness — the racism within me that makes and consumes that neutral (white) version of myself, that allows me the sad privilege of being, in this white white world, not the target but the gun. (138)

The writer-subject of *Diamond Grill* holds a tenuous position as a mixed-race figure whose chameleon-like markings produce a subjectivity that oscillates between the minor and majority chords of social formations. His situation is especially telling because his imagination is an effect of that gap between the discursive production of the Asian/Chinese body and the visual codes attached to the Asianized body. As "Wah," he is identified as Chinese and as such inherits the legacy of "yellow peril" in the construction of a white, Anglo/European Canada, whereas his body as mixed lacks the visual signs that would fix him as Chinese (or Asian). This dichotomy between his name and his body has been the impetus for numerous moments of mis-identification — those very moments that expose the undercurrents of racialization and that, as a writer, he taps into with a kind of second sight. As he informs his readers:

The name's all I've had to work through. What I usually
get at a counter is the anticipatory pause after I spell out
H. Is that it? Double U AY AYCH? I thought it might be
*Waugh*. What kind of name is that, *Wah?* Chinese I say,
I'm part Chinese. And she says, boy you could sure fool
me. You don't look Chinese at all. (169)

The exposure — the lighting up of the social terrain and the
imprint on consciousness — performs the incommensurability of discourse and visuality that allows for or otherwise
necessitates a critical awareness of the unequal relations of
power embedded in signs of racialization. What position
does an "I" as metaphoric "gun" occupy when it both sites
and sights its "target"? What has the seen become when
it functions as the "end" of the desire for ownership that
copyrights the "I"? Is it then not a "sad privilege," from
the enclave of King's restaurant, to be the vehicle through
which otherness is made into an extension of the same?
But how, to think otherwise, can the racialized domain of
King's speak its singularities from its position as "target"
in a "white white" nation? And even if it did, what would
be visualized in its institutional re-dressing?

## THE CALL FOR CRITICAL READING PRACTICES

What is remarkable in Wah's text is the performance of the
position in between — for him the position of the hyphen —
which the powers of social normalization cover over. When
the writer enters the imagined community of King's Restaurant, he remains conscious of the privileges encoded on

his passing body. It is this awareness that foregrounds a relationship of complicity: the dominant subject situated at the normative centre of social and cultural formations in which a racialized/Asian minority is configured.

Institutional formations, themselves extensions of existing relations of power, can be seen to play out a homologous dynamic, as variously positioned readers interact with what are assumed to be Asian Canadian textual formations in order to produce critical representations that are tied to disciplinary values. Institutionally sanctioned reading practices in these formations are dependent on a reader who has the capacity — indeed is accorded the role — to enter the text to see through its representational frames, and who is thereby accorded the critical authority to construct interpretations that situate the texts within the constituted fields, such as those of nations, genres, periods, histories, and identities. Yet the positivism of such a model has not necessarily accounted for the effects of unequal relations of power and privilege that precede the event of reading to compromise its critical language. What often remains unaddressed is the instability of the reader as a site of a performance that is aligned with the very discourses constitutive of a field of knowledge. The reader, in other words, performs a double (or doubled) function: as the one whose subject formation translates the material conditions of the text into a representation and as the one who represents the position out of which the subject formation is itself enabled. In this compromised situation, the scene of reading Asian Canadian has the potential to become the "seen" of reading.

In this "seen," the referentiality of Asian Canadian, as embodied in diverse cultural works, may be limited by the social construction of the Asian figures who have been the constituted others of the Canadian nation and who, for this reason, always remain in tension between incorporation and externalization. The movement into the frameworks of disciplines such as CanLit changes both its valences and its values. The object of knowledge produced loses its singularity and takes on appearance through the already-established categories of literary studies. In this transaction the problematic representational displacements in a text such as *The Concubine's Children* may not be seen.

In such a field of reception, an unreflected critical practice may very well encounter an already-minoritized text as constituted by a lack that requires compensation through the production of positivist meanings. The substitution of the cultural, for instance, may provide an alibi for eliding the racialized effects of a text. Signs of difference can then be attributed to cultural elements, a character's Chineseness or Japaneseness or Asianness as explanatory codes that domesticate what is already construed as foreign. As the "interested" voice in Safeway exclaims to the narrator of *Chorus of Mushrooms* discovering a Japanese eggplant, "How wonderful! This is what our eggplants look like. They're so different!" (90). Such a translation into already-constituted critical discourses may then close down the capacity of Asian Canadian texts to perform a resistance with the potential to inject more radical alternatives into institutional frameworks. Incorporated as a component of disciplinary boundaries that reconstitute the text (in its own image?), the asymmetrical conditions of textual production become invisible. What is seen as Asian Canadian can then be categorized as an addition to CanLit, a kind of Asianized modification of Canadian through which cultural difference (or the multicultural) stands in for the racialized subject. In this process, the Asian Canadian subjects who created the works can subsequently be (re)produced in the language of specialization that is pressured to hold allegiance, not to the site-specific conflicts and contradictions of textual production, but to the authority of institutions — institutions that are themselves extensions of frameworks in which Asian continues to be a term of outsiderness.

Critical reading practices that are wary of institutional boundaries can help negotiate the tensions between the material nitty-grits of language and form that give a text the singularity of its power to see and the expectations of reception that shape the subjectivity of readers and thereby influence what gets to be seen. As the writer of *Diamond Grill* discovers, the limits of critical frameworks are influenced by the always shifting and shifty contexts of racialization processes. All of these, and more, come into play in the field of conceptual variables and patterns of non-equivalences that are the ingredients of literary and cultural representations. Reading for signs of Asian Canadian in such conditions should push for interventions that move against the grain of institutional practices — seeking instead to yield critical reading practices with the power to provoke crises of representation that challenge and transform our social and cultural relations with each other.

Being open to cultural difference entails the inherent risk of the radical transformation of the language and structures by which we recognize ourselves. We risk losing the vision of ourselves in the mirror of our cultural organizations and ministries. But perhaps the risk of being open to the views and sites of 'others' is the ethical origin of democracy.

**MONIKA KIN GAGNON + SCOTT TOGURI MCFARLANE,**
"The Capacity of Cultural Difference"

## *"Inside the Black Egg"*
### CULTURAL PRACTICE, CITIZENSHIP, AND
### BELONGING IN A GLOBALIZING CANADIAN NATION

In the nation-building agenda that underwrites so much of Canadian history, the cultural has been simultaneously the most visible and most invisible of processes. Its presence is often the most acute when presumably absent. This syndrome has complicated and compromised public discourses that have circumscribed the formation of the citizen as one who performs the power and the limits of the cultural. Here, I would like to approach the cultural as a matrix for the social imagination of embodied subjects. It assumes that these subjects engage in a never-ending process of making significations and being made by signifying systems in local sites of lived networks that fan outward and move inward to include national, transnational, and global interactions. From this standpoint, the cultural needs to be distinguished from culture as an achieved state to be possessed, commodified, or otherwise treated as a privileged container that subordinates individual agency to pre-emptive frames of already-constituted identities. Culture is more likely to be found in complicity with political and economic regimes in power, whereas the cultural, operating out of the material exigencies of daily lives, can be read as a variable complex of signs, unpredictable in the multiple affects generated in subjects who process them. I want to explore this speculation through a short story that works as a social parable. For me, Winston C. Kam's "Inside the Black Egg" can be read as a cultural performance that localizes the problems to be addressed before questions of belonging can be negotiated in critically informed ways.

## START WITH THE NATION AS A BLACK EGG

When the story begins, its loner protagonist, Stephen Shih, is cooking dinner. It is Christmas season in Toronto, a quintessential time for the nation. However, as he savours his Trinidadian meal "of curried chicken on rice, fried plantains, eddoes and cassava," his body — without warning — craves a taste his memory traces back to his origins. Unable to suppress his desire, Shih sets out on a quest through the ubiquitous "winter slush" of an urban space that has taken on a decidedly multicultural air, one that Stephen himself performs as he makes his way. He wants to acquire a "Chinese side dish" in the form of a "preserved egg," and so he mulls over "what kind of egg he might buy" (90).

As this inner drama unfolds, Stephen finds himself at one of numerous green grocers in his neighbourhood. It is at this precise moment that he overhears (in a kind of fatal attraction) "a white couple, middle-aged . . . looking completely out-of-place in Chinatown"; they are talking about the "black eggs" (aka "one-hundred-year-old eggs") talked about on a TV cooking show, the ones that the ethnic Chinese enjoy during *their* New Year (91). Torontonians on their own quest, they have adopted a touristic gaze in crossing the border into Chinatown. Unlike Stephen Shih, for whom the black egg signifies sameness, they seek an exotic commodity that signifies difference. What Stephen craves they want to purchase for its foreignness, in other words, for its multicultural difference from the norms that govern the perceptual frame of *their* city's Chinatown.

Unable to maintain his distance from this frame — after all, he understands English and genuinely wants to be helpful — Stephen quickly surmises that the elderly couple lack the cultural knowledge needed to distinguish between two kinds of eggs. On the one side are the eggs that are black on the outside but yellow inside; on the other are the eggs that are white on the outside but black inside. Stephen recognizes that they cannot tell the difference, even though ironically they are seeking difference. Becoming aware that the couple are on a quest for the latter, he kindly offers his assistance. Of course, a simple exchange of information could have occurred and they could have all gone their separate, merry ways. The trouble brews — and here the drama shifts to a more layered social register — once Stephen gets entangled in the framework of culture brought to bear on the scene by the couple. While only a moment before a private citizen savouring the thought of a "preserved egg," he has been transformed into the object of the liberal multiculturalism that Chinatown and Chineseness signify. For his part, ever resourceful and quick-minded, Stephen Shih cannot be contained and managed so easily. Instead, in his determination to help the couple, he dissolves the boundaries of the frame and produces a social anxiety that lights up the differential relations of governance in Canada as a racialized nation. All he does is open his mouth and make audible the slanted English of his "thick Caribbean accent": "'Oh Lord, lady, dem ain't de hundred-year-old eggs, yuh know!'" (91).

This close encounter of the cultural kind is also a social event, and it reveals the incoherence and irresolution of the plethora of mobile identity formations that implicate the nation as a performance. In these instances the power of difference is played out in multidimensional and conflicting scales that produce social anxieties; the lack of communicability clashes with representations that work to contain and manage the hierarchic structures producing the social relations of subjects. Let's leave Stephen Shih in his interventionist moment to broaden the scope of this outbreak of anxiety in the marketplace.

## LOCATE THE ANXIETY OF THE NATION, PLEASE

While this reading of "Inside the Black Egg" seeks to draw attention to the cultural practices of those who fall under the signs of difference and difference-making that have preoccupied the so-called liberal multicultural Canadian state, it also argues that these practices can function to render indeterminate, uncertain, and unpredictable its systems of order and administration. Contradicting the unquestioned assumption that all citizens are equal in this state, these practices come to visibility on the threshold of an ensemble of policies, discourses, and determinations that work to maintain the security and stability of the state and the nation-based identity formations that further these ends. At this juncture in its history, the Canadian state, in line with other capitalist-obsessed states in the global economy, is driven by its desire to situate itself as opportunely as possible in the multifaceted processes of economic globalization. These are processes that have brought into the cultural spaces of its citizens a pattern of anxieties—in a continuum, for instance, that brings into tension the relentless pressure of what John Agnew and Stuart Corbridge have called "market idolatry" (qtd. in Penrose 34) and the financialization of the private sphere, the runaway technologies of the producers of mass media, and of course the unprecedented commodification of everything including "life" itself in the discourse of biotechnology.

Cultural processes, moreover, are constrained in being embedded in further anxieties specific to Canadian circumstances. Although Canada has benefitted from the imperial and colonial scripts that have provided the templates for settler-society formations in North America, its troublesome contiguous relationship, first and foremost, remains with the US border, and behind this are the equally troublesome symbolic linkages to a valorized United Kingdom. Both in tandem have generated what I would call an alibi for not being accountable for its own actions. Cultural nationalists, for instance, have often fixated on Canada's apparent position of subordination to the extent that the Canadian state's own internal colonization has been glossed over. Yet, as itself a construct, Canada has been complicit with an originating dissimulation in which its evolution is read as an ordained unfolding. The violence of appropriation and territorialization that secured its ownership of spaces it did not own is mediated in the narrative of the nation as a progressive formation. Legitimacy derives from a liberal discourse of rights and citizenship based on the overarching notion of property rights with its sacrosanct relationship to the liberal "I" of its citizens.[1] From a broader historical perspective, the making of the Canadian nation-state is not a unique phenomenon. Its colonial moment, a part of British expansionism, remains another example of the ascendancy of nation-states in the west from the seventeenth century on. As Stephen Castles and Alastair Davidson point out in *Citizenship and Migration*, "Colonialism was crucial to the emerging nation-states: exploiting the natural resources and the labour power of dominated peoples made industrialization possible" (3). This exploitation rested on a "dialectic of progress and violence," which, in turn, accounts for the "ambivalences inherent in the nation-state model" (3). The ostensible "progress" that served the interests of modernization, in other words, relied on the "violence" of exploitation through which the others of the nation-state were both constructed and incorporated as a constitutive outside.

In specifically Canadian terms, the founding moment out of which the state derived the parameters of its potential identities over time was enabled in the very discourse through which it had become itself. Tellingly, the language of the constituting document, the 1867 British North America Act, produced "Canada" in a declaratory act, as we read in section 4, "the Name Canada shall be taken to mean Canada as constituted under this Act." Once constituted, this "Canada" covered over the violence of its origins by naturalizing itself as a nation whose properties could be inhabited through the institution of a settler-society and appropriated as the material basis for its cultural representations. This is evident from the outset in the most tangible of all means — the direct act of naming (or more precisely, renaming) the lands taken from the indigenous or native collectives that were already there (or more precisely, here). In the colonial forgetting of the violence of arrival, these collectives were also re-identified, as "Indians." And they were declared not to have legitimate ownership of the lands in order that the nation could be deemed to have started with *terra nullius,* an "empty land." Patrick Macklem, in *Indigenous Difference and the Constitution of Canada,* explains the historical dimensions of this fiction of ownership:

> During the period of initial European contact and colonial expansion in North America, it was accepted practice among European nations that the first to discover vacant land acquired sovereignty over that land to the exclusion of other potential discoverers. With populated land, sovereignty was acquired by the discovering nation not by simple settlement, but by conquest and cession, but such land could be deemed vacant if its inhabitants were insufficiently Christian or civilized. International

law subsequently deemed North America to be vacant, and regarded the acquisition of territorial sovereignty by European powers as occurring through the mere act of discovery and settlement. (91)

It was this "vacant" land that was anthropomorphically remade as an animate presence — "Not written on by history, empty as paper" in the words of modernist poet F.R. Scott in his poem "Laurentian Shield" (58) — and it is perceived as waiting for the cultural imagination of the settler-colonist "I" to language it into existence. Much of the thrust of nationalist Canadian literature owes its impetus to this narrative of conquest and settlement that appropriates the nativization process to acculturate the lands taken. This complexity explains what Scott McFarlane has identified as "the haunt of race" (18) in Canada. There persists an acute anxiety — often ready to explode in reactionary gestures — that the making of a (white) liberal nation cannot ameliorate the violence of its origins in colonial racialization. In the continual production of this nation, or as a consequence of the internal contradictions in its history, the violence is constantly sublimated through shifting mechanisms of management and control.

It is out of this matrix that the category of *citizen* has issued and been accorded a privileged status in the shaping of the Canadian nation-state. As a prime signifier, citizen connotes both inclusion (or belonging) and rights (primarily the right to vote, to hold public office, and to own property). For the first hundred years of its history, the rights of citizenship and the ability to become a citizen were systematically guarded to protect the authority of its ruling group (white male, English and European identified) at the expense of women and those racialized in relation to an ascribed otherness. And when the latter were incorporated into the nation's body, they could do so only through the shadows of difference—shadows that marked their distance from a normative whiteness. Such subjects came to be positioned and came to position themselves as racialized minorities (aka "visible minorities," in the Canadian state's language).

A "minority," in this instance, is not an identity in the strict sense of the term. It is, instead, a complex manifestation of a double-edged cultural condition: on the one hand, the effect of a naming through state-endorsed constructions of difference, and on the other, the demarcation out of which the individuals and groups who have been identified as such have produced affects. This condition— "minority" as both effect and affect—has made it difficult to see the ideological seams that suture the two in often-irresolvable contradictions. David Lloyd has pointed out that the distinction between "ethnic subject" and "minority" status has created a specific kind of doubled tension in the "writings of minority intellectuals," and I would also include the work of writers and artists, especially in Canadian contexts. As Lloyd argues, they position themselves

> around the relation of the minority subject to the ethnic community and in the long-standing political problem of articulating the bases for solidarity between distinct groups while respecting the specificity of their own

"Inside the Black Egg"

histories and projects. Both kinds of tension are the source of painful affects and political difficulty, but exactly in so far as they derive from contradictory formations have the capacity to become the ground for a far-reaching critique of the state formation itself. (221)

Produced by the nation-state, "minority" subjects, in discursive terms, at least, are ostensibly situated on its social and cultural margins, but this spatial fiction, reifying as it does a centre-margin binary, belies their more internal connections to the nation's identity as the constituting difference through which the same—the coherence of "the people" as unified—is enabled. In what is perhaps more appropriate terms, these marked subjects come to appearance in the interstitial sites of its body politic.

## MEANWHILE, BACK TO STEPHEN SHIH

When we circle back to Stephen Shih's dilemma, we see that he has been drawn into a social confrontation at the grocery store. In this scene, he performs a doubled space in which he both acts as a social agent and is acted on as a racialized minority through the gaze of the white couple. But revealingly, as they themselves enter what is for them the marginal space of Chinatown — where their reach exceeds their grasp — they are confronted with an otherness they cannot process according to their multicultural assumptions. Stephen initially destabilizes them in not speaking the requisite broken English of those with the mandatory Chinese identity. For his part, Stephen acts as a "good" citizen. He empathizes with the couple's ignorance, even taking time to explain the distinction between the two types of quite different eggs. In the liminal space of their encounter, he thus takes on the role of both native informant, in a parody of the anthropological transaction common to colonial encounters, and of the liberal subject of the nation who conveys "cross-cultural" knowledge to fellow citizens. From this pedagogical vantage point, he offers a contradiction that can educate them on the limits of their social frameworks. What you see is what you do not get. The "black egg" they desire, the one seen on TV, is white on the outside and black inside.

Say what? The couple, apparently in control of their shopping when they arrived at the grocery store, are suddenly asked not to trust the logic of empirical evidence, the same logic, incidentally, that has scripted social subjects like Stephen Shih in the racialized codes of skin colour. Who the social heck is this strange figure? So when Stephen is asked by the woman why he does not speak Chinese to the Chinese grocer and he confesses that he cannot speak the language, she sounds relieved: "'Ah! I see. Well now.' She turns to her husband. 'That explains it. I dare say it makes our task easier'" (92). But what does she see? And what does she not see? And what is the "it" she refers to?

While the couple scramble to fit their ignorance to their assumptions, the scene of cultural encounter intensifies, with more humour, of course, through the intervention of the grocer who does speak in the requisite broken English. Are these the black eggs? "'Yes, brack. You tly'" (92). The kicker, though, is that the grocer reacts to poor Stephen as an other, recognizing in his alien accent that he is not performing a normal Chinese Canadian ethnocultural identity. This intersubjective gap between them, the splitting of difference in the social seams, remains completely invisible to the white couple. They cannot see "it" because of their own struggle to maintain the frame of a homogenized minority group — members of a "visible minority," a term in the discourse of multiculturalism through which, as Himani Bannerji has written in *The Dark Side of the Nation*, "peoples from many histories, languages, cultures and politics are reduced to a distilled abstraction" (111), out of which various "appellations follow suit — immigrants, ethnics, new Canadians and so on" (121).

The unfolding exchange at the grocery store in Chinatown captures the material conditions of identity production in a heterogeneous nation such as Canada — a scene of misrecognition and misrepresentation, of contradiction and incommensurability. The middle-aged couple find themselves caught between two overdetermined social frames, both of which they have brought (as ideological baggage) to the scene and see enacted there, but which clash to generate anxiety in and around them. Should they believe the ethnicized/racialized grocer in their multicultural imaginary, who cannot understand the nuances of English but who has identified the empirical black egg as the object of their quest? Or should they believe the equally ethnicized/racialized, but for them abnormal customer, who seems to understand them but speaks with an unrecognizable accent and who cannot even speak Chinese? Before they can make a decision based on some serious ratiocination, the drama erupts in a verbal cacophony between Stephen and the grocer:

> "That no brack. This is." The clerk held up the salted egg with its black coating.
>
> "No."
>
> "Yes."
>
> "No."
>
> "Yes."
>
> "Inside. Inside not brack . . . I mean black!" Stephen shouted excitedly.
>
> "Is brack egg."
>
> "Outside, yes." Stephen desperately tried to explain. "Buh not inside. Inside! You unnerstan'? Inside? Dese people interested on'y inside. Not outside. You see on'y outside. Not inside. They wan' inside." (93)

Immediately after this rapid-fire interchange, Stephen actually demonstrates his knowledge by purchasing the two different eggs and cutting them in half to show the couple precisely what he is saying. But the conversation ends abruptly. The grocer walks away thinking Stephen may be "a little tetched" (93), and the middle-aged couple hurry away, "but not before throwing him chilly glances as they disappeared into the crowds." Stephen goes elsewhere to buy his eggs. Later, back in his apartment, he remains puzzled by the couple's reactions to his offer of knowledge. He wonders why they did not "acknowledge that they had almost made a mistake. That's the proper way of doing things, isn't it? Especially here in Canada where people like to get to the core of things. Hadn't he done just that? Gotten to the very core?" (94).

Well, yes and no. Yes, Stephen's gesture did set off a train of events that got all of them to the "very core" of the Canadian nation, but no, getting to the "core of things" is not the way things are done "here in Canada." Between this yes and no, though, there emerges those interstitial spaces where the destabilization of norms suggests the translation of difference into alternative configurations. A playful sign of such a state, perhaps the effect of strangeness to the couple who inhabit a state-inflected multicultural imaginary, is a whiff of a new cultural lingo emerging, as the narrator seductively says, "The muffled sounds of 'Jingle Bells' in Cantonese came from a passing car" (92).

## THE TIMELY ARRIVAL OF THE MULTICULTURAL

As a shorthand means of locating the destabilized cultural contexts "inside the black egg," we need to be reminded of the critical intersecting scenes of nation-making that coalesced in the brief period from the mid-1960s to the early 1970s, a period that may very well have been formative for both Stephen Shih and the middle-aged couple in the story. It was a period when the dominant power of Anglo-conformity, more or less secure from Confederation on, began to waver, generating a narrative of a "crisis" of nationhood. In this crisis, the nation was seen to be caught in a moment of transition from an (old) colonial to a (new) national identity, necessitating the formation of the Bilingualism and Biculturalism (B&B) Commission to determine new policies to protect the legitimacy of the nation's founding groups, the English and the French.

Most revealing in the cultural politics that characterized Canadian public life during this period was the obfuscation of culture as both real and unreal, both substantial and insubstantial, in relation to the heightened status given to citizenship—the rights, responsibilities, and privileges that were supposedly available equally to all Canadians. But as the framers of the bilingualism policy that became official at the time knew well, language remains fundamental to the integrity of culture. According to Richard Day, the members of the B&B Commission recognized clearly "the links between language and culture," noting that the Commission "concluded that 'the vitality of the language is a necessary condition for the complete preservation of a culture', and that 'the life of the two Founding cultures implies in principle the life of the two languages'" (182). The same links were denied to those who were not part of the two founding groups. By protecting the language rights of the English and French, privileging them as the founders of the nation, everyone else is relegated to positions in what was aptly identified as "the others," for whom a new policy would be established.

The multiculturalism policy of 1971 would declare that Canada did not have an official culture, but only a multiplicity of "cultures," and that these "cultures," which supplement the identities of individuals from non-founding groups, are a private matter. In other words, the others were told that, for them, language and origin are not important for their ethnic identities. What mattered was their private membership in an ethnocultural group. Indeed, so the logic of the policy went, the same components constitutive of the identities of the two founding groups could be a hindrance for them. How so? Here is a snippet from Prime Minister Trudeau's statement from October 8, 1971:

> The individual's freedom would be hampered if he were locked for life within a particular cultural compartment by the accident of birth or language . . . In conclusion, I wish to emphasize the view of the government that a policy of multiculturalism within a bilingual framework is basically the conscious support of individual freedom of choice. We are free to be ourselves. (qtd. in Fleras and Elliott 281, 283)

The liberalization process promoted by Trudeau denies the give and take of cultural processes, including conflicts and contradictions, as a source of the nation's values. Culture, even in its supposed pluralized form as the fabric of multiculturalism, remains aligned with ethnicity as something that is non-essential, what one chooses for purely private reasons, and therefore of secondary value to the more crucial status of the individual as citizen. As this notion of culture disappears as integral to the nation, the cultural values inherent in the (official) languages — and thus of the founding groups — resume the position of the norm.

I came to social consciousness in the nation described above. Variously designated as "of the Japanese race,"

"Jap," "Japanese," "Asiatic," "Asian," "Japanese Canadian,"
"Canadian of Japanese Ancestry," "racial minority," and
"visible minority," like so many not-whites who were born
into the nation, the social "I" that I performed functioned
as a kind of labyrinth of qualifications and descriptors
for bodies marked by difference. The social and cultural
transformations that would complicate the boundaries of
my subjectivity, and would as well enable the appearance
of a figure such as Stephen Shih in Toronto's urban landscape, were triggered, at least in part, by the points system
for immigration. Once the more explicit racist barriers
were lifted, immigration from various Asian countries, for
instance, from Taiwan, China, Hong Kong, India, and the
Philippines, which had been negligible up to then, increased
dramatically in the decades to come. During the period
from 1946 to 1955, as charted by Peter S. Li in *Destination
Canada: Immigration Debates and Issues*, of the total number
of immigrants admitted (1,222,319), 87.1 percent were from
Europe (including Britain) and only 2.2 percent were from
Asia; during the period from 1968 to 1970, immigration
from Asia made up 21.1 percent of the total; but from 1979
to 2000, the percentage jumped to 53.8 percent of the total
admitted (3,794,009). In total, then, 2,039, 479 people came
from Asian regions, the largest number settling in large
urban centres such as Vancouver and Toronto. According
to Li's figures, "42 per cent of Canada's 3.2 million visible
minority members resided in Toronto [in 1996], and they
accounted for 32 per cent of Toronto's population. Visible
minority members also made up 31 per cent of Vancouver's
population in 1996" (36).

This large-scale demographic shift has led to the perception, especially by Anglo- and Euro-Canadians, that the "Canada" they had known has been destroyed by these new others who were less assimilative and more insistent on the recognition of their own ethnic histories and values. But in reality the transformations are far more complex, motivated as they are through a confluence of both internal and external pressures. As the nation shaped through the liberalizing discourses of the 1960s unravelled (as it has done) in the arrival of the neoliberal discourses of globalization and all it brought in its wake, the culture that once was the desire of state policies has been retooled to accommodate new expectations. In place of a highly state-constructed national identity are the signs of another Canada coming to visibility. This one is configured in the global networks of a corporate commodity culture in which representations of difference take on value as a supplement to economics. Culture, then, abstracts itself from the cultural as the performance of the nation. Even the political system is abstracted from the materiality of the quotidian lives of its citizens. In turn, they are rearticulated in the language of consumerism.

It is this kind of complicated notion of the citizen as consumer, which seems to replace the older notion of the citizen as a free-thinking liberal subject, that makes me uneasy with liberal theorists of multicultural citizenship, such as, for instance, Will Kymlicka in *Multicultural Citizenship*. Although his reconceptualization of the liberal state to incorporate what he calls "differential citizenship" is understandable, given the so-called ethnic make-up of its citizenry, the integrationist model that he proposes still raises questions: integration into what? Under what conditions? The ethnic subject who is drawn in enters the system as one already marked as a minority whose visibility is determined by the representational schemata that preceded him. The problem he signifies, then, has been produced by the same system that apparently enables him to overcome it. His difference, on the surface, is seemingly accommodated (Kymlicka provides the example of the Sikh wearing the turban in the RCMP), but his difference is also constituted in relation to the unmarked centre that is the space of the same. In this system the differential relations of power remain more or less intact. According to Kymlicka, however, the system is strengthened because the minority subject who is given the space is glad to belong. Kymlicka's "differential citizenship" assumes that a liberal political system can accommodate ethnocultural identities because its dominant forms are not undermined: "Most polyethnic rights . . . take the authority of the larger polity for granted. They assume that immigrants will work within the economic and political institutions of the larger society, but that these institutions must be adapted to reflect the increasing cultural diversity of the population they serve" (181). This view is a familiar one, and while, of course, no one would want to discourage policies that might ease the burden of representation placed on minority shoulders, the violence of naming is reinforced rather than ameliorated. In return for the recognition of their "cultural diversity," these ethnics — who also go under the name of immigrants — are expected to work in tandem with mainstream institutions of the "larger society" (read: the dominant groups in power).

Coming from a position that sees more of the same in such a model, Smaro Kamboureli, in *Scandalous Bodies: Diasporic Literature in English Canada*, comes up with the challenging critical term "sedative politics." She offers a necessary critique of Canadian multiculturalism as an ideology that lulls citizens into states of complacency and complicity. In the fantasy that the liberal nation welcomes "cultural diversity," the legacies of trauma, racialization, and containment visited upon its marked subjects—its scandalous bodies within—are rendered inarticulate and invisible. Kamboureli proposes a critique of the liberal accommodational approach to the politics of difference: "The goal . . . is not to construct a reality of comfort, but rather to view comfortable positions with suspicion . . . not to capitalize on the currency of diversity, which would amount to fetishizing minoritanian identity, but to resist designing boundaries that would discipline diversity and to reconsider the overdetermined value assigned to it" (130).

## STEPHEN SHIH TO THE RESCUE, AGAIN

Kam's story ends with Stephen Shih reflecting on, but not resolving, what had happened to him in the mundane encounter: "And for days, then weeks, the ineffability of it all troubled him, and because it went unresolved he began to believe that, perhaps, he was the fool. An old fool at that" (94). Unable to figure out how to read the event, Stephen begins to internalize its "ineffability" and assume the burden of blame for the effects of miscommunication, even though, as readers well know, he had spoken the "truth" of the black egg. He even begins to think of himself as an "old fool" for assuming he could assist the couple. The lack of receptivity — that is, the lack of social ears to recognize the specificity of his discourse — continues to haunt him long after the event has passed into history. I am taken by the unresolved condition of Shih's ponderings, a condition of affect that is all too often lost in critical efforts to understand the knots of identity-making in nation-state formations such as Canada. While holding this condition in suspension, I would add that the obsessive drive towards a resolved state, what Richard Day describes as the "fantasy of unity which underlies both the problem of diversity and its solution" (4), has restricted the social imagination of subjects whose lives are always in excess of the boundaries of governance and policy.

From his own subject positioning, Stephen, who had simply dropped by to satisfy his private craving, has been initiated into a profoundly disturbing public event. One might say that he has encountered the live contradictions that constitute the seams of an internalized Canadian nation-state but which gain their efficacy through a process of erasure. How, then, to begin working out the critical terms to read these contradictions? The story ends with the protagonist in an intellectual quandary trying to un-riddle what he has just gone through. Occupying its interstices, or what Fred Wah in *Diamond Grill* exposes as the fraught zones of the "noisy hyphen" (176) in the nation, he is a figure who does not fit the normalized ethnic subject in the framework of a dominant multicultural ideology; rather, in his actions, he performs the material conditions of cultural difference in the making. The distances separating him from the couple bespeak the incoherence suturing the relations that differentiate social subjects in specific Canadian locations.

To take the specific to the level of critical reflection, we can turn to Aihwa Ong's proposal that the term "cultural citizenship" refers to "the cultural practices and beliefs produced out of negotiating the often ambivalent and contested relations with the state and its hegemonic forms that establish the criteria of belonging within a national population and territory" (264). The negotiation process is never one-dimensional but operates at several registers simultaneously, more often than not in hierarchic relations that remain largely invisible as such. The critical challenge for those of us who look towards more inclusive forms of cultural belonging is to make these relations visible through critical methods that can account for these different registers without resolving them into a foreordained unity.

## WHITHER THE NATION²

When seen through the lens of capital expansion, the now-dominant language of globalization raises the possibility of an increasing homogenization of cultural forms, particularly as these forms come to service the ever-proliferating powers of commodity production and consumption. In this scene, the earlier politics of difference that caused such havoc in the sociocultural spheres of the nation-state in the 1970s and 1980s is retooled in the faces of an ethnicity that is all the more appealing as a performance of commodity acquisition and/or consumption. The danger in all of this is that the cultural can become merely an adjunct of capital production, and not a medium of resistance to its reductive values whereby human exchange and representation are measured according to market conditions and expectations. The critical potential of cultural performance, then, is absorbed in the logic of profitability and loses its function as the practice of a cultural critique.

I was made aware of this danger while attending the 2003 Minister's Conference on Cultural Diversity in Ottawa. This state-sponsored event was costly (rumoured to have a budget of over $2 million), dressed up in all the glittering signs of celebration rather than serious introspection on cultural problems. Numerous cultural events were inserted between presentations and discussion sessions, featuring writers and musicians from so-called "diverse cultures" (the government's euphemism for racialized groups). All of these events were carefully choreographed to move the participants swiftly through the packed agenda. This conference was portrayed as the culminating "consultation" session in a series that was intended to assist the government to formulate policies that would transform Canada into a model nation of "cultural diversity."

I had no more than anecdotal knowledge of the behind-the-scenes processes leading up to the conference, but I was struck both by the familiarity and the incongruity of the framing language. The terminology that had defined the liberal multiculturalism of the postwar era, especially in the period between the early 1960s and 1988, the year the Multiculturalism Act was passed, was the medium of representation. Government voices, including two ministers, Sheila Copps of Canadian Heritage and Jean Augustine of Multiculturalism and the Status of Women, affirmed diversity and expressed pride in Canadian ethnocultural identities. There was also talk of building a more humane country based on disseminating "stories" reflecting the diverse backgrounds of the citizens, and so on. But the incongruity became evident in the distance of this language from the material conditions of the everyday lives of Canadian citizens in their continuing struggles against racialization, poverty, classism, and the continuing exclusion of many disadvantaged citizens from the dominant cultural institutions of the nation. With no effective mechanism provided for recommendations and accountability, the discussions produced more anxiety than hope. In the end, the conference, while having some entertainment value for the participants, did not allow for the more urgent tensions to emerge between the pedagogical drive of the government to manage its people and the conflicted and layered cultural desires of its citizens.

This conference did demonstrate, however, that culture has always had a political function in the hands of the state. The appropriation of culture to serve economic (rather than social and nation-based) ends is evident in the government's discourse in its publications. For instance, on the website of the Department of Canadian Heritage, the policy on cultural diversity is tied to marketplace values — in contrast to the use of culture as a realm separable from economics in the nation-building strategies of the postwar years. In one of the Department's sites, "Frequently Asked Questions: The International Cultural Diversity Agenda and a New International Instrument on Cultural Diversity," readers are told that their government's policy on cultural diversity has the following objectives:

- ensuring a place for Canadian stories in the domestic and global marketplaces;

- supporting business and investment opportunities while ensuring consumer choice and a diversity of voices and opinions; and

- providing Canadian creators and entrepreneurs with the skills they need to be successful both at home and abroad.

*     *     *

In a critical examination of the recent history of the nation-state from the Cold War era to the era of globalization, from "then" to "now," Barbara Godard posits

> a shift from a concern with establishing sovereignty over a physical space through communication technology to securing the symbolic space of the nation in formation through a government apparatus of culture and, more recently, to securing the global markets for the export of Canada's "knowledge industries." The shift in cultural values and national definition is not the consequence of some essential economic rationality but the effect of political strategies that aim to restructure the social and

political dimensions of capital so as to ensure the continual reproduction of the Canadian state. Such 'structural
readjustments' have profound implications for literature
and for literary criticism in Canada in both material and
formal terms. (214)

Godard's analysis of the effects of corporate capitalism
on literary studies in Canada calls for critiques of a state-
endorsed culture that threatens to cover over its attachment
to mechanisms of management and power.

In the midst of a massive drive to capitalize culture,
the challenges to cultural creators who remain committed
to the critical potential of democratic processes have been
enormous. Who can resist the lure of commodification? Of
significant capital gains for products that can achieve global
circulation? Of global/capital spaces in which diversity
signifies a consumerist understanding of cultural difference? Or where difference has been reduced to the food we
eat, the clothing we wear, and the media we absorb? Such
speculative questions bring us into the arena of globalized
culture.

Despite the announcement by many cultural theorists that globalization has grown at the expense of the
declining power of the state to govern its real and symbolic borders, it seems more accurate to see the relations
between them as more porous and complicit. The category
of culture, which serviced a particular mode of nationalism in the Cold War era, can be remade to become an
instrument of economic expansion and a means to enter
the global network of mobile capital and the production of

commodities. As a mode of intervention, we are called to rethink the cultural practices that have issued from creative sites of critique, particularly from the work of so-called minority artists and writers, such as Winston C. Kam's "Inside the Black Egg."

How voice the silent dash? Say blindfold, hinge, thorn, spike, rope, slash. Tight as a knot in binder-twine. Faint hope. Legally bound (not just the feet), "Exclusion Act," head tax, railway car to an internment camp, non-status outskirts of town nomad other side of tracks no track. Mi-nus mark, not equal sign. A shadow, a fragile particle of ash, a residue of ghost bone down the creek without abridge for the elusive unacknowledged "im" of migratory tongue some cheek to trespass kick the gate the door the either/or, the lottery and the laundry mark, the double mirror, the link between. How float this sign, this agent of the stand-in. Caboose it loose and let it go, it's "Not in Service" anymore.

**FRED WAH**, "Hy (briti) Tea," *Faking It* (94–95)

## A Poetics of the Hyphen
### FRED WAH, ASIAN CANADIAN, AND
### CRITICAL METHODOLOGY

## ASIAN CANADIAN FORMATIONS

If we were to begin by saying that the creative writing of Fred Wah is "where we're at," how would we set out the terms of the present implicated? There are always potential barbs in the discourses that are invoked to explain or otherwise account for the regulation of social and cultural formations that determine the limits of bodies moving through its networks. In the passage cited on the previous page, Wah offers up a sort of inventory of Asian Canadian bodies, and more specifically Chinese and Japanese Canadian bodies, that have been managed and contained by state-ordained histories of othering (the alien-Asian), exclusionary immigration polices, and internment. Though hardly a consolation, more a necessity, the Asian Canadian "silent dash" operates as a sign that embodies subjects who

**145**

have been produced as the outsiders in the interstices of the nation—and who the state has used not only to exploit their labouring bodies but also to legitimize a ruling regime of whiteness. These subjects, in turn, accrue a public presence as voices that emerge through processes of endurance, resistance, critique, and creativity. This particular Asian Canadian writer, Wah, sets out to undo the fixity of that sign and to "float" it, so that its mobility will be able to circumvent or otherwise exceed the political and linguistic categories that have cordoned him off in their alienated spaces within the nation. As Wah sets out on a textual journey, he announces to his readers that the sign—perhaps of his racialized body as well as his racialized subjectivity— is no longer in service to the social formations that marked the framework of its troubled history. But then again, he issues a declaration that in letting the "caboose . . . loose" in his train of thought, his writing will take on new energies and possibilities.

The kind of liberation from a history of sustained racialization for Asian Canadian subjects that is the intent of Wah's work—and to which I will return—raises questions before the present that critical thinkers, particularly those in institutions that produce interpretations of Asian Canadian literature, including Wah's own provocative text, *Diamond Grill*, need to acknowledge and address, especially since these institutions are themselves entangled in the effects of the state language historically used to restrict the rights and movements of Asian Canadians. In attempting to figure out "where we're at" in the critical methods we apply to Asian Canadian textual formations, we may find ourselves in the thrall of critical language that cannot catch up to the loose caboose in Wah's writing. For those who may have been educated to think that academic studies constitute a kind of trans-conditional sphere of research objectivity, if we remain open to the mobility of creative texts, our readings may very well undermine the assumed stability of knowledge formations. In doing so, they may offer up critical methods that refuse the language of appropriation and containment familiar to disciplinary models and provoke crucial questions around relations of power and representation in our interpretive methods.

Consider here an anecdote the writer of *Diamond Grill* presents about his Chinese Canadian father's dicey and troublesome negotiations with the English language, a language with its roots in the very British imperialist legacy that has marked Fred Sr. as Chinese/Asian, even though he is part British himself. Being incorporated into the dominant business society of his community, the Lions Club, he is required to give a banquet speech. But in the performance of his speech, sure enough, he falters in pronouncing the simple word *soup*, which he calls "sloup," exposing the common difficulty native Chinese speakers have with the "l" in English. In missing the mark in his speech performance, he opens a yawning gap between himself and his all-white audience. Instead of capitulating to the embarrassing moment in front of his so-called peers, he quickly improvises a linguistic means of transforming his mistake into a joke, as his writer-son explains:

he does what he has learned to do so well in such instances, he turns it into a joke, a kind of self put-down that he knows these white guys like to hear: he bluffs that China-men call soup *sloup* because, as you all know, the Chinese make their cafe soup from the slop water they wash their underwear and socks in, and besides, it's just like when you hear me eating my soup, Chinamen like to slurp and make a lot of noise. That's a compliment to the cook! (66)

This on-the-spot recuperation — through a bluff — of what could have been a devastating event depends on the quick mind of Wah Sr., who is so adept in the English language he has adopted that he creates a hybrid word out of a combination of *soup*, *slop*, and *slurp*, in effect resorting to a sophisticated use of a portmanteau form to translate his slip into a creative performance of *sloup*. Here, then, is a methodological model for Wah Jr., a witness to this agility of intellect. What does he take away from his father's quick mindedness?

So he fakes it, and I guess I pick up on that sense of faking it from him, that English can be faked. But I quickly learn that when you fake language you see, as well, how everything else is fake. (66)

When Wah Jr. published his critical essays, he titled his book *Faking It*, perhaps a reminder to his readers, many of whom would be affiliated with institutions where *Diamond Grill* is studied as an example of both Asian Canadian and Canadian literature, that the terminology of literary interpretation is also another form of faking it.

Before we jump up and down in exasperation at Wah for using such a loaded term for both language and "every thing else," we need to consider its implications. He is not simply being cynical and calling everything a sham, but instead is calling into question essentialist approaches to language and form. The underlying assumption is that values, meanings, and methodologies are provisional formations, which depend on a complex of uncertain and unpredictable contingencies that are as immediate as the local and as variable as transnational and global flows. Some years back, Pierre Bourdieu commented that "there are no longer any innocent words" (40); language is heavily invested with the power-suffused networks of production and consumption that mark both the intimate and broader currents of our lives. Here I agree with Smaro Kamboureli's understanding of the trope of faking it as enacting a "blurring of disciplinary knowledge and formal disjunctions." Such an effect, she writes, initiates "a coming into words and a field of action that may otherwise be foreclosed, a potentiality of entering a site of critical junctures where the writing generated by this encounter at once speaks of influence — influence as both continuity and departure — and of the critique of history, an intervention into the present cultural moment, in other words, a critical gesture that allows someone like Wah a point of entry into culture" ("Faking It" 115). This critical gesture, in turn, enables us, Wah's readers, to comprehend how crucial an awareness of interpretive limits has become in shaping the intellectual sites of our research and writing. No point in the trajectories of our scholarship is free from the ensemble of forces and conditions that influence, in specific ways, our formation as social and historically situated beings.

A Poetics of the Hyphen

This speculation around fakeness in Wah's writing takes us to the always-slippery nitty-gritty question of what constitutes critical agency, especially if we can no longer continue with our work as "business as usual." Once we attempt to account for elements of confluence in the forces shaping our critical methods, the importance of critical pedagogy takes on more urgency. In saying this, I suggest that the term *pedagogy* be approached as broader than the institutional confines of our teaching and research, and that it encompass a movement back and forth between the confines and the contingencies of local/global networks — or the elements of "glocalization" [1] — that cannot be grasped in their totality. The event of reading cultural texts, in the classroom and in our studies, brings into play a vast complex of interrelationships that incorporate, close by, the biological and social semiology of our living bodies in specific time and space, but fan out to interact with the local, national, and global conditions of all the material and symbolic values attached to the reception, containment, and interpretation of the diverse range of cultural productions.

It is because of our inability to totalize without, in effect, closing off contingencies that we need more than ever to understand the specific boundaries making possible what we know and therefore to leave open the spaces of elsewhere to what we know. Working in the midst of the social and cultural formations that produce indeterminacy and uncertainty in our positioning vis-à-vis a desire to engage in progressive scholarship, the epistemological and social implications of pedagogy have moved directly into the foreground of our work as academics who are also social subjects. Disciplinary positioning and declarations of neutrality and objectivity are no longer—and never really were—a guarantee that the effects of our research will not feed into hierarchic relations of power. Attention to the pedagogical scene of our practices would help us account for the contingencies of our own location(s)—whether in the classroom, in our research and writing, or in our social and cultural relations with each other. It is at this location that we might be able to envision more malleable methods to negotiate the intellectual and social shifts occurring all around us and, at the same time, to prompt us to rearticulate the nation-based formations whose very limits have become the disturbances brought to prominence by the influx of transnational flows.

## APPROACHING ASIAN CANADIAN LITERATURE

Although all texts, minority or otherwise, are subject to the knowledge power of institutionalization, the stakes can be high for texts incorporated through discourses of ascribed difference. In making such a statement, I acknowledge my own complicit relations with Asian Canadian writing over many years and, along with those with whom I have shared this history, I can even take some pleasure in the signs of arrival. But then again, arrival on what shores? And what are the consequences of landing? The normalization of Asian Canadian in the sphere of CanLit, while something to be desired, could make less tangible the vulnerability of its textual body and critical endeavours to mediate its ephemeral conditions. Enter here the poetics of the hyphen.

On the way to Fred Wah's writing, and more specifically to *Diamond Grill*, I found myself pausing on one critical essay that attempts to anticipate the development of Asian Canadian literary studies. Donald Goellnicht is a specialist of minority literatures who, in a recent book he co-edited with Eleanor Ty, *Asian North American Identities: Beyond the Hyphen*, aligns himself with a formation called "Asian North American Literature." Goellnicht's more detailed critical approach to Asian Canadian is worked out in "A Long Labour: The Protracted Birth of Asian Canadian Literature." In this essay, Goellnicht adopts the trope of birth to explain the so-called long delay in the arrival of Asian Canadian literary studies. Its "protracted birth" is the consequence of its lack of cultural visibility in comparison to the much earlier birth of its Asian American counterpart. Not surprisingly, in constructing his argument through the paradigm of origins, Goellnicht resorts to an account of historical contexts, precedents, and comparisons, all understandable strategies to institute the order and coherence that are associated with a field of specialization.

But a problem arises in the blurring of boundaries between Asian Canadian literature—which implicates whatever identity formations are tied to that literature—and Asian Canadian literary studies. The latter cannot be divorced from the former, but "literary studies" nevertheless gestures towards critical concepts, assumptions, frameworks, and interpretations, all of which condition knowledge production and its institutional investments. At one point, Goellnicht does qualify by telling his readers that he does not use the term "Asian Canadian literature" as a reference to "the literary texts themselves . . . rather I mean the clear identification of an ethnic minority literary tradition in English and the academic study of it as such" (2). But then, he does not use "literary studies" in the subtitle of his essay, and he does not strictly maintain the distinction between "literary" and "academic" in his essay. When it is blurred, the term Asian Canadian is collapsed into a representational frame that depends on unqualified assumptions. First, there is the valorization of "birth," that origin out of which "Asian Canadian" can be said to issue; and second, there is the strategic comparison with "Asian American" temporality. Consequently, when measured against the emergence of "Asian American" studies out of a strong "national-political-social movement focused on identity politics or the politics of difference," the only conclusion he can draw is that "Asian Canadian literary studies have languished in the wilderness" (3). Aside from the disturbing colonial echoes in the Judeo-Christian trope of wilderness, the argument is that the construction of literary history, which is the project the essay seeks to further, constitutes the necessary first step in bringing Asian Canadian criticism out of the wilderness. While referencing discussions of "Asian Canadian" by Guy Beauregard and Glenn Deer, Goellnicht sets out his own difference:

> Neither of these most recent examinations of an area of cultural study labeled 'Asian Canadian' attempts to trace the historical contours of this literary academic field in any detail, however; it is this gap that I am attempting to fill here in the belief that we will be able to understand the full implications of this term only after we have begun to understand its institutional history. (2)

Here "Asian Canadian" becomes an "area of cultural study" and the implication is that it can include cultural concerns that extend to subjectivity, identity, and the production of literary texts. But more, the privileging of "institutional history" as the means through which "Asian Canadian" can be understood raises serious questions of management and containment. How, then, are we to read the "gap" that is being filled? Will the rise of Asian Canadian literary studies be at the expense of Asian Canadian writing? To his credit, Goellnicht goes on to chastise the academy for not opening spaces for Asian Canadian studies, which would have given these studies a "necessary stage of its development: the state of structured interdisciplinarity that challenges conventional disciplinary boundaries and forces the academy to rethink the ways in which it organizes knowledge and uses its knowledge base to tackle social problems and injustices" (27).

## THE WRITING ACT IN DIAMOND GRILL

Wah's writing in *Diamond Grill* issues from encounters with gaps in history and memory, gaps that implicate Asian Canadian as a form of writing. Asian Canadian textuality is performed in the material conditions of graphic signs that function as an enactment of process — of lived time as a movement that is constituted on waves of change:

> ready Freddy, open up with a good swift toe to the wooden
> slap that swings between the Occident and Orient to break
> the hush of the whole cafe before first light the rolling

gait with which I ride this silence that is a hyphen and
the hyphen is the door. (16)

The hyphen is the most appropriate sign for a text that
performs the critical limits of socially sanctioned identity formations, even while it opens the door to cultural,
familial, and personal narratives that have been silenced
by racialization, displacement, and colonial histories. Elsewhere in *Diamond Grill*, the writer blasts the mandatory
"ethnic" identities of Canadian liberal multiculturalism, and
by implication the literary representations that reproduce
its assumptions. Go ahead and don whatever identities are
available, he says, "But stop telling me what I'm not, what I
can't join, what I can't feel or understand . . . Sometimes I'd
rather be left alone" (54). But this is a big problem for the
vulnerable bodies that signify as Asian Canadian. While
they may have been invisible, ignored, or even shunned, they
have never been left alone. Once they take on visibility in the
spaces of creative writing, they are willy-nilly woven into the
processes through which Asian Canadian is produced. And
for better or worse, the ties that bind them to the Canadian
in this formation have often been, to cite the epigraph by
Wah in this chapter, "Tight as a knot in binder-twine."

Unlike the literary texts that speak for the cultural
dominant, which can enjoy a more transparent relation to
the goes-without-saying public, minoritized texts, including Asian Canadian ones, have often come to social voice
through allegiances to groups that have undergone traumatic
histories. In Wah's poetics, instances of painful subjugations
are invoked through the signs of the hyphen as noted in the

passage cited above — "Legally bound (not just the feet), 'Exclusion Act', head tax, railway car to an internment camp, non-status outskirt of town nomad other side of tracks no track. Mi-nus mark, not equal sign." In this inventory of unjust policies and actions carried out in the name of the Canadian state, the Asian as hyphen has been subject to extreme forms of policing, expulsion, and abjection. Yet it is through this response to brutality that resistance is born in Wah's "migratory tongue some cheek to trespass kick the gate the door the either/or"; the site of writing opens the door to possibilities denied by the regulatory apparatus of the state: "How float this sign, this agent of the stand-in. Caboose it loose and let it go, it's 'Not in Service' anymore." "High (bridi) Tea," the title of Wah's prose poem, riffing on the hyphen, playfully invokes the empire's culture of leisure, its "high tea," which has been riven by the force of hybridity, at which point the marked writer sees through the systems that have produced him. As the medium of his (limited) agency, writing becomes a site of floating signs that exposes the fakeness or the constructedness of the nation wherein the once used (and misused) Asian body is no longer in service to the state.

> This is what little Freddie and then a more mature Fred Jr. figures out in *Diamond Grill* and what, in turn, the text of *Diamond Grill* figures for the reader. Thus in its opening section the performance of the imagined becomes a kind of heterocellular recovery [that] reverberates through the busy body, from the foot against that kitchen door on up the leg into the torso and hands, eyes thinking straight

ahead, looking through doors and languages, skin recalling
its own reconnaissance . . . mouth saying what I want to
know can feed me, what I don't can bleed me. (1)

In Wah's writing the vulnerable body becomes a resource
for memory and history, its movements carrying the residue
of the personal, familial, and social anger that has long been
covered over, suppressed, and rendered mute, but now finds
an outlet in the writer's voice — the mouth a gap out of
which language issues. It is the sensate body, in its singular
rhythms and desires, that opens pathways for the writing
of *Diamond Grill*, as for instance in one of many heightened
moments when the writer is able to enact "a kind of hetero-
cellular recovery." He had been searching for years for a food
taste, "not in the mouth but down some blind alley of the
mind" (67). Then, one day, in a seemingly banal occasion in
a grocery store he comes across some Chinese turnips, and
when he asks a women beside him how to prepare the food
he "knew instantly [he] had found a lost taste" (67).

   Both a graphic sign and a metonym of minoritized
and/or racialized groups, and even more pointedly in Wah's
poetics, of mixed race subjects, the hyphen — "that marked
(or unmarked) space that both binds and divides" (72) — carries a heavy load in being open to misleading conclusions.
This is the case when it is tied (like a caboose?) to the notion
of hybridity, as Wah does in having the "bridi" perform as a
hyphen between "high" and "tea." If, for instance, the hyphen
is read as a hybrid state that covers over the contradictions
of the social markings of difference, it then gets recontained
(and tamed) as simply another version of the hyphenated

identities of multicultural discourse. In a clarification of the hybrid "I" of the writer in *Diamond Grill*, Julie McGonegal has argued that Wah's "use of hybridity does not make him overlook the experience of psychic pain and confusion that more triumphalist investigations of hybridity typically leave out," and that his approach to it in *Diamond Grill* "enables its readers to imagine hybridity, first, as a metaphor for the racially mixed subject's transitions and translations between racial, cultural, and linguistic identities, spaces, and struc-tures, and, second, as a 'poetic tool' with which to dismantle official literary models and practices" (178).

The operative words here are "transitions" and "translations," both of which have to do with the movement of the body among things as well as the shifting contours of the imagination. Brian Massumi, in his discussion of the body's movement through geographical spaces, distinguishes between a navigation process based on "bodily memory" (*Parable* 178) and one based on "visual form" (*Parable* 179). In the latter, we make our way through spaces using visual cues to create "cognitive maps" of the environment to ori-ent us, whereas in the former we make our way through a proprioceptive sense, which he defines as "a self-referential sense, in that what it most directly registers are displace-ments of the parts of the body relative to each other." In a proprioceptive condition, the imagination produces the dimensions of spaces, not through external reference points, but through physical "contortion and rhythm," an internal sense that is akin to what has been called "dead reckoning," a nautical term that describes a method of spatial orientation through the movement of the body. In such a process, then, position does not determine movement but is an effect of movement. "Movement is no longer indexed to position. Rather, position emerges from movement, from a relation of movement to itself" (*Parable* 180).

The notion of dead reckoning explains why a pivotal act for the writer in *Diamond Grill* is kicking the swinging doors — another version of the hyphen — that mark the boundary both binding and dividing the primary spheres of his subjectivity. The movement of his body generates the imaginative act of invoking the figural elements of his history and memory. Going through the doors — "Fish an! Side a fries! Over easy! On brown! I pick up an order and turn, back through the doors, whap! My foot registers more than its own imprint, starts to read the stain of memory" (1). And when the writer allows free rein to writing as a performance of language, as he does in certain islands of improvisational riffing, we glimpse bodily memories emerging in trans —:

> whisper of tires down the distant freeway, ciped tableaus of voyage forgetting, the raiments of message or the caprice of house grammars, smell the meltdown, remember the pear tree, are the membranes paper thin, are the layers of dream time disappearing, these are the details under foot, this is the soil the clay the mud, this is the dirt of dying. (121)

In this passage, a passage of text and a passage through text, the movement of the body in the world interferes with the markers of spatial orders, such as the "tableaus of voyage" which are forgotten and the "house grammars" whose "caprice" is revealed. As the writer in the writing emerges from the frameworks that have organized his consciousness, he becomes acutely aware of the immediate finitude of things, the "details under foot" that are part of the "dirt of dying." Here, we might argue, the movement of the body precedes the positioning of the autobiographical self, translating Wah's writing into a version of a process in which the unresolved resources of the imagination and its memories, including memories of being marked as a racialized subject, are encountered, contested, absorbed, appropriated, and negotiated. And it is this activity that takes on positioning in the representational frameworks of a literary text such as *Diamond Grill*. The disjuncture between writing and positioning accounts for the gap between the writer speaking in the unfolding time of composition and the formal boundaries of the text that produce the writer as an embodied consciousness. As Hall commented some years back, "though we speak, so to say 'in our own name', of ourselves and from our own experience, nevertheless who speaks, and the subject who is spoken of, are never identical, never exactly in the same place" ("Cultural Identity" 392).

## ASIAN CANADIAN AS A LITERARY FORMATION

Although the gap in *Diamond Grill* between speaker and subject, or writing and the written, could be understood as a general condition of literary texts, for Asian Canadian writing it brings out the complicated internal dynamics of the shifting constraints — historical, aesthetic, intellectual, and cultural — out of which this writing appears. These constraints have incorporated, as Wah's narrative reveals, the legacies of intense periods of racialization, repeated attempts by dominant groups to expel the marked bodies of Asian Canadians from the territorial boundaries of the state, and a barrage of social nomenclature that has instilled fear and resentment towards them as the face of "yellow peril." Long before the ascent of the fear-based language of security in the post-9/11 era, Asian Canadians have been the victims of social and cultural assumptions that have categorized their visibility as alien/Asian bodies as a threat to the whiteness of the body politic. In the face of this condition, Wah's *Diamond Grill* is paradigmatic in its insistence that the materiality of the body not be contained, or otherwise defined away, by a positioning that is complicit with racialized norms. The disjuncture between the movement of writing and the representational frames of the writer as subject allows for the simultaneous recognition of social and cultural inequities and the material conditions of the body that exceed those inequities.

This textual condition helps account for the often unnoticed but troubling tension between critical expectation and textual specificity, one identified by Rey Chow in Asian American literary studies: on the one side are literary theorists whose poststructural lens can valorize such phenomena as mixed or hybrid identities, boundary crossing, and mobile or nomadic stances, and on the other are the Asian American writers who see these same elements as limits that signify alienation and abjection, of not quite belonging anywhere (see "The Secrets of Ethnic Abjection," in *The Protestant Ethnic and the Spirit of Capitalism*). In *Diamond Grill*, the tension is played out in the pull between an assumed identity and the conditions of the writer's subjectivity, dramatically so in one painful textual moment. Scanning and reflecting on his own property, the writer sees himself as a "trespasser" on "this land secured through my wife's British heritage" (124). While recalling his children's ritual claiming of place, as much as he desires to do so, he is unable to claim the security of belonging because of his complicity with the racialized contexts that have framed his subjectivity and that continue to frame his body: "The problem here is that I am an obstacle. I can't get out of the way now that I've stepped into the frame" (134). For the reader, the problem here is the destabilizing conjunction of "I am" (an affirmation of existence) and "obstacle" (a negation of autonomy), which together raise a haunting question: what kind of frame would produce the writer's choice of "obstacle" to identify himself? His agency in imagining himself as "obstacle" implies a recognition that he cannot simply remove himself from the frame; his subjectivity, the very medium through which the text of *Diamond Grill* has taken form, has been constituted by the trajectories of colonial histories. He has, as he says, been "interloped" so that he becomes "the echo of an old empire heaven" (134).

This acknowledgement, I would suggest, cuts to the heart of the kind of self-consciousness and critical intensity that have marked the textual exigencies of Asian Canadian writing, and that make *Diamond Grill* a model text for speculations on what might be taken as the need for Asian Canadian literary studies. Here its writer addresses, plays with, and transforms the temptation of a transparent identity — "I am a Chinese Canadian writer who etc. etc. etc." — through an attention to the hyphen as simultaneously a sign of visibility and invisibility; an effect that is relative not only to the subject's positioning but also to the critical capacity to read the social and cultural codes of difference making that are operative in context-specific instances. The shiftiness of this double-edged condition is best exemplified in his own ability to pass between Chinese and Canadian identity constructs that have threatened to contain him. This ability, a kind of "sad privilege" (138), enables an in-betweenness that he embodies in the language play of the word "transpicuous," which, as I suggested earlier, linguistically performs the difference between "conspicuous" and "inconspicuous" (136), the "trans" making all the difference. As his body becomes "transpicuous," or not seen through racializing codes, he is able to see through — that is, by way of — the hyphen, and in this process becomes conscious of the ethical call of the other in all transactions of difference in the "contact zone" of cultural processes. Wah cites Louise Pratt's well-known definition of the term both in *Diamond Grill* (69–70) and at the conclusion of his essay "Half-Bred Poetics":

> By using the term "contact", I aim to foreground the inter-active, improvisational dimensions of colonial encounters so easily ignored or suppressed by diffusionist accounts of conquest and domination. A "contact" perspective emphasizes how subjects are constituted in and by their relations among colonizers and colonized . . . not in terms of separateness or apartheid, but in terms of copresence, interaction, interlocking understandings and practices, often within radically asymmetrical relations of power. (*Faking It* 95–6)

If the cultural spaces of Canada are seen as contact zones, as the writer of *Diamond Grill* proposes, its citizens engage in ongoing and always negotiable relations with each other as their subjectivities are formed and reformed, according to Pratt, in terms of "radically asymmetrical relations of power." Privilege and subordination, along with being visible and/or invisible, become conditions performed in tandem with the relations of power that underwrite institutional norms. As the textual drama of *Diamond Grill* reveals, in performing a poetics of the hyphen, Wah remains critical of a multicultural politics that packages ethnic identities, and in one provocative rhetorical instance he appropriates the hyped discourse of capitalist spin doctors to mock its market ideology. "The return on these racialized investments," readers are told, "has produced colourful dividends and yielded an annual growth rate that now parallels blue-chip stocks like Kodak and Fuji, though current global market forces indicate such stocks, by their volatile nature, will be highly speculative and risky" (83). The potency and, given the threatening escalation of global conflicts over differences in subject position—from radical fundamentalist premises to the market-centred dogma of corporate capitalism—the prescience of the hyphen reside in its critical flexibility and acumen. As a poetic tool, the hyphen exposes the fake front of liberal discourses that cover over the traumas endured by minoritized subjects who have been "in service" to their constitutive outside, though even multiculturalism is "risky" in the face of unpredictable transnational variables, such as war and terrorism. The mediation that Wah offers to readers, and the hope as well, is performed in the "eth" movement proposed in his essay "A Poetics of Ethnicity" — from "ethos" to "ethnic" to "ethic" (*Faking It* 56–57). While ethos and ethnic do not share the same linguistic root, Wah transgresses normative etymologies and, in a sense, takes poetic license to posit a linguistic slide from "ethos" to "ethnic" that yields a concern for "ethic" as attention to the play of otherness in constructions of difference. If ethos is read as the space of the imaginary, and ethnic as the complex specificity of embodied beings, then ethics becomes the necessary critical consciousness of the "radically asymmetrical relations of power" that constitute systems of representation and interpretation. Wah devises a cryptic phrase for an ethics appropriate to contemporary contact zones, "synchronous foreignicity," which in the density of its linguistic form resembles the graphic surface of an ideogram. In "Half-Bred Poetics," he defines this phrase as "an ability to remain within an ambivalence without succumbing to the pull of any single culture (resolution, cadence, closure)" (*Faking It* 83).

Synchronous foreignicity could be considered a version of the trans that has to do with the ability, while passing through contact zones, to look both ways at once "without being appropriated" (*Faking It* 90). In other words, as a stance towards writing as a creative means of resisting "the stasis of identity" (*Faking It* 92), it points to the capacity simultaneously to recognize the limits of representation in containing the body's movement and to affirm the right to enact textual manifestations that are open to the influx of otherness. The turn to a preoccupation with change and transformation in recent Asian Canadian texts, such as Hiromi Goto's *The Kappa Child* (2001) and Larissa Lai's *Salt Fish Girl* (2002), extends the formal possibilities of Wah's poetics of the hyphen. These texts do so not by directly taking on the burden of representing the nation's racist history, as Wah does through his personal and familial memories, but by moving into the more fictive potential of writing. When transplanted in local sites of Canadian cultural formations, the figure of the kappa in Goto's novel allows for the living body—akin to Wah's mobile hyphen—to become the constantly changing medium of language and narrative. Its life-affirming water, carried in a bowl-shaped space on its head and contained in the cucumbers it craves —as does the unnamed narrator of the text—becomes the reservoir out of which Goto's narrator draws the agency to move beyond imposed myths of patriarchy, colonialism, and heterosexism. She learns to trust the dead reckoning of her bodily desires so that she can determine ethical directions for her will. Once she overcomes the closed shop of solipsistic individuality, her body becomes the medium of new consciousness: "My head spun dizzy with a flash of memories not mine. An unknown ache twisted my heart. Tears filled my eyes and longing rose, not from my stomach, but from the belly of my soul" (146).

The drive to reclaim the body from the overdetermination of racialization and sexism, specifically by Asian Canadian women, is also an urgent aesthetic and theoretical concern for Larissa Lai. In her writing, Lai recognizes the debilitating legacy of trauma in the history of Asian Canadians, yet she insists, and her novel *Salt Fish Girl* bears this out, that the writing negotiating this history needs to reject mere reaction and, in its critical reach, become resistant, oppositional, and transformational. "To react is to reproduce" (21), she says in an interview with Robyn Morris, echoing an earlier comment by Goto in a critical statement: "I find it troubling when my writing is reacting. When I would much rather act." Goto goes on to say, in a comment that could be applied to a reading of *Diamond Grill*, "Yet in writing, I can empower my reaction as a simultaneous resistance/empowered celebration. Language, the site of colonization, becomes an instrument I use to try to dismantle it. It's very difficult. This negotiation between freeing from oppression with that which oppresses" ("Translating the Self" 112).

For Goto and Lai, as well as Wah, reactive writing reproduces the expectations of normative assumptions and forfeits its potential to exceed or otherwise change the repercussions of historical trajectories, especially those that are the effects of racialized identities. The figure of Nu Wa in *Salt Fish Girl* emerges from the writing process as a matrix that is implicated in the management of the body, but which exceeds its containment through imagined sites wherein binary modes of containing bodies, as in colonial and/or corporate forms of authority, have been drained of their power. These are textual sites that reclaim the vulnerability of the body in conditions of change. As Lai says in her essay "Corrupted Lineage," Nu Wa "is a figure of corruption . . . For the place of rot is also a fertile place, a place of new beginnings. The goddess of the straight line is both the pen and the mark it makes on paper. She is also the spark of story that glides between the two" (51).

That "spark" functions as the hyphen in Lai's writing practice, a creative power that the nameless narrator of Goto's *The Kappa Child* comes to claim only after she painstakingly decolonizes the racialization of her body that she has internalized from childhood. The self-destructive perceptual frames through which she has seen her body as monstrous (as, in effect, the alien/Asian of a white-dominant social space) begin to dissolve as the figure of the kappa takes shape in her body. That this has to do with learning how to act — that is, how to live the full life of the imagination — comes through in one of the pivotal scenes in the novel. Undergoing a deformation process as her consciousness begins to see through the internalized structures that have prevented her from performing desire, the narrator encounters an "Asian" stranger with a shopping cart cleaning a street. In her hyper-conscious state she immediately thinks he is a homeless man, but it turns out that he is a retired English professor named Jules, who is accompanied by a dog named Grace, a loving and trusting companion. They begin a friendly conversation over a cup of tea, and Jules then gives the narrator some advice having to do with methodology and critical consciousness, elements that have been missing in her life: "if you want to believe badly enough, you make your need real. A physical articulation. And live your life accordingly. The results of your choice will affect everyone you come into contact with" (186–187). When the narrator responds that such attentiveness necessitates assuming responsibility for one's actions, Jules acknowledges the absence of such self-consciousness: "Many people," he tells her, "enact their lives without understanding the consequences of their choices" (186). The gem of wisdom that Jules offers the narrator has to do with the simultaneity of creative and critical procedures — in writing as well as in life. It also has to has to do with a respect for the processes of becoming that constitute the fullness of her embodied life, which are all too often covered over, or occluded, in the language of racialization that has categorized her Asian-identified body out of existence and which, until her now-not-so-chance encounter with Jules, she has internalized as a mode of self-colonization. "A physical articulation" also encapsulates the writing act in Wah's *Diamond Grill* and by implication in the call for Asian Canadian writing.

## THE FUTURE OF WAH'S POETICS OF THE HYPHEN

In all three works — *Diamond Grill*, *The Kappa Child*, and *Salt Fish Girl* — the socially and politically contained Asian body, the subject of so much regulation by the Canadian state, exceeds its historical boundaries to reclaim its consciousness of embodiment in always ongoing life processes. In the "physical articulation" of writing practices that align with these processes, the somatic condition, what we have referred to as the "dead reckoning" of the imagination, is apprehended as a creative force that can be drawn upon to critique the closure of the play of otherness. In all three works, as well, the more homogenous (read: white) nation produced through the management of its alien/Asian subjects loses its coherence through the emergence of transnational and diasporic flows — the site of Wah's hyphen — that allow for more fluid Asian Canadian formations.

These are formations that offer a critique of hierarchic cultural categories — the "fake" structures of racialization — while simultaneously generating a matrix for the creation of Asian Canadian works.

Asian Canadian literary studies, if such an entity were to find a place within institutional frameworks, would do well to develop its critical pedagogy by drawing sustenance from the poetics of the hyphen in Wah, following his awareness of the always-potential barbs in the discourses that are invoked to explain or otherwise account for the regulatory networks of social formations. In the passage from *Diamond Grill* used as an epigraph for this chapter, as we have seen, Wah takes stock of the racialized history of Asian Canadians in which Chinese and Japanese Canadian bodies that have been rigorously identified and controlled.

Larissa Lai's *Salt Fish Girl*, following on the example of *Diamond Grill*, is an Asian Canadian novel that performs the poetics of the hyphen in seeing through — that is, by way of — the in-between spaces where the creative can circumvent the closure of oppositional thought in times of escalating global tensions. Her futuristic work functions as a critical frame through which the consequences of the capitalist appropriation of living matter — with human cloning as the horizon of its reach — are played out in its narrative. An important strand of Lai's narrative is set in the future, between 2044 and 2062, a time when the local geography of Vancouver and the west coast of BC has been completely transformed. Not only has the nation become obsolete, but its space is now also divided up by a handful of transnational corporations that control their own territories, outside of which exists an unstructured or wild local site that the novel calls the "Unregulated Zone where law-abiding corporate citizens . . . are not supposed to go" (14). Born into this precarious world, its central character, Miranda, carries in her body the genes of a Chinese fruit called the durian and, for this reason, emits its stinky smell. Her smell alienates her from other children and even from her family, so that she grows up marked with all the signs of difference. When she begins her narrative, Miranda lives with her mother, father, and brother in a place called Serendipity, a "walled city on the west coast of North America" (11). When her family is forced to resettle in the Unregulated Zone, Miranda begins to develop a critical consciousness of her own history, and in the process comes to realize that her world is being managed by large corporations that have resorted to human cloning in order to produce a cheap labouring class. A crisis erupts when there is an outbreak of what is called the "dreaming disease" (243) that strikes certain individuals and makes them prey to strange past memories. Lai has commented that this disease in her novel is related to her "attempt to think through a North American relationship to the past, one that is repressed and broken but keeps surging violently to the surface precisely because we try so hard to hold it back" ("Fish Talk").

Although set in the future, Lai's novel performs a critique of the global present, a time that she has described as "capitalism-on-steroids" ("Fish Talk"). In the empowerment of one group of clones, the Sonias, who have learned to break the power of their masters, Miranda begins to envision a new form of social agency, one that can transform binary structures of power in which the ideology of commodification, extending to the human body in biotechnology, for instance, is generated. The realignment of Miranda's critical consciousness with the deeper history of global exploitation, the novel posits, opens up an ethical response to the present drive to cover over the past through the neoliberal language of global capitalism. Lai's novel, then, draws attention to the local conditions of embodied lives and the need to remain conscious of the precariousness of social relations of power. It calls forth the urgency to forge cultural frameworks in which the local and the global can coexist in non-violent forms, where the legacy of colonial histories is recognized as manifest in present conditions of inequality, and where the imagination has the opportunity to invent new democratic modes of governance.

Today, as we struggle to find ways of countering the invasive language of securitization and racial profiling, we find ourselves asking, more frequently than ever before, to what extent the products of our labour—in the classroom, in our relations with colleagues, and in our social interactions—compromise the integrity of a critical relationship to systems of dominance and privilege. When the knowledge we produce loses the stability of referenced certainties, then the "truth" value of our work translates itself into discourses that can no longer be trusted to carry out the effects of our intentions. When every word, or at least the prime words in our academic language—the medium of our articulations—begins to be seen and heard in scare quotes, we quickly sense that it has taken on the quality of counterfeit bills. I'm drawing on Leslie Hall Pinder's essay in which she posits the incommensurability of applying, in the time-space territorial demarcations of a Canadian courtroom, the colonial discourse of laws based on property rights to the "land" as imagined by First Nations subjects who had been displaced. The language, in this instance, takes on the aura of fakeness and therefore becomes untrustworthy as a medium for equitable social transactions and intersubjective exchanges.

The potential duplicity of the discourses that represent our social and cultural spaces creates the sense of precariousness that produces anxiety and uncertainty, and brings the threat of global conflicts over land and resources home to roost in our everyday lives. What is at stake, even in the relatively humble realm of Asian Canadian literature, is the enabling power of the creative imagination in the face of the violence and militarism that haunts the cultural representation of global processes. The conjunction of rapid capital expansion, the relentless drive on the part of corporate interests to maintain their furious pace, and the increasingly omnipresent sense of a "terrorism" spreading beyond the borders of nations are producing a global consciousness of a highly fraught and unpredictable network of interdependencies. These are interdependencies that do not obey simple cause-effect relations, but consist of crisscross effects, where seemingly benign actions in one place can wreak havoc in another. This also leads us to ask to what extent the corporate push to globalize all things marketable has not called forth a growing and often-retaliatory animosity towards capitalist commodity values, thus transforming the world into a minefield of clashing ideologies based on religious and ethnic fundamentalisms.

Consciousness of the precariousness of our embodied lives has to do with a critical understanding of the multilayered contexts within which subjectivities are formed and performed. Such an understanding necessarily rejects the binary of fundamentalism—the we/they syndrome—in favour of conceptual approaches that can account for what is provisional and contingent. These, then, are approaches whereby social and cultural formations are assumed to be embedded in networks of differential power relations—relations produced through inequities of economic resources, cultural authority, and neocolonial privileges. Literature with this kind of critical edge, as I suggest Asian Canadian writing can possess, may be distant from the binary forces now emerging in global politics, and for this reason may be seen to be inconsequential or otherwise powerless vis-à-vis these forces, but ultimately this may be its advantage. Paradoxically, its lack of overt power allows for an awareness of the precariousness through which its readers can imagine ethically—in other words, to apprehend and to build on a sense of otherness as always in conditions of mediation and negotiation.

The peril, as the work of Wah, Goto, and Lai reveals, is that writing that resists and exceeds regulatory systems, including social identification, disciplinary discourses, and aesthetic expectations, can be stripped of its affectivity when conceived through predetermining social and cultural norms, for instance, in redemptive terms such as "atonement for past wrongs" (41), to recall Goellnicht's conclusion. Other variations could follow or complement the notion of redemption. Asian Canadian literary studies could be seen as a corrective for the exclusive boundaries of mainstream Canadian literature, or as a colourful (pun intended) adjunct to that literature, or as a racialized cultural identity that is distinguished primarily through its difference from a normative whiteness. What is questionable in these frameworks is the reliance on the critical model of "progress" in which the conditions producing Asian Canadian have been overcome. If Asian Canadian, as evident in Wah's poetics of the hyphen, operates in always-provisional negotiations with its vulnerable body, then any disciplinary management of that body risks losing the very entity it seeks to know. Literary studies needs to develop reflexive modes of thinking that can account for the normativity of institutional representations, but at the same time can remain open to Asian Canadian writing *as* writing. In the dynamics of the contact spaces between these two elements of interpretation, it might thankfully never reach — indeed might even breach — its institutional ends, thereby allowing the hyphen to do its creative and critical work.

"Every day that the war goes on, raging emotions are being let loose into the world."

**ARUNDHATI ROY**, *Power Politics* (139)


"Writing is an act of hope."

**RITA WONG**, "Consensual Practices"

*Are You Restless Too?*
*Not to Worry, So Is Rita Wong*
TOWARDS A POETICS OF THE APPREHENSIVE

PREFACE: THE HORIZON

At the outset of *The Natural Contract*, Michel
Serres recalls Goya's painting *Single Stick Duel*. Two men,
each wielding a stick, are fighting until death do they part.
All the while they remain oblivious to their legs sinking in
the shifting medium of quicksand. The image captures the
futility of wars between enemies who share the contexts of
natural forces that will eventually swallow up both of them
together. The combatants are so self-consumed that they
lose consciousness of the earth force — "the abyss" (1) — that
responds in its nature to the militarism performed in their
bodies. The drama of the scene prompts Serres to ask: "In
what quicksand are we, active adversaries and sick voyeurs,
floundering side by side? And I who write this, in the solitary
peace of dawn?" (2).

In "Re Sounding Dissent in a Time-and-Space of Imperial Delirium," Rita Wong comments, "[w]e are living in dangerous times, in a world where ongoing economic violence and military violence are systemically normalized." Such normalization makes it exceedingly difficult to ascertain the equally systemic effects of violence, and specifically how violence in one region of the world has both covert and overt effects and affects in other regions, often across large geographical and cultural differences. As readers of literature we may resemble "voyeurs" who witness life and death dramas in representations that we interpret in the peace of domestic and institutional spaces, but, for Wong in her latest book *Forage*, we are also restless social subjects who are implicated in conflicts between adversaries that dominate contemporary scenes of violence. As she says in "value chain," "the internal frontier: my consumer patterns . . . / military industrial complex embedded in my imported electronics" (11). If, as consumers, we are willy-nilly bound into patterns of exchange that are complicit with global violence and the inequities caused by unequal relations of power, how can we tell where the quicksand might lie?

Think here of the precipitous drama of citizens in Tuvalu, a country that consists of nine atolls, or coral reef islands, in the South Pacific. A small nation with a population of 11,000, Tuvalu seems as if it is destined to disappear as a causality of global warming. In their essay "Globalization, Vulnerability to Climate Change, and Perceived Injustice," Bradley C. Parks and J. Timmons Roberts point out that "Tuvalu's extreme vulnerability to sea level rise makes it one of the coastal and island 'canaries in the coal mine' of global warming," and because of this precariousness the country "has been attempting to locate a nation willing to resettle the entire population of the islands in case water should overtake it" (350). On Tuvalu's website, Prime Minister Saufatu Sopoanga is cited as informing the United Nations in September 2003: "The threat is real and serious, and is of no difference to a slow and insidious form of terrorism against us." Such a site-specific crisis, as we see distinctions between nature and culture become increasingly blurred, calls for a rethinking of accountability on a global scale. If we accept as true the link between human consumption and such natural phenomena as hurricanes and floods, including the coming of Katrina to US shores, what are the consequences for determining responsibility and accountability for the human suffering caused by them? Moreover, is it possible that the large increase in industrial output caused by the production of armaments for the War on Terror was one of the factors in the severity of Katrina's force, so that the war came back home in another form? Or moving outside of US territories, what about the effects of pollution by the largest producers of greenhouse gases on parts of the world that are differentially situated in the scale of polluters? Is this where the quicksand lies?

## A SIGN OF THE TIMES

During a 20-day period in October and November 2005, large groups of restless youths, the French-born children of Arab and black African immigrants, exploded in outrage against the systemic racism of their society. The outburst was sparked by the deaths of two innocent individuals, 15 and 17 years old, respectively, in a power plant. They had mistakenly been chased there by the police. Reports later revealed that the police knew the boys had entered the dangerous building, but did nothing to warn or assist them. The anxieties over the deaths were exacerbated by earlier taunts by Nicolas Sarkozy, who was then the strident minister of the interior. Sarkozy "had brutally announced that he would 'cleanse the neighbourhood with a *Karcher*' (high pressure hose)" (Fassin 1).[1] When the government failed to offer any "gesture of compassion or respect towards the grieving parents and relatives of the boys," rioting broke out in cities all over France, though the Paris crisis received the most media coverage. As the daily news and images of the social upheaval were documented on the internet, 10,000 cars and many public buildings went up in flames. Photos framed the crowds of police and the defiant bodies of the racially marked youth. The targeting of vehicles functioned to combine the most tangible sign of capitalist consumerism with their own beleaguered bodies. Their actions, in this sense, expressed in highly visible — as well as visceral — signs a resentment towards a capitalist social system that professes democracy and equity, but then covers over the racialized hierarchies on which it maintains its status quo.

But these youth were not simply taking an anti-capitalist stance. Their anger exposed years of frustrating confinement in racially marked ghettos, years of enduring poverty, unemployment, and alienation. The signs of their identification with black US youth, and the otherness this identification created in French society, brought out the global inflections of their actions. In one account, for instance, reporter Jamey Keaten was candidly informed how French-style racial profiling works on their bodies: "'You wear these clothes, with this colour skin and you're automatically a target for police,' said Ahmed, 18, pointing to his mates in Izod polo shirts, Nike sneakers and San Antonio Spurs T-shirts" (Keaten, "Anger"). The specificity of their clothes, and the inventory of brand names, exposed the more trans-local implications of their restlessness. Marked and visible — resistant and expressive — their bodies performed the systemic inequities that constitute the infrastructures of Western capitalist regimes. Their bodies finally had enough of the "groundless identity checks and . . . searches carried out systematically" (Fassin 2) on them.

—

*That body, awakening to oppressive conditions.*
*That body, the terrain of biopolitical violence.*

—

THE BODY AS ALPHABET

These days the body — in all spheres, from the local outward and back — is undergoing new configurations through networks of proliferating and often predatory signifying systems. As embodied beings, we are moved by a sea of external forces that are internalized, even as we move to externalize what is internal. Ceaselessly in process, we cannot resist being moved, even as we move ourselves through volition. In more stable social circumstances, bodies might not be as restless as they are, or appear to be, in their current encounters with the vicissitudes of capital accumulation and the global struggle for power generated on its behalf. After all, this is also a time of well-publicized medical breakthroughs and biotechnological wizardry that promise the second coming of disease-free bodies — and bodies that will out-manoeuver the mortality that marks the temporal limit of organisms. But the trouble is that bodies remain subject to violent confrontations over land, resources, and imagined identities. Bodies are called to defend territories, to flee territories, and to invade territories. Even if we seem to have moved beyond the so-called identity politics of the era of more stable nation-state formations, the body these days is passing through the uncertainty of apprehensive spaces. Surveillance technologies monitor its movements in social and domestic spaces. The seductive codes of commodity culture continually populate its idealized forms in all the seams and folds of mass media with its hunger to spawn a profusion of information and images. Genetically modified foods that line our supermarket shelves now pass through its biological network on a daily basis. And more and more, as the body becomes the dominant contact zone of the bio-political machinations of the strongest nation-states (think here of the US in relation to Canada), citizens have to confront the effects — and the more unpredictable affects — of new forms of governmentality that see threats to security around every corner.

What might this all mean for those of us who work with the shifting language of literary texts that perform the exigencies of the body? In her poem "open the brutal" (35) in *Forage*,[2] Rita Wong tells her readers:

> your body's
> alphabet encrypts the message. rising,
> sigh the silent letter that alters the
> sound around it.

Wondering about the encrypted message of the "body's / alphabet," as a reader I am struck by the flitting body that I had processed without knowing so. There, still in a previous moment in the poem now recalled, is the "squirrel running across the / grass, a living question mark," outrunning the "guard dog." This figure of the "living question mark" brings into nervous view the field of tensions that the body performs: as mark the body signifies, and as question it is always unsettled. The body, then, at least in one of its manifestations, gives way to what might be considered a poetics of the apprehensive — which may be the screen out of which the poet advises her readers to

> loosen the
> literal to littoral, slippage is better than
> nothing . . .

The slippage of letters that gives way to figures is better than the nothing of ignoring the affective reach of the body's restlessness.

The regulatory system called the dictionary — in this instance *The Free Dictionary* online — offers two standard definitions of *apprehensive*: 1) uneasy, or anxious or fearful about the future; and 2) capable of understanding and quick to apprehend. The two definitions offer up a binary zone in which the nervous condition arising from insecurities that exceed control and threaten the well-being of the body exists alongside the vital capacity in the human organism to manage its conditions, including those conditions that might otherwise overwhelm its will to exist. A poetics of the apprehensive would dissolve the binary by negotiating the in-between relations that would embody a liminal process — an enactment that Wah has delineated in the hyphen, a graphic sign of division and connection that also signifies the instance of transition in which the one and other interface with each other. Not itself sensible, the hyphen is "silent," and according to Wah in *Diamond Grill*, it is also "the door" (16). In this figure of a threshold space, the hyphen as door becomes a figure of that "turn" we associate with poetic verse, a turn that enables the two aspects of the apprehensive to be constitutive of the poetic act.

—

*Do you ever, in the course of a day, find your mind drifting along a side trail of linguistic associations?*

—

## "NERVOUS ORGANISM"

Rita Wong doesn't just talk about being apprehensive in the face of new corporate capitalist technologies that have their sights on the inner workings of the body. She walks the talk in the linguistic body of writing — at what bpNichol once called the letteral level of language where the signifier slides out of the scope of the signified. Where it matters the most, as it does in the opening lines of "nervous organism"(20) [3]:

> jellyfish potato/ jellypo fishtato/ glow in the pork toys/
> nab your crisco while it's genetically cloudy boys/
> science lab in my esophagus/ what big beakers you have
> sir/ all the better to mutate you with my po monster/

In these lines — of shifting letters and syllables, riotous rhymes, and jittery voicing — the poet's "I" addresses the scientists who are engaged in genetically modified (GM) food production. In performing her apprehensive state, Wong adopts the nervous voice of a consumer and mistrusts the motives of those who profit from the transgenetic production of new living forms. The text transmits the poet's anxieties, calling attention to the pacing of her voice through the placement of slashes, graphic marks that the reader cannot hear but sees. The use of the slash is perhaps comparable to Wah's hyphen, a graphic mark that functions, as we have seen in his writing, as a "space that binds and divides" (*Faking It* 72). Gene splicing, a technique carried out in the controlled environment of corporate laboratories, is mimicked in the syllable splicing that "binds and divides" to create new entities ("jellyfish potato/jellypo fishtato") that could have monstrous consequences. The references are to a potato the genes of which have been spliced with the genes of a jellyfish, as well as future pigs that may be modified to glow in the dark. For the GM potato that has already been developed, its leaves glow when the plant needs water, and this of course makes it easier to grow, thus making the GM plant more profitable as a commodity.

Still, what does "jellypo fishtato" do to the body? The bodies of consumers who lack knowledge of genetic alterations become a medium of experimentation. Here fear as affect generates the spectre of scientists as wolves disguised as benign grandmother figures to the Little Red Riding Hoods of consumer capitalism. But the poem does more in the sonic propulsion of its letteral "o" that attaches to a variety of consonants to project the rhythm of a voice resonant with somatic impulses: *po, to, ow, oy, yo, co, clo, bo.* The "po monster" that is the object of experimentation also invokes the literary technician of horror, Edgar Allan Poe, as well as the notion of Frankenstein Foods (see Vandana Shiva, *Tomorrow's Biodiversity* 79). The cumulative textual effects of the sound, rhythm, and popular cultural allusions operate to provoke a response in the reader. If she has been moved so far, she is drawn into a close encounter with a social world in which the body has become prey to systems of knowledge that, as well intentioned as they may seem to be, could irrevocably undermine its well-being.

We then arrive, in the course of this poem, at the opacity of the phrase "jellypish for tato smack." In this nonsensical phrase, the syllables—bless them—take on a life of their own, as if they were organizing to resist the reasonably proper meaning of scientific language. Sound precedes sense, though the "smack" (created through the consonantal drift of the "n" in "snack") strikes the nervous system of the reader, prompting the last two lines of the poem:

> slugfish arteries
> brain murmurs tumour precipitation whack

The "slugfish" that appears to be invented in the space of the poem verifies the poem's creative power, a power that has been mobilized by the poet's critical engagement with systems of knowledge under corporate control. The nervousness over the potential effects of the biotechnological production of food plays out in the body as its "murmurs" translate into the "tumour" that precipitates the "whack." Is this "whack" a wake-up call, or the end of the line? Is this end the blow that is deadly, or is it the jolt that restores life to the organism? The questions linger.

—

*Do you have this apprehensive curve in your image field that begs to differ?*

—

## "DOMESTIC OPERATIONS"

The post-9/11 production of fear is a concern in Brian Massumi's reading of the US government's "color-coded terror alert system" ("Fear" 31) that uses different colours for different levels of alert from "low" (green) to "severe" (red). This system, which has permeated all areas of public life, enabled the government to manipulate fear as an affect in "each individual's nervous system," Massumi argues, so that its citizens became "a distributed neuronal network registering en masse quantum shifts in the nation's global state of discomfiture in rhythm with leaps between color levels" (32). The nervousness of these same citizens was compounded through the strategic insertion of manufactured news — that is, news that promoted the "War on Terror" — directly into the most influential mass media outlets. Numerous reports are now available that document the US government's clandestine operations to shape the affective responses of its citizens: for instance, by producing and choreographing the dissemination of misinformation; by paying journalists to say the right things; by approving the staging of events to bolster the US allegory of might as right, such as the rescue of 19-year-old Private Jessica Lynch and, most likely, the capture of Saddam Hussein; and by composing a string of fake articles with good news about the US, translated and planted in Iraqi news outlets, some of which found their way back to the US through its national media (see the websites for Free Press [www.freepress.net] and the Centre for Research on Globalization [www.globalresearch.ca]). On the domestic front, then, US citizens were subjected to a barrage of warnings about terrorist threats that implanted a climate of fear. The effects of this climate were intended to instill a visceral patriotism that stoked the desire for revenge and that ruled critique and dissent as out of order.

In her poem "domestic operations" (42), Wong worries about the language of vengeance that saturated US mass media following 9/11. She sees the manipulation of affect as itself an invasion — an invasion of the "neural network" of bodies — that complements the military invasion of foreign territories, Afghanistan and Iraq, which was scripted through televised reports by so-called embedded reporters who worked alongside the military. Massumi comments on the power of TV in the wake of 9/11, a moment that extended into the War on Terror: "In a time of crisis, television was once again providing a perceptual focal point for the spontaneous mass coordination of affect . . . Television had become the *event* medium" ("Fear" 33). TV then became a powerful means for the propaganda machine of the government to plug into and occupy the intimate domestic spaces of its citizenry. In this way, the boundaries of perceptions about the war were formed through the narrative constructs that reflected the position of the US administration and military working in tandem.

Wong's poem juxtaposes two voices, one in roman type and the other in italics. The former, in a state of heightened apprehension, imagines the invasion of the domestic through the power of TV, whereas the latter assumes a critical edge that apprehends the consequences of the invasion, for example in its opening lines:

the home's plaintive cry
upon being invaded by CNN:

*When the rich declare war, it is the poor who die.*

unable to bear the wart on error,
war-torn era, warped shorn blare on
living room as fractured as the globe
in the hands of the arms manufacturers
running the commercial breaks

*nuclear spectres*[4]

The poem projects a vision of a world of living beings "blown-apart," of the "wails of orphans," and of "corpses" that "democracy" does not see in the "glazed look called mass media." What the poet sees in what she calls the *"walled mind"* of a militarist mentality is its refusal to acknowledge contingencies. It is a mentality that frames everything on the other side of its wall as objects to be appropriated, controlled, or otherwise destroyed. Such a closed system of power becomes a *"coffin"* that is divorced from the creative resources of embodied life. Opposed to the engineering of affect in the government's representations, the poet apprehends a generative vision of collective possibilities. Her poem ends with the resonant phrase *"all our relations,"* a phrase that invokes the ethical call of the other as a "relation" that needs to be addressed. In his introduction to an anthology of Native literature that uses the phrase "All my relations" for its title, Thomas King identifies it as "the English equivalent" of a Native phrase used to "begin or end a prayer or speech or a story" (ix). He explains further that it serves to "remind us of the extended relationship we share with all human beings" and the "web of kinship" that humans share with all living beings, a point that the poet emphasizes with her more emphatic use of "our" in the last line of the poem.

—

*Does it appear at times that some larger network
is using your imagination as a sounding board?
Do you feel at times that you're being played?*

—

"Once war begins," Arundhati Roy has written, "it will develop a momentum, a logic, and a justification of its own, and we'll lose sight of why it's being fought in the first place" (106). Say it isn't so, but US audiences are being targeted in the "Boots on the Ground" campaign promoted by the Canadian Embassy in Washington DC. The campaign figures prominently in the embassy-sponsored website Canadian.Ally.com, which represents Canada as a nation that supports the US war. An insert box of the "full-colour banner" shows a Canadian flag unfurling over a lightly fluttering US flag, and viewers encounter the body of an armed soldier with dark glasses, who can be imagined as voicing the subtitle of the ad: "US-Canada Relations: Security is Our Business" (Alberts, "Washington"). Behind this soldier are other soldiers. They appear to be in friendly conversation with three locals, one of whom holds a young child whose back is to the camera. At the bottom of this grouping of figures, viewers see the official seal of the Government of Canada. What is so disturbing about this banner is its intended audience — the US public. Despite the Canadian government's decision not to support the US invasion of Iraq, and despite the so-called peacekeeping role of the nation, there it is. We are at war, and what causes more apprehension is that US viewers are being assured that Canada is taking on the US cause. In a news report on the banner, Lt. Col. Jamie Robertson, a military attaché at the Canadian Embassy in Washington, is quoted as saying, "We are on the front line of this war [on terror]" (Alberts, "Washington").

What is troublesome, particularly in Canada, is that the language associated with the US War on Terror, like a river flooding its banks, has been spreading through the social and political airwaves of our communications systems, simultaneously situating us in the pathway of its power and alienating us through its imperialist reach. Such alienation, in a sense, may be salutary in demarking differences that matter. But, of course, it's not all straightforward. The contradictions become apparent. The Canadian state chooses not to support the pre-emptive US war on Iraq, thereby distancing Canadians from its imperialist aspirations, yet in the past four years the state has sent more than 7,000 troops to Afghanistan. In the latest move alone, the government is deploying 2,300 troops there. The Afghanistan war budget is well over $2 billion, not including costs for these additional 2,300 troops (Pugliese, "Afghanistan Costs Hit $2B"). So while Canadians identify themselves as a peacekeeping nation, the Canadian state supports the War on Terror by fighting indeterminate enemies of the US state. The Canadian state thereby becomes an accomplice in US imperialist narratives that demonize any forces that are opposed to its self-interests.

—

*That body, the object of corporate biotechnology.*
*That body, the matrix of desire, language, and hope.*

—

"CHAOS FEARY"

What can poetry — or literature — do to intervene at this critical moment, a moment that strangely brings together threats, including of nuclear weapons, that could irreparably harm both human collectives and the earth? Recognition, or more precisely, re-cognition of interdependencies, opens up the possibility of negotiating alternative ways of mediating dissent and difference. In the shifting signs of the literary, the states of apprehension that produce nervous organisms are also potential sites of immediacy, hence sites that make visible the embodied modalities of the imagination.

Wong's poem "chaos feary" (37) offers a paradigm of a creative/critical practice. In this practice, affective responses are generated that call for both resistance and transformation in forming the terms of peaceful coexistence in a world seemingly spinning out of control. In this poem readers witness the turn from crisis into agency. The title itself sets up the action to come through a linguistic display of meanings: "chaos" is a conventional word for disorder, which is normally read as the antithesis of rational order, but its radical or root sense connects it not to the opposite of rational order but to the absence of such order, or to what the alchemists used to call *prima materia* ("prime matter"), the stuff out of which living forms issue; "feary" contains fear but also invokes the power of both fire and creative energy. Taken together, or as the words are set by each other and in relation to each other, the reader encounters a liminal site — the site of a threshold betwixt and between — where the apprehensive signs of social and political disorder become the medium through which forms of resistance and agency can arise. To underscore the importance of reading as a critical practice, the poet acknowledges that her poem is a response to Vandana Shiva's *Biopiracy*, a book opposing the appropriation by transnational corporations of traditional knowledges, medicinal plants, and genes of indigenous peoples. Through patent laws and intellectual property rights that serve the capitalist interests of powerful Western states, with US corporations at the forefront, biopiracy strips less-powerful groups of their most precious resources.

For her part, the poet enacts a complicated process of syllabic, sonic, rhythmic, and homonymic turns, as she calls attention to textuality as a critical articulation of the current state of things:

> pyre in pirate bio in bile
> mono in poly breeder in
> womb pull of landrace allo
> me poietic auto me diverse
> trans over genic harassment
> over seas genetic as pathetic
> as engine of disease.

In its dis-ease, the poem connects the dots of a series of flashpoints that expose the bonds of complicity connecting patent and copyright laws, transnational corporations, biotechnology, genetically modified foods, political confrontations over resources, the US military, and neocolonialism. These together constitute a network of states and institutions (think also of the World Trade Organization and the International Monetary Fund) that seek to manage and capitalize on an escalating biopolitics. At stake is the ownership of the body as an object of commodification and control, including as its prize the power to manipulate its genetic make-up. Moving in a linguistic rush as she takes in the massive changes taking place all around her, the poet appropriates the language of these changes to expose their representational limits — "organ as an ism," "patent as in lies." She is conscious that "pollution erodes these lines," and that her own text issues from the very conditions she deplores. This recognition of complicity calls for what she terms a "soma ethic," an ethics that propels readers towards a consciousness of the current social crisis:

> hubris as in corporate
> coalition as in american
> military as a choking tentacle
> as pollution erodes these lines
> no sense in food or rhyme
> resistant as in herbicide or
> people lost and found field a
> factory dinner a roulette
> conquest as in seeds hands as in fist

Wong's poem rehearses the conjunctions that corporate agendas and their valorization of market values strive to keep under wraps: that is, the ties that bind militarism, pollution, global warming, biotechnology, monopolies, biopiracy, and neocolonialism. The fist is not armed, but it resists social injustices through the dissemination of words as seeds.

—

*Do you suspect, in moments, that your image generating capacity is much deeper than the rationality of events?*
*Yes, please do.*

—

Organizations such as the Project for the New American Century reveal the imperialist ambitions of the inner cabal of the Bush administration long before 9/11. Its June 3, 1997 "Statement of Principles" is signed by a group of hard-line believers in US might, including Jeb Bush, Dick Cheney, Francis Fukuyama, Dan Quayle, Donald Rumsfeld, and Paul Wolfowitz, more or less a who's who of the Bush circle that took power in 2001. In this statement, these men affirm that they seek to "shape a new century favorable to American principles and interest" through the use of military force. They also say that "we need to accept responsibility for America's unique role in preserving and extending an international order friendly to our security, our prosperity, and our principles." "Our" is the operative pronoun in the whole statement. Thus, as David Harvey writes in *The New Imperialism*, "9/11 provided the golden opportunity, and a moment of social solidarity and patriotism was seized upon to construct an American nationalism that could provide the basis for a different form of imperialist endeavour and internal control" (193).

The question of the connection between neoliberal globalization and military imperialism has been muted in the post-9/11 era, as all attention has been refocused on the so-called War on Terror. At first, it appeared that the capitalist agenda of free trade, global financialization, and property values would be disrupted by the neoconservative agenda of religious fundamentalism, and there were some ominous fluctuations in the financial markets after the collapse of the Twin Towers, but there was no immediate economic collapse. Indeed, the military ventures, while costly by any standards, have also stimulated US financial markets, particularly in the arms industry and all of its subsidiaries; moreover, the imperialistic ambitions of the government at the time have been aided by the religious fervour of the neoconservative right, a group that supports the increasing militarization of US social spaces. The rebuilding processes of the regions decimated by US militarism also harbour golden opportunities for US corporations to profit from these processes, which simultaneously may enable the reshaping of these regions to bolster US consumer products and the capital expansion that is so much a part of "our security, our prosperity, and our principles" (Project). The extent to which this may come to be is highly unpredictable, given the wave of anti-US sentiments that its militarism and its ideology of US exceptionalism has generated, but clearly there are deep alliances connecting the military control over territories that may harbour anti-US groups, the global expansion of US capital and its corporations, and the US-centred religious right that seeks to defend and promote its Christian fundamentalist values.

In light of the imperialist motivations of the US, Canada's complicity with the War on Terror needs to be questioned. Will Canada become an accomplice to new forms of governmentality that will use this war as a pretext for ruling out peaceful modes of mediating differences? Will the expansion of the US power place Canada in the role of a subordinate whose own security laws and policies will be dictated by the US government? Will the ideology of might as right then infiltrate the political agenda of the Canadian state, as is perhaps already evident in the Canadian Embassy's website in Washington? Will the escalating militarism of

US corporate interests soon be reflected in Canada's defence budget? We see signs of a government that seeks to align itself with US security initiatives. Soon the border—what Roy Kiyooka once called the "49th Peril" (*Transcanada Letters* 2005, 289)—will be much more intensely policed as bodies crossing either way will be subject to electronic surveillance, which may soon include such biometric markers as retinal imprints, fingerprints, and DNA.

From the Canadian side of the border, in her poem "domestic operations 2.0" (43), a companion poem to "domestic operations," Wong raises the spectre of US imperialism as an ideological structure, one that is prone to internal weaknesses because of its failure to interpellate all of its subjects, in fact, generating powerful forces of resistance and hope for a future that witnesses its collapse. Appropriating the language of militarism in its title, Wong draws the reader's attention to the maternal resources in the US that have the capacity to speak back to the masculinist imperialist ambitions of its current political leaders, as in the opening lines of the poem:

> the eagle will plummet if one religious wing refuses to hear the other religious wing. intimidated by the testosterone in suits but refusing to back down

The dedication to the companion poems, which frames the poems with handwritten text, acknowledges the antimilitarist actions of three heroic American women—"Carol Gilbert, Jackie Hudson, Ardeth Platte, three Dominican sisters who disarmed a missile silo in Colorada on Oct. 5, 2002, the anniversary of the US bombing of Afghanistan." Drawing on religious values of compassion, creativity, and the relationality of all living forms to protest the testosterone-laden posturing of the US government, these sisters "spread their blood in the sign of the cross on the silo tracks and completed a liturgy." Their critique consisted of a creative performance in which they mimicked their government's search (ultimately a failure) to find weapons of mass destruction (WMD) in Iraq. In exposing the presence of WMD in their own country, they also exposed the complicity of a social and political system that benefits from its militarism. That they were willing to accept imprisonment to voice their opposition to their government's actions, while obviously a painful ordeal, is also a sign of hope — hope that others may follow their example to encourage the imperialist eagle to "plummet" once it recognizes the brutality of its own violence.

Energized by the possibility of domestic hope in the face of the US War on Terror, the poet moves from a somatic moment of awareness to the more public rhetoric of the manifesto, in particular invoking the collective spirit of women:

> wet earth calls forth my maternal instincts. do the suits
> have maternal instincts? sure could use an estrogen bomb
> aimed at the pentagon right about now. a betty crocker
> takeover even. housewives of suburbia unite, you have
> nothing to lose except your lives if you wait any longer. an
> apron of discontent. a whole refrigerator full. replace the
> steroid-laden steaks with happy cows and more vegetables.
> replace cancer with sinewy health.

For Wong, we are what we eat in both material and figurative terms. If we consume what the suits serve up with their imperial hardware, we will be left with nothing but aprons of discontent. In the same way, we have a responsibility to divest ourselves of the need to be told what to think and how to behave and move instead, as she says letterally, "from apathy to anarchy in a few consonants." Creative anarchy is not disorder but the absence of dependency on a ruler to rule over us. So much depends upon the critical consciousness we bring to bear on the collective conditions that mark our daily lives and that we mobilize in our social practices. "[S]inewy health," not only of bodies but also of social formations, depends upon the transformation, as the poet says, of "property into commons." The distinction raised here reflects the poet's desire for collective spaces and discourses that circumvent the language of ownership and commodities. Such spaces and discourses would respect the nature of the body's drive towards self-preservation and the nature that suffers at the hands of cancerous forms of rule. The War on Terror, as a reaction to the bombings of the Twin Towers in New York, has garnered its power through an extreme restriction on the freedom of critical reflection and the suppression of social and artistic dissent.

Indeed, what has become clearer in the years following 9/11 is that the US transformation from the subject positioning of a victim to that of a warrior[5] engaged in a global War on Terror would have not have been possible without the constituting moment of "terror" that took on spectral proportions because of that event. Critical thinkers, such as Judith Butler in her book *Precarious Life,* have argued that a healthy response to the event would have been to ask what role the US played in the attack on its symbol of corporate wealth and power, the Twin Towers of the World Trade Center. Such questioning, she says, would have led the US to "think about how its own political investments and practices help to create a world of enormous rage and violence" (14). The pre-emptive war ruled out such an awareness, and this foreclosure accounts for a public sphere in which critiques of US policy are defused by being read as acts of disloyalty and sympathy with the enemy. In the banishment of grief through the normalization of violence, the complexities of negotiating across and within differences were also ruled out. The scenario has been ripe for the emergence of fundamentalist binaries in which the War on Terror could be narrated in the sleazy language of self-righteous moralism. Racialization and demonization, the familiar techniques of maintaining asymmetrical power relations in colonial regimes, become common practice in the design and execution of security measures and policies.

Thus the US administration, acting in tandem with the military, was able to translate the widespread shock of being victims into a national discourse of revenge.[6] It was the hypocrisy of this discourse that was exposed by the three activist nuns who pointed to the presence of WMDs on domestic soil. In his exploration of the public's psychic reactions, François Debrix argues that in the initial shock of the bombings people experienced a deep sense of abjection, which provided the impetus to throw their support behind their government's War on Terror. Militarism became its own end as the elusive cause of their abjection, now

Are you Restless Too? Not to Worry, So is Rita Wong

personified as terror, was given narrative form in extreme security policies, including the suspension of civil rights. In this narrative — a fundamentalist allegory of US goodness against the evil lurking everywhere *out there* — the military was handed an astronomical budget to purchase a gigantic arsenal of weapons, bombs, and fighting bodies to hunt down the perpetrators of terror. But as the war in Iraq dragged on, the terror that was the object of the war has not been captured, and of course it never will be.

▬

*Shifting sands. Sand boxes. Sand castles.*
*Sand dunes. Sand in your pants.*

▬

## A PROVISIONAL CONCLUSION

In thinking through the body's restlessness in the face of global conflicts and contradictions, we can follow the lead of Wong's double-edged apprehensiveness, which functions as both affect and effect, invoking the conditions of fear and uncertainty, while simultaneously mounting an alternative to systems of power that appropriate and contain the creative force of the imagination. In her poems, forms of social violence and forms of economic privilege are intertwined in such ways that implicate all subjects, herself and her readers included. In "reverb," she writes that "annoyance is a warning signal" (60), reminding us that we are all of us the medium of social discontents. Here the quicksand of the affects of the angry youth of Paris, on the one hand, and the effects of global warming on the island of Tuvalu, on the other, come home to roost. Adapting her letteral poetic practice, we might ask, is this where (t)here is t(h)ere? It comes down to the body and its continual becomingness in local networks of global relationships.

William E. Connolly, in *Neuropolitics: Thinking, Culture, Speed*, identifies a "somatic marker" as a "culturally mobilized, corporeal disposition" (34), which, as a poet, I understand to be akin to somatic signs generated in the molecular field of the body, as it undergoes its everyday existence in a vast mobile infrastructure of material and discursive exchanges. These markers or signs form layers of sensations, inchoate feelings, images, thinking processes, and affects (fear, nervousness, joy, disgust) that interact with the limit frames of social contexts to create the sensory images, consciousness, and assumptions that we associate with the becoming of subjectivity. As a material process, this becoming accounts for acts of the imagination—those acts that operate in a complex continuum: simultaneously connecting to affects outside the boundaries of conscious knowledge and yielding the material conditions for thought and action in the form of willful movement, gestures, speech, and also writing. Readers of literature who focus exclusively on signification at the expense of somatic signs may foreclose the affective dimensions of writing—and the poem in particular—as a linguistic performance of critical thinking. In this sense, maintaining a dichotomy between nature and culture becomes an anthroprocentrism (i.e., a human-centred frame) that denies the limits of human formations and their ties to the finitude that constitutes all material processes. This is a cover up that has worked to benefit the technological agenda of corporate capitalist discourses that frame nature as merely raw data that is appropriated to serve its rapacious consumerist interests.

Even though a poetic act may not appear to make much happen, it remains a potent model of a creative form that attends to the ethical call of otherness. Whether we acknowledge it or not, we are, all of us, woven into the social contexts that limit our bodies and influence what we feel, think, and do in our reading and writing practices. The critical obstacles we face in our struggles to create alternatives to closed systems of power may appear formidable, but they are never inevitable. The vulnerability of our bodies demands that we develop critical practices with the capacity to nurture the power of creative acts in our embodied lives.

In her analysis of subject formation as an extension of dominant power relations, Butler raises a crucial question: "Is there a way," she asks, "to affirm complicity as the basis of political agency, yet insist that political agency may do more than reiterate the conditions of subordination?" (*Psychic Life of Power* 29–30). A negative answer, of course, would mean the impotence of any notion of the creative, since responses to existing power relations would simply reproduce, even reinforce, the same conditions. But Butler proposes a discontinuity between the power that conditions the subject and the forms that power assumes in the agency of the subject. Relative to the poetic act as performed in Wong's poems, it is precisely in the discontinuity that a turn occurs. The power that conditions the subject turns against itself in the linguistic agency of the textual act. In this act, an openness is created that calls forth a critical moment — a moment of crisis — in the reader as both a somatic and social being. The textual act, then, functions as an ethical site for a negotiation of self and other that circumvents the closure of violently positioned binaries. The desire for becoming inheres in the creative as always in excess of regulatory mandates. In this way, "the poem," as the production of desire, aligns itself with the creative push of the body.

In her essay "Consensual Practices," Wong cites a hypothetical scene constructed by Chinese writer Lu Xun. A group of people, or most of them, are fast asleep in an "iron house without windows, absolutely indestructible," unaware that they are going to "die of suffocation." If one were awake, and had become conscious of the dire situation, Wong reflects, should that person alert the others? Or is it better to let them remain unaware? While this is an extreme analogy for the vast majority of writers, Wong still approaches textual praxis as a means of awakening her critical consciousness and that of her readers to the anxieties posed by the "iron house" of closed systems of power. Writing poems and other creative works necessarily aligns itself with "an ethics that attempts to relate with other restless bodies who cannot or will not sleep." Poetic texts, and specifically Wong's poems, show us that we are always in states of apprehension — if we are willing to listen. In "in the teasing of a cellular dream," a poem from her book *Monkey Puzzle*, Wong advises her readers to "follow the wind's clues yet bear steady in changing currents" (85). Pretty good advice to get us through the day.

"What do you tell the dead when you lose?"

**JOHN W. DOWER**, *Embracing Defeat* (486)

## Rewiring Critical Affects

### READING ASIAN CANADIAN IN THE TRANSNATIONAL SITES OF KERRI SAKAMOTO'S ONE HUNDRED MILLION HEARTS

In the nation-based assumptions that have underwritten the emergence of Asian Canadian as a cultural and literary area, Asian remains a highly fraught abstraction. Produced under colonial-settler relations in Canada, it has been used to stand in for specific groups that trace their origins to countries as diverse as Japan, China, India, Korea, Vietnam, and so on. Although Asian, when set alongside Canadian, has generated proliferating cultural works, as evident in the surge of Asian Canadian literature in recent years, the term Asian Canadian carries the burden of histories of racism in which Asian has been aligned with alien or minor status. Writers who are identified, or who self-identify, as Asian Canadian often find themselves having to negotiate the effects of this contradiction in their work. How they account for or otherwise represent the subjective coordinates of racism will influence the aesthetic dimensions of their work.

The integral connection between subject formation and aesthetics in Asian Canadian writing has meant that its cultural content has been largely a function of its highly mobile and indeterminate critical formation, and not vice versa. The term Asian Canadian makes its appearance out of an ensemble of contingencies that embody the uncertain effects and affects of both elements in its formation, the Asian and the Canadian of which it has been constituted. Since it is produced out of constantly shifting boundaries of identity and power, it can be read as a limit term that simultaneously references groups identified under its aegis — that is, groups tracing their ancestries to a host of Asian regions with highly differentiated histories, languages, and cultural values — and nation-states that have been at odds with each other through long histories of colonialism, as well as cultural and economic competition. In the more restricted arena of Canadian liberal multiculturalism, the modifier Asian has provoked complex and multifaceted effects and affects in those subjects, in most cases citizens, who have had to contend with a national discourse that produced the Asian as an internal outsider, at once a threat to its racialized body politic and a presence to be reckoned with. In this drama of effects and affects, the Japanese Canadian redress settlement of September 22, 1988, which redressed injustices endured during and after the Second World War, remains a visible sign of the malleable — and always potentially transformative — nature of Asian Canadian formations.

Such is the case for Kerri Sakamoto's novel *One Hun-dred Million Hearts* (2004), a work that exposes the shifting boundaries of Asian Canadian literary production under the current literary, cultural, and institutional conditions governing the study of Canadian literature. In Sakamoto's narrative, a nation-based Japanese Canadian network of affects is rewired to encompass its complicated ties with a Japan that apparently got lost in the internment of Jap-anese Canadians. When stripped of their citizenship rights and branded enemy alien by their own government, many Japanese Canadians demonstrated their loyalty to Canada, the country of their birth, by disavowing their transnational connections to Japan. The novel's critique of a Japanese nationalism in which the aesthetics of cherry blossoms is used to glorify Second World War *kamikaze* pilots, whose deaths are ritualized in the controversial Yasukuni Shrine in Tokyo, points to the potential of Asian Canadian to move beyond its nation-based borders to speak back to the trans-national contexts of its cultural formations. The limits of Japanese Canadian subjectivities within these borders had precluded such speaking back.

## THREE POINTS OF ENTRY AS DEPARTURE

One: During a childhood in Winnipeg, Manitoba, where my family resettled after the mass uprooting of Japanese Canadians from the BC coast in the 1940s, I found myself in an identity conundrum, one shared by others of my gen-eration who grew up in the aftermath of internment. In the dispersed sites of forced relocation, living among white majorities, we were consistently framed as Japanese, even though we were Canadian by birth. At the same time, as Japanese Canadians whose loyalties were always suspect, we encountered the internalized pressure to disavow relations to Japan, even though we had familial and cultural ties there. The pressure to disavow — "I am not Japanese" — in the face of the social condition — "You are Japanese" — gave rise to the qualified drive to excel at becoming Canadian, becoming, in this sense, more than Canadian in what became a model minority syndrome. In the qualification, though, there was nestled a restless curiosity about Japan, an exotic place portrayed in the Canadian media as rich in aesthetically refined cultural practices, yet a nation whose fanatical military government had caused such pain and suffering to others and who, in return, had suffered horrendous mass deaths in Hiroshima and Nagasaki. This curiosity got the upper hand during the late 1960s and 1970s, the search-for-roots era, when a number of *sansei* (third-generation Japanese Canadians), myself included, set out to live in the land of our ancestors. But it did not take long to realize that we would never be seen and accepted as genuine Japanese. The strict identitarian borders of Japan as a nation-state, seemingly homogenous to the core at that time, refused to yield to our desire for a connection.

Two: There was the conundrum that 4,000 Japanese Canadians, over 75 percent of whom were Canadian-born, faced when they were exiled from Canada near the end of the war. The Canadian state represented their journey to war-torn Japan as "repatriation," but similar to other state-manufactured words, such as *resettlement* and *evacuation*, this one too, was a euphemism for expulsion or deportation. The bureaucrats who administered the policy of repatriation never questioned the reality that one could not be repatriated to a country to which one had never belonged. One member of this group, Irene Tsuyuki, was categorized as enemy alien, that is, Japanese under the Canadian federal government's racialized policy of treating her as "of the Japanese race," despite her Canadian birth. When she landed in Japan, she was also categorized as alien, but there it was because of her Canadian nationality. An alien in the regulatory discourses of the two nations, Irene became stateless for several years, until she was eventually able to return to Canada.[1]

Three: Immediately following the Japanese Canadian redress settlement, many of us were surprised to learn about large numbers of Japanese Canadians in Japan who were not acknowledged during the movement itself. The NAJC, the organization that negotiated the settlement, had been so intent on impressing on Canadians the hyper-Canadian nature of its human rights cause that it had unintentionally disavowed its responsibility to the Japanese Canadians living in Japan. We had missed the transnational implications of redress, not recognizing those who had been trapped in Japan during the war, many of whom never returned to Canada. When the question of their exclusion arose, the NAJC and the Canadian government established a Redress Advisory Committee, under the authority of the Secretary of State for Multiculturalism, to determine on a case-by-case basis their eligibility for the redress compensation received by other Japanese Canadians. I served on this committee and remember many heart-wrenching stories of children separated from their families, of families unable to return to their Canadian homes, and even of young men who were conscripted into the Japanese military, and I also learned that in some instances they had joined voluntarily. The stories told in the applications confirmed the complicated and at times highly conflicted transnational ties that Japanese Canadians had with Japan prior to the war. Many had sent their children there to be educated and acculturated, and one of the reasons was for security. Many feared that the anti-Asian forces in Canada could one day succeed in expelling them. Their children would at least have a chance to work in Japan.

## TRANSNATIONAL DILEMMAS IN ONE HUNDRED MILLION HEARTS

Kerri Sakamoto's novel *One Hundred Million Hearts* is insightful in its narrative handling of the transnational dilemmas often elided in representations of Japanese Canadians that deal with the traumatic effects of race assumptions, injustice, and internment. Her protagonist Miyo Mori inhabits an uncertainly disabled body, a condition that mirrors her relationship with Masao, her Canadian-born father, whose secret life in wartime Japan has sealed them in a psychologically debilitating bondage to each other — until Miyo's father dies. She then discovers from her father's former lover, Setsuko, that she has a half-sister in Japan, Setsuko's daughter Hana, who had been given up at birth for adoption by Setsuko's Japanese sister. In what is her first decisive act, Miyo travels to Japan to meet Hana, but also to investigate her father's secret past, which is mysteriously tied to Japan's wartime military regime.

Arriving in Tokyo, Miyo is drawn into the ghostly landscape of wartime memories through Hana's large, obsessively created visual collages that project the figures of the infamous *kamikaze* ("divine wind") pilots. Hana initiates her into the lives of some Japanese who continue to relive the permeating ideological injunction of the wartime imperial nation—that all Japanese subjects were expected to sacrifice their lives to the one body of their divine emperor. This expectation, translated into belief, is captured in the well-known Japanese phrase that Sakamoto cites in her novel's title: "one hundred million hearts beating as one." By dying for the emperor, the *kamikaze* would become gods (*kami*), and as *kami* they would become immortal and be remembered each year at Tokyo's Yasukuni Shrine during the season of falling cherry blossoms (*sakura*). The blossoms themselves would embody their sacrificial act for the emperor. In the wartime refrain, "See you at Yasukuni," the *kamikaze*, or the soldiers of the Special Attack Force, the *tokkotai*, went to their deaths with the thought that they would return as gods to Yasukuni Shrine.

I have to confess that on first reading *One Hundred Million Hearts* my impulse was to shy away from the figure of a Japanese Canadian *kamikaze*. This affective response to the figure was difficult to accommodate for me, evoking as it did a tangle of nerve endings associated with its history in the imagination of North Americans: the *kamikaze* suicide bombers as the epitome of the fanatical and maniacal enemy whose sole intent was to destroy all whites. Becoming the face of military Japan, the *kamikaze* were represented in popular culture through newsreels, cartoons, and Hollywood films as the incarnation of "yellow peril," a discourse that referenced the "Asiatic" as an alien-other that had to be expunged from the Canadian nation. For Japanese Canadians, the figure conjured shame and fear through its association with their own ascribed status as enemy alien in the country of their birth. For someone whose subjectivity was influenced by the anti-Japanese propaganda in Canada, the media-produced faces of *kamikaze* bombers—their compassionless eyes riveted on their target—descending on a US warship typified the racialized other as a diabolical threat to security.[2]

However, in drawing attention to the history of the *kamikaze*, Sakamoto's novel challenges the more familiar nation-based Japanese Canadian narratives of the internment, and this creative intervention on her part provoked a rewiring of my own critical affects. The *kamikaze* may have been the product of Japan's military machine, but the "yellow peril" images generated in response to them in Canadian contexts expose a transnational dimension to Japanese Canadian history previously covered over. In transgressing the limits of strictly nation-based representations of Japanese Canadians, *One Hundred Million Hearts* can be read as a post-redress literary work: that is, a work that seeks to move beyond the vestiges of the shame of being identified and interned as Japanese by the Canadian state.[3] Sakamoto suggests as much in an interview, when she comments that her "parents' generation felt a sense of shame by association. There was an impulse to distance oneself, especially because the whole internment was perpetrated because Japanese Canadians couldn't be distinguished from Japanese. But we need to get past that. The redress movement brought Japanese Canadians a kind of re-enfranchisement and a reaffirmation of citizenship, so we can be more bold and speak out" ("Surviving History" 140). If the redress movement gave permission to "speak out," then it also gave permission to "speak back" to the Japanese wartime conditions that left their marks on the memories of Japanese Canadians. While their citizenship connects them to the Canadian state, the achievement of redress can henceforth function as a critical frame that brings into relief the politics of memory in Japan around the question of responsibility for the massive injustices the Japanese state inflicted on others. Among the groups, as listed by Laura Hein in "War Compensation," are

> women who were forced to provide sexual services to the Japanese military forces (the "military comfort women"), Asian men who were compelled to perform other kinds of slave labor, Chinese people subjected to chemical or biological experimentation, and Western POWs who were mistreated, starved, and forced to work in contravention of the Geneva Conventions on Prisoners of War. (127)

Although compensation for past injustices remains an important component of calls for redress from the Japanese government, acts of acknowledgement and remembrance are also crucial for those directly affected, just as these acts were for Japanese Canadians in their redress struggle.

Steven Okazaki's *White Light/Black Rain: The Destruction of Hiroshima and Nagasaki* (2007), a film that presents the memory of fourteen atomic bomb survivors (known as *hibakusha*), begins with a select group of iconic images that encapsulate Japan's war years: Japanese troops in 1931 leaving for the conquest of Manchuria, the bombing of Pearl Harbor in 1941, the US president's declaration of war on Japan, massive bombings of Japan by the US in the final year of the war, and, finally, the atomic bombings of Hiroshima and Nagasaki in August 1945. When we cut to the present, we encounter a bustling street scene with a two-person street band dressed in red, and lines of pedestrians passing them. The scene, which could be in Tokyo or any large urban centre in Japan, serves to situate viewers in Japan's present. We are witness to a highly developed, technologically sophisticated consumer society, which is a radical contrast to the utter violence of the war years. We are told on-screen that "75% of the population of Japan was born after 1945," after which the filmmaker enters the crowd to ask a number of twenty-something Japanese, "What historical event occurred on August 6, 1945?" In a succession of responses, they all say they do not know, and the implication is that there has been a systematic forgetting, even suppression, of their nation's dark wartime history, both its aggressive imperialism and its defeat following the atomic bombings of Hiroshima and Nagasaki.

As Miyo, the protagonist in *One Hundred Million Hearts,* enters the urban street life of Tokyo, she, too, becomes conscious of the amnesiac relationship that the younger generation has with the war years and, as a consequence, their indifference to the subject of her trip: the exploits of the *tokkotai*, otherwise known as the *kamikaze*, a group of young Japanese, her own Japanese Canadian father among them, who sacrificed themselves to the emperor and his war machine. In a scene that reveals not only the distancing from but also the pop cultural transformation of the fanaticism that fuelled the ideology of Japan's military government, Miyo drops into a crowded and noisy bar with a fast-talking turntable DJ, the new centre of youth culture. Miyo's sister Hana yells to her, "He's our Emperor," adding: "DJ Atomic . . . who can make them do anything" (79). This sensory-saturated space of commodity culture typifies the new dominance of electronic forms of social mediation, suggesting the extent of the modernization process that began in the rubble of defeat, a process made possible by the technological bubble that fuelled Japan's economy from the 1970s on. On the other side of this mass amnesia among the youth generation we encounter Hana's small band of elderly women, who faithfully mourn the war dead at the Yasukuni Shrine during cherry blossom season in April, a highly ritualized time of Japanese cultural life.[4] The mourning enacts the identification of fallen cherry blossoms with the fallen soldiers of the *tokkotai* who sacrificed their lives for the emperor, thus fulfilling their sacred duty as honourable Japanese subjects.

But in the mourning process for the war dead, no questions are raised about the indoctrination of the young soldiers, particularly the military government's propaganda that linked the aesthetics of falling cherry blossoms — a highly charged affective image in Japanese culture — with the act of becoming one with the so-called divine body of the emperor. The *tokkotai* were not instrumental in the military's war strategy from the outset; the concept of the unit was manufactured in late 1944, when military leaders knew that the defeat of Japan by superior US forces was imminent. The suicide missions were a last-ditch effort to inflict as much damage as possible before the inevitable happened. In her impressive book on the *tokkotai*, *Kamikaze, Cherry Blossoms, and Nationalisms*, Emiko Ohnuki-Tierney provides convincing evidence to support her claim that young, untrained, and inexperienced soldiers were exploited by the military leaders: "When the operation was instituted, *not a single officer* from the military academy volunteered to sortie as a pilot; they knew too well that it was a meaningless death. Those who 'chose their fate' consisted of teenage soldiers, university students whom the government graduated early so that it could draft them" (4). The propagandistic conjunction of suicidal violence for the sake of the emperor and the ephemeral beauty of cherry blossoms proved to be a lethal medium for attracting, and more often than not coercing, young idealistic university students to join the *tokkotai*.[5]

In *One Hundred Million Hearts*, Hajime is one of the young men. It is through his wartime letters to his then-young lover Kiku, which she reads from as a ceremonial act at the Yasukuni Shrine, that Miyo learns an awful truth: Hajime had taken the place of her father Masao. Why? Because Masao was ostracized for being Canadian. We also learn that Hajime had serious doubts in the belief that the *kamikaze*, in death, would become one with the body of the emperor. In his letter, Hajime goes so far as to confess that he has chosen to die for Kiku, not for the emperor. For her part as the dutiful survivor, Kiku has carried this knowledge forward to the present, but she is tormented because it was her love for Hajime that drove her to insist that he die for the emperor. Both got tangled in the inconsistencies of an ideology of sacrifice that left little room for critical reflection of its consequences. Moreover, Kiku's will to continue the mourning process so many years after the war is a testament to the power of the belief in sacrifice in the general population. The dogma that sent the *kamikaze* to their deaths saturated the daily lives of Japanese subjects. They were persistently called upon to support the war and to honour the dead as resurrected gods at Yasukuni Shrine. Indeed, as David C. Earhart argues, the government instituted an overall "kamikazefication" (570) whereby all Japanese were expected to sacrifice their lives for the emperor. In effect, they were required to emulate the actions of the *kamikaze* in what was a "state of Total Warfare," and this, Earhart says, resulted in a traumatic period "of self-censorship, self-denial, and self-annihilation" (576). The will to honour the sacrificial acts demanded of them during the long period of war (1931 to 1945), despite the lethal nature of these acts, would persist in the decades ahead in the continuing nationalization of memory.

## THE CONTEXT OF THE ASIA PACIFIC WAR

The history of the *kamikaze* becomes a major component of the narrative that Sakamoto constructs to make the transnational dimensions of Japanese Canadian identity formations visible prior to and during the Asia Pacific War (what we normally refer to as the Second World War). In her novel, not only Miyo's father, Masao, but also another central figure, Buddy (Koji) Kuroda, both Japanese Canadian *nisei*, get swept up in the wartime mandate to die for the emperor. During April, the designated month for commemorating falling cherry blossoms, Buddy recalls being attracted to Japan's colony in Manchuria (or Manchukuo in Japanese), China. Compared to the racialized conditions of life in Vancouver's Japanese Canadian ghetto community around Powell Street, his life in Manchukuo seems full of the promise of freedom derived from his imagined Japanese identity, which he acquired through a process of mimicry. In his body movements and especially in his use of Japanese, he does everything he can to become transparent, though in his consciousness, where English continues to circulate, he knows he is an alien and will be an alien forever. It is through Buddy's double consciousness that the novel exposes the constructedness not only of Japanese Canadian identities but also of Japanese identities built on essentialist premises that foreclose an awareness of Japan's culpability for its war crimes in the Asia Pacific region.

Historian John Dower, among others who have studied the US occupation government from 1945 to 1953, has noted that some of the ways in which the Japan government came to "embrace defeat" in response to the occupation produced the conditions that subsequently enabled it not only to evade taking responsibility for its wartime actions, but also to reconstruct the nation as peace-loving, democratic, and unique in being the first victims of the atomic bomb. It is as if, in the bombing of Hiroshima and Nagasaki, which led to the surrender on August 15, Japan was relieved of making amends for its own actions. Reinforcing this lack of responsibility was General MacArthur's actions to protect the emperor from blame for Japan's imperialist atrocities. Even though he legally divested Emperor Hirohito of his divine nature, MacArthur allowed him to retain symbolic status as the centre of Japanese society. This may have been a pragmatic move, a response to the fear that removing the emperor would cause uncontrollable social unrest. But by exonerating the emperor while retaining his symbolic status, MacArthur also relieved the people as a whole from having to face their own accountability. Instead, blame was transferred to a small, identifiable group of military and government leaders, who were then charged, convicted, and sentenced to prison or hanging in highly publicized war trials. The demonization of a named group of war criminals offered the alibi that those responsible for Japan's actions had been officially punished. Although many Japanese writers and social critics would call for more accountability from the Japanese as a whole, the government was not compelled to acknowledge and redress the injustices it had caused—in a trail of bloodshed that cut through the colonization of Korea, the vicious treatment of women used as sex slaves (the "comfort women"), and the massacres in Nanjing.

Despite the illegality of ties between state and religion in the US-produced Japanese constitution, Yasukuni Shrine was not dismantled, nor were its close affiliations with the emperor disrupted. While officially no longer aligned with the state, in the inner confines of Yasukuni Shrine the business of worshipping and commemorating the dead soldiers as national heroes went on as usual. Eventually, starting in 1975, various prime ministers quietly began visiting the shrine to commemorate the day of surrender, August 15 — in Japan, marked as the end of the war — claiming that they were doing so as private citizens and not as state representatives. Then, in 1978, without public notice, fourteen Class-A criminals who had been executed for war crimes were inducted into the shrine, joining all those, such as the *tokkotai*, who had sacrificed themselves for the emperor. Against highly vocal international opposition to the ceremonial visits to Yasukuni Shrine by successive prime ministers, the visits have continued, a sign of the continuing influence of conservative groups who have balked at any form of apology or acknowledgement and who continue to valorize Japan's imperial past.

Without diminishing the threat of the Japanese conservative right, at a deeper level the ritual commemoration of the wartime dead may be symptomatic of a nation in a state of arrested mourning, fixated on an unresolved relationship to the Asia Pacific War. As Haruko Taya Cook and Theodore F. Cook propose, because the Japanese government had failed to assume responsibility for the wartime atrocities, it has not had to script a postwar language of accountability and acknowledgement, a language that might have mediated the humiliating and shameful affects of defeat and surrender. Instead, in the absence of such a language, the war continues to be remembered in the language of the pre-surrender period, when the myth of sacrifice for an essentialized nation (the Yamato nation) was the norm. That myth, they say, portrayed the soldiers as "'the emperor's soldiers', [who were] willing to die for the Imperial Nation, secure in the belief that, should they fall in battle, their spirits will be enshrined and honoured by their families and even by their Emperor in the Yasukuni Shrine" (576). In their interviews with ordinary Japanese survivors, the Cooks have noted how quickly the survivors use the language of the military government to frame their private experiences: "So little in the public sphere stands between their war memories and the moment of their telling decades later, that the language of those war years comes immediately back to their lips" (577). In Sakamoto's novel, Setsuko informs Miyo that her father's last words for her were "endure the unendurable" (42), quoting Emperor Hirohito, who, in his surrender speech, told his subjects to do the same. Even in death, Masao has no intimate words to offer Miyo; instead, he performs the language of the past, just as the elderly women at Yasukuni Shrine do in their yearly gatherings to mourn their loved ones during cherry blossom season.

The death of loved ones includes both civilians and soldiers, and it is here that Hiroshima, the other site of mourning in the politics of memory that structures the novel, gets linked with the ritualization of remembering at the Yasukuni Shrine. Rather than confronting the atomic bombings of Hiroshima and Nagasaki as one of the consequences of its own militarism, mourning the bomb victims at the shrine produces a memory field antithetical to the process of acknowledgement and redress. It is as if the US bombings, which led Emperor Hirohito to tell his subjects that they must "endure the unendurable," were of such enormous proportions, with such a high death toll, that — in a stroke — their effects and affects somehow counteracted the horrific record of bloodshed and brutality left in the wake of the Japanese military's imperialist drive to territorialize much of East Asia. Without eliminating the question of the US's own motives in singling out the Japanese people as the target for the unprecedented use of nuclear weapons, the bombings propelled Japan into the atomic age as its first casualty, and it was not long before the images of mutilated and deformed bodies became the dominant representation of Japan as a defeated and deflated nation. The fact of the victimization of innocent civilians in Hiroshima and Nagasaki was and is undeniable, but the critical problem is that the victimization would overshadow the broader question of responsibility and accountability. It would result in what Lisa Yoneyama in *Hiroshima Traces* has identified as "amnesic elisions" (4), a condition in which "Hiroshima memories have been predicated on the grave obfuscation of the prewar Japanese Empire, its colonial practices, and their consequences" (3). The forgetting of Japan's role as victimizer in the ritual memorializing of Hiroshima resulted in covering over — or otherwise excluding from public recognition — the violence endured by countries that were subjected to its imperial ambitions. From the context of China, for instance, the affects were radically different and remain so up to the present time. In *The Age of the World Target*, cultural theorist Rey Chow has recalled that

> As a child, I was far more accustomed to hearing about Japanese atrocities against Chinese men and women

during the war than I was to hearing about US atrocities against Japan . . . It is as if the sheer magnitude of destruction unleashed by the bombs demolished not only entire populations but also the memories and histories of tragedies that had led up to that apocalyptic moment, the memories and histories of those who had been brutalized, kidnapped, raped, and slaughtered in the same war by other forces. (26)

In mediating the cataclysmic effects of the atomic bombings, postwar Japan could transform its national image of militarism into one that projected its peace-loving nature and its achievement of normalization (after the so-called madness of warfare). This new, more gentle nature, according to Lisa Yoneyama, was part of the postwar construction of a "feminized memory" (193) that coincided with the democratization of gender instituted by the US occupation government to counter the severe patriarchy of the wartime government. With the rising stature of women in the public sphere, the figure of the mother was used to generate "memories of innocence, victimhood, and perseverance with regard to prewar and wartime women, Japanese and non-Japanese alike." The mothers of Hiroshima, more specifically, "are remembered as victims oddly similar to those who suffered from Japanese colonial and military rule," and this sense of equal modes of suffering enabled "a forgetfulness about how Japanese women's feminine subjectivities were, and have continued to be, interpellated as imperialist and militarist" (196). In Sakamoto's novel, Kiku and the other women in her group are unable to break the spell of mandatory mourning for the sacrificial war dead, even when they intuitively sense not only the futility of their actions but also their own complicity in maintaining the very imperial values that condoned the deaths of their loved ones. The melding of victimization by bombing with a deep cultural impulse to honour those who sacrificed themselves for the war would buffer, even preclude, critical awareness of responsibility for atrocities the Japanese military government inflicted on others when they acted, in the memory of Kiku, as "crazed monsters" (258). Refusing the myth of sacrifice, the Japanese American Rinzo tells Miyo he feels no sympathy for Japanese mothers who gave up their sons "in the name of their emperor," adding: "No one dares speak of this today. Only Hana and a few others. Everyone would rather forget" (118–119).[6]

Near the end of the novel, at Yasukuni Shrine, as Kiku reads from Hajime's letters, we witness the power of the myth of sacrifice in her, but we also recognize the state of arrested mourning that it instills in those formed in its crucible. Despite Hajime's doubt that he is giving his life for the emperor, and then his confession that he is undertaking the suicide mission out of love for Kiku, and despite Kiku's love for Hajime and her insistence that this love is manifest in giving Hajime's body up to the emperor, there is finally no consummation. Nothing has come of his actions. Japan was defeated, the country devastated, and all the expectation of a nationalism full of meaning had collapsed into "All . . . gone" (247), as one of the survivors says. Although, as Harry Harootunian has argued, "Yasukuni provided the site . . . where the aura of the past coexisted with the present, through acts of public mourning and remembering the dead" (151), in Sakamoto's novel these acts demonstrate the larger cost of the inability to move beyond the stage of mourning—because the beyond only invokes the spectre of defeat, failure, and an overwhelming sense of emptiness at the core of Japanese ritual practices stemming from the war years.[7] While the posture of mourning the war dead is maintained, the liberation possible through taking responsibility is seemingly forever deferred. As Hana tells Miyo, "We don't want to say what we've done" (72).

By exposing the contradictions inherent in the injunction to sacrifice for the sake of the emperor, Sakamoto's novel opens up a critical space that speaks back to its ideological underpinnings. In their failure in consciousness to carry out the mandate, the members of the *tokkotai* reveal that they were not passive and compliant subjects but that they acted out of motives other than utter devotion to the emperor. To the extent that many of them were critical of the mandate, or at least were self-conscious of being used by the military machine, the rituals of commemoration at Yasukuni Shrine are exposed as a religious and cultural form that forecloses a critical awareness of the injustices perpetrated by the Japanese government, even on its own subjects.

Such a foreclosure may be symptomatic of a reaction in the present to a government-perceived crisis in national unity—in other words, a reaction to the fragmentation of Japan's formerly more homogenous identity formation. The conservative re-appropriation of the wartime discourse of sacrifice then becomes a political strategy to shore up an essentialized Japanese subject. This is a subject who is rapidly achieving obsolescence, as it confronts, on the one hand, the disappearance of its past in the hyper-mediated electronic gadgetry that dominates its youth culture and, on the other, the emerging voices of minority groups within (Korean, Okinawan, Ainu, and Burakumin), who are demanding policies and changes in consciousness that respect principles of equality, social justice, and redress.[8] These voices make evident the development in Japan of what Jennifer Henderson and Pauline Wakeham identify as "the culture of redress," a social medium they associate with efforts to redress historical injuries and to reconcile "social divides framed as stemming from those injuries" (7). As in Canada, the calls for redress in Japan have not been "borne of reflexive state initiatives but, rather, by the ingenuity of citizens" (6).

What is telling is that the same memory politics that has allowed many in Japan to distance themselves from responsibility for the wartime atrocities has fostered the oppositional and transformative work of social justice advocates and peace activists, many of whom, for instance, have coalesced to oppose the rescinding of article 9, the "renunciation of war" provision in the constitution drafted during the US occupation. Philip Seaton issues a warning that the dominant or "orthodox" representations of Japan from the outside — his example is the British media as reflected in BBC reports, but he includes the US and Australia — dwell so much on the Japanese state's "war responsibility" that they tend to ignore acts of resistance and opposition within the Japanese body politic (288). As one example, he notes that there is strong opposition to textbooks that whitewash or otherwise excise Japanese war crimes, and that some 40 percent of those polled about Prime Minister Koizumi's 2001 visit to Yasukuni Shrine opposed his action (304). As a site of war memory, the Yasukuni Shrine generates complex and often-conflicted memories in individual Japanese, and these memories are often out of sync with those who subscribe to the nationalism of the past. The artistic work of Hana in the novel suggests that the subjective responses to the wartime sacrifices, while still unresolved, point towards the possibility of reclaiming responsibility and therefore of creating affects that foster critical reflection and redress.

## ASIAN CANADIAN LITERARY FORMATIONS

In her narrative treatment of Japan's unresolved relationship to its past, Sakamoto reinforces the potential for Asian Canadian literature to go transnational without abandoning the critical concerns that underwrote its formation within the nation. To appreciate the critical relevance of this continuity, we need to remind ourselves that Asian Canadian has always been, from the outset of its use in the 1970s, a shifting formation with referential limits that have varied according to critical assumptions and presumptions. The very notion of Asian in its Canadian contexts has a long history in the belly of a nation that constituted itself through privileging its colonial ties to British imperialism — an imperialism that was seen as parallel to Japanese imperialism at the outset of the twentieth century. The social figures identified as Asian gestated inside the nation, and for a long period of time suffered a barrage of exclusionary state policies, including disenfranchisement until the late 1940s. By then, the Chinese Canadians, Indo-Canadians, and Japanese Canadians, who would finally be able to act as citizens, had already struggled for decades to show their loyalty to Canada, even through military service. Such service proved that many were willing to sacrifice their lives to protect the security of a nation that had not granted them the right to determine its political representatives.

What remains crucial is how Japanese Canadian literature and, I would argue, Asian Canadian literature came to appearance in the history of those categorized as Asian. The initial literary efforts to redress the racism of this history came, not surprisingly, in the form of representational spaces that demonstrated how Asian Canadian subjects had been integral to Canada's social and historical development. In speaking back to the normalization of colonial history in English Canadian literature, the first Asian Canadian novels to receive institutional approval, Joy Kogawa's *Obasan* (1981) and SKY Lee's *Disappearing Moon Cafe* (1990), adopted a genealogical form that mirrored the nation's generational history, while going further to expose the anti-Asian policies and assumptions that framed Chinese and Japanese Canadians as alien-others.

In contrast to the nation-based narratives of Kogawa and Lee, which emphasized the claiming of place within the nation, the more current focus on the transnational has generated interest in flows and exchanges — on mobile rather than settled identities. The so-called globalization of cultural production seemingly opens up more expansive contexts for creativity, but it also raises, once again, the question of what constitutes the intentionality of Asian Canadian cultural formations. The presence of an imagined Japan in Hiromi Goto's *Chorus of Mushrooms* (1994) and *The Kappa Child* (2001), an imagined China in Larissa Lai's *When Fox Is a Thousand* (1995) and *Salt Fish Girl* (2002), novels that are still set in local Canadian sites — though a futuristic Vancouver in *Salt Fish Girl* — and even more recently, an imagined Malaysia in Madeleine Thien's *Certainty* (2006), all point towards a spatialization of narratives quite different from the genealogical structures of *Obasan* and *Disappearing Moon Cafe*. Although the notion of moving beyond, in this case beyond the boundaries of the nation, has a positive ring to it, this shift brings into play a new binary that needs to be questioned. On the one hand, there is the apparent loss of urgency for nation-based cultural production, which signals the passing of what has been called the literature of identity politics. On the other hand, there is the apparent gain in visibility for Asian Canadian literature, as it finds a niche in the broader transnational spheres of cultural representation. This assumption of discontinuity, of Asian Canadian literature moving on from the confines of its nation's borders, risks the loss of connection with the collective struggles and the critical reflexivity inherent in its literary formation within the nation. Severed from its local contingencies and the specific histories in which it has been produced, the Asian in its formation can easily become another sign in a global market economy of a consumable commodity, on a par perhaps with the popularity of Japanese *obento* as a form for both food and software. In other words, transnational stories, comparable to transnational commodities, are more amenable to commodification for a readership that expects fiction to reflect the cross-border traffic in goods and services.

Sakamoto's novel may appear to fit this model of cultural consumption, but the critical nodes of its narrative resist such expectations, projecting instead the effects of transposing the conditions of Japanese Canadian redress to contemporary Japan. Here, the narrative itself is crucial, and it is one that Miyo, a third-generation Japanese Canadian, performs in body and imagination as she travels to Japan to meet her Japanese-raised sister Hana, an artist obsessed with stories of the *kamikaze*, one of whom was their father, Masao Mori. This transnational familial structure complements Miyo's ambiguously disabled body, a condition that bound them together in a disempowering cycle of mutual dependency. At one point the Japanese American Rinzo even suspects that Miyo's condition may have been inherited from her mother, as if she had been a *hibakusha* ("those affected by the bombing"). He draws from speculations that *hibakusha* women may give birth to deformed children. In an interview with Pilar Cuder-Domínguez, Sakamoto admits that she inserted this slight possibility—it turns out not to be true—in her story, perhaps to draw out the problematic connection between the suffering at Hiroshima and during the war as analogous in Japanese national memory. The suggestion is that Miyo's knowledge about the debilitating consequences of the ideology of sacrifice, the "secret" of her father's inability to move beyond his wartime experience, constitutes a rewiring of affects that helps to heal her body.

In the narrative, signs even appear that Miyo's condition may be largely psychosomatic. We see her gaining new psychic energy and physical mobility as she unravels her father's secret life in Japan before and during the war.

Considered as a novel that comes after the redress settlement, *One Hundred Million Hearts* is one example of what can happen when Asian Canadian literature goes transnational while recognizing its contingent relations with the fraught social and historical conditions of its nation-based affiliations. Consciousness of these relations in the novel functions as a powerful critical screen to make visible similar processes in other national contexts, such as in contemporary Japan, where cultural homogeneity leads to the denial of full rights and equality to the minorities in its midst. Adopting for Asian Canadian cultural work what Kandice Chuh says about Asian American studies, we can mobilize the transnational "as a critical frame attuned to bringing to surface the practices of life and culture that unfold beneath the radar of state power" (14–15). For Asian Canadian writers, these practices can expose often-fraught ties to Asian ancestries that have been underrepresented in nation-based formations and thereby open up new modes of representing the imagined Asia of their own social and cultural subjectivities. In mediating the Canadian in its formation, Asian Canadian writing has been woven into the dynamic power relations of settlement, citizenship, and representation, but by entering into critical engagements with its transnational ties, as Sakamoto does in *One Hundred Million Hearts*, it can extend its constitutive drive toward redress to cultural spaces beyond—yet of—the nation.

"To be in any form, what is that?"

WALT WHITMAN, *Leaves of Grass* (53)

## Doing Justice to CanLit Studies
### BELIEF AS/IN METHODOLOGY AS/IN FORM

In one of many talks on poetics that bpNichol gave during the 1970s and 1980s, he returned to a preoccupation, perhaps more tellingly an obsession, with the question of form, not limiting himself to the practice of creative writing, but also taking into consideration the somatic conditions of the human organism in its production of the spatial and temporal boundaries of its enactments. When asked to explain a phrase he had once used, "syntax equals the body structure," Nichol referred to the emotional and psychological processes by which we "armour the body, the easiest illustration of which is: if I live in a house with a low doorway, I'm probably going to end up walking like this a lot. (Hunching)" (276). In thinking about this deformation of body structure in relation to the restricted spaces of syntax in his writing, he says that he discovered that "the order in which I wrote my poems allows certain contents in and keeps other content out, i.e. the syntax I choose, the way I tend to structure a piece, form per se, permits some contents and excludes others." For a creative writer to maintain a vital and generative relationship to form, then, the trick is to "keep moving the structure of the poem around," so that "hopefully I can encompass different realities and different ways of looking at things." What is revealing in Nichol's practitioner's notion of form are the intimate connections he draws between the body of the writer and the "body of the poem," both constantly engaged in a somatic process where form is crucial to the workings of our consciousness. If the body of the poem, and by implication other forms of writing, can undergo "hunching" by restrictive forms, then readers who inhabit these forms will be subject to the same limits. And even if their bodies will not be physically hunched, their consciousness may be by the formal restrictions of the texts.

Taking Nichol as a cue, then, we can assume that writing, and specifically our writing as intellectuals and researchers, has worldly effects and consequences that necessitate ongoing self-reflection as well as reflexivity of form. This writing will vary according to the contexts of its unpredictable circulation in networks of often conflicting and asymmetrical discourses, as well as the assumptions we bring to the moment of composition. The interplay of the networks and the assumptions constitutes a basic operation of our work in literary studies, an operation that, to a large extent, helps establish the agenda of our institutional affiliations as custodians and interpreters of creative texts.

With the ascendance of transnational and global discourses, we have witnessed the unravelling of coherent external frames of reference, such as the nation-state and its attempts to produce a coherent subject. We have also undergone, and continue to undergo, the absorption of a common discourse broadly neoliberal in its valorization of an individuated subject-as-consumer, who inhabits a vast field of market financialization that produces what we experience as an omnipresent commodity culture. The reach of this social and economic model, so the language of the neoliberal would have us believe, is everywhere and nowhere simultaneously, located in monetary networks and free floating across borders and boundaries, as fluid as oceanic bodies. Nevertheless, the recent economic meltdown, which caused the internal hemorrhaging of those large US institutions whose sole purpose is to profit by credit, made tangible the always-potential void at the core of finance capitalism. The fear is that the whole free enterprise scaffolding could collapse in a heap of bankruptcies. The frantic action of national governments to shore up the very institutions that created the collapse with huge infusions of capital exposes the political fantasies that are necessary to maintain neoliberal economic policies.

But even if we, in CanLit studies, have little influence on the economic crisis, the destabilization of the machinery of finance capitalism makes visible the extent to which commodity culture has infiltrated, on the one hand, the nooks and crannies of our daily lives and nightly dreams and, on the other, the spheres of knowledge production where economic and increasingly market-driven forms of knowing are endorsed and critical forms are dramatically under-funded. As the state of things has come to be measured according to the dictates of commodity consumption, the "personal" itself, once distinguished as "private" in relation to "public," has become a central site of appropriation. As Yasmin Ibrahim writes, "The recognition and perhaps the celebration of the body as a site of consumption has witnessed an array of technological and mobile artifacts designed to lure its cognitive senses away from the communal and into the personal. The personal space is a coveted commodity in which new technologies, innovative designs and convergence occur and coalesce." We have gone far from that older mantra, "the personal is the political," to the more in your face(book) condition, "the political is the personal," a condition that is associated with the heightened status accorded to the mobile bodies of individuated consumers.

Of course, we're not on a one-way street. The same technological devices that reshape the body according to their forms have the potential to empower those consumer citizens who are able to use it to form new collective possibilities and identities to institute changes in social relations. The Barack Obama camp demonstrated this in mobilizing campaign-changing support through the Internet, taking the political to the personal with a flourish. But as Ibrahim cautiously notes, "The counter-gaze of the technologically connected bodies presents the potential for empowerment and connection with wider society, yet it inadvertently raises new conundrums in which the politics of gazing present new ethical and moral dilemmas for humanity." For this reason, as our bodies are increasingly technologized, we need to pay attention to the impact — both direct and subliminal — of this rapidly transforming condition on our consciousness and its manifestation in our relations with each other. At the social level, for instance, the personalization of technology helps account for the simultaneous fragmentation of once-mainstream media and the rapidly growing power of highly decentralized modes of communication, such as cell phones, Facebook, and Twitter, to produce the news, and with the arrival of the latter we are witnessing the possibility of a "personal" consumer/subject with no recognizable location and therefore no containable circumference. In large measure the power of commodity culture is derived from the convergence of overlapping surfaces — of mobile bodies, advanced technologies, particularly the increasingly widespread use of wireless devices that suit those bodies, of a dizzying supply of goods to consume made possible by the technologies, and all the seemingly endless supply of commodities that personalize the consumer according to styles, trends, and brands.

While the dangers of over-consumption are always nearby, the perils of commodity culture do not reside so much in the pleasure of consumption and the desire to possess trendy and glitzy goods, but more in the mode of relationality instituted by neoliberal beliefs. Jeremy Gilbert has argued in "Against the Commodification of Everything" that these beliefs pose a threat to democratic processes when they impose the mode of "marketization and commodification" with its "seller/buyer paradigm on every possible set of social relationships" (562). In this mode, all things, including life itself, are rendered as commodities to be bought and sold. For this reason, so much depends on the actions of consumers who perform the language and mobility of commodity culture, which includes the production of a proliferating array of personalized images, news stories, and commentaries. Part of the attraction of commodity culture is the excitement derived from a sense of drama of the presentness and connectedness in the interplay of mediated surfaces — of voices, images, videos, texts, and chat sites — all of them converging in the style and technology of techno-gadgets worn on mobiles bodies. These devices become narrative and aesthetic sites that situate the consciousness of the user in the midst of unfolding dramas that are affective whirlpools of desire. The ubiquity of wireless devices that offer the conjoining of computers and phones has also contributed to a sense of the speeding up of time and the compression of space.

Does this mean there is no elsewhere to commodity culture? This closure may reside in the dreams of diehard neoliberals, but the spell cast by commodification has it limits. A great social urgency remains to provoke our imaginations to create forms of coexistence that respond to asymmetric systems of exchange and consumption. The void at the centre of capitalist logic — the secret that all its bells and whistles are merely technologies that treat the earth as mere matter to be appropriated as property — exposes an elsewhere that its representational schemata cannot finally capture and contain.

So yes, here, in the midst of the corporate push to transform the personal into a site of commodification, there is the potential to take advantage (yes, I said *advantage*) of life in neoliberal times by transforming the personal (yes, I said *the personal*) into a site of ethical reflection and practice. It may be paradoxical, or not so depending on methodological assumptions, that the reduction of everyday life, especially in North America, to the dominant refrain of buy, sell, exchange, and consume (the more the better) has supposedly freed the subject/consumer to identify themselves through what they consume, rather than old-style ethnicity, geography, and lineage, at the same time opening up creative and critical spaces where such conditions raise questions of accountability and responsibility. The very neoliberal assumptions that say, hey, everything is governed by personal choice place the burden of ethical questions on those same individuated subjects. In other words, although the language of commodity culture has become a pervasive force in representing what it means to live in current times — that is, times of currency in both senses — it is not only possible but also necessary for those of us in literary studies, and in CanLit studies in particular, to work through this language to imagine life-affirming and life-respecting alternatives. To do anything less, I would suggest, is to abandon the necessities out of which creative and critical work arises, and therefore to default to the position of being only a transfer point in systems of economic exchange, even when those transfer points are wealth pools stocked with exotic fish.

If anything was revealed in the heady era of identity

politics in a more immediate nation-state formation, it was that the imagination is always already inflected by the conditions of its emergence, so that the forms it creates are never free from normalized regulations and assumptions, even in instances when it transgresses, resists, and opposes them. While the imagination remains a force for inventing new forms that exceed the boundaries of given norms, its actions are nevertheless implicated in the relations of power it negotiates through its forms. For literary studies, this often-fraught combination of inventiveness and complicity makes the activity of reading more than simply the consumption of texts but a site of multiplicity and heterogeneity, of identification and estrangement, of insiderness and outsiderness—in short, a site in which the self and other are brought into the domain of ethical acts.

How we can move from commodity culture to the imagination and to creative reading practices is more difficult to track through the logic of institutionally sanctioned discursive modes than it is to propose the connections thereto, and to do so would move us well beyond the limits of this essay. Can we then imagine that we have entered a discursive stream that meanders in a space-time field of energies that shifts as we move, a field that projects our desires even while it mediates the reach of our terminology? Such a field is both personal and social, and to the extent that it modulates the boundaries of the imagination it also generates different forms of consciousness. With this thought before us, I want to return to one of the key moments in the history of CanLit studies.

In thinking though the implications of form and the formations to which they give rise, it is revealing to turn to Northrop Frye's essay, a constituting document of CanLit as an institution and one that has received ongoing attention since its first publication.[1] In Imre Szeman's recent engagement with his "Conclusion to a *Literary History of Canada*," published in 1965, a period of the Cold War era when a powerful cultural nationalism ascended, Frye's essay is described as "an unavoidable text, the Urtext for the critical analysis of Canadian literary criticism" (176). He resituates Frye's reading of the Canadian literary scene in relation to "nation" as a formation in Canadian literature and criticism. Criticism receives more attention because, according to Szeman, it is primarily in its development "the nation has become the concept around which every other consideration revolves" (176). By literature, Szeman thinks primarily of fiction, and there he sees the absence of national cultural preoccupations, which leads him to argue that the valorization of the nation by critics goes contrary to its exhaustion as a vital force in the two major intellectuals whose work has been generative for criticism: George Grant and Northrop Frye.[2]

In his essay, Frye says (famously) that the "forms of literature are autonomous" (232), but since Canadian writers, as part of a colonial society, are so distant from these forms, they necessarily encounter a disconnect between reference and these forms, which have become foreign, or back there in a pre-colonial space and time. Consequently, writers of British or European origin in Canada have no choice but to represent their experience of place through foreign forms. Supposedly, we would get the kind of hunching that bpNichol says is the result of forms being imposed rather than created out of the actual conditions of existence. Having established a cultural and historical context for his imagined Canadian writers, Frye concludes with a Cartesian flourish, but with little sense of doubt: "The separation of subject and object is the primary fact of consciousness, for anyone so situated and so educated" (233). We have moved from a particular instance of an alienated condition, the result of colonial displacement, to a general state of consciousness.

Frye qualifies his assertion somewhat in acknowledging that some writers have overcome the shortcoming of their colonial situation to access "the real headwaters of inspiration" (234), but the general rule is that Canadian literature begins in its estrangement from its literary roots, which accounts for the "separation of subject and object." If left untended, such a fraught, even traumatic state could become unbearable. What is needed is the invention of tradition, and this calls for his central notion of the "pastoral myth" (238) that functions as the origin of Canadian literature. Leaving aside for now his use of this myth, what remains exceptional is the way Frye strategically frames the inaugural power of this literature's dislocated state. Applying the metaphor of organic growth in cultural formations, he proposes that, unlike American literature, Canadian literature did not undergo a historical phase during which a "social imagination can take root and establish a tradition" (219). English Canada went from being "part of the wilderness, then a part of North America and the British Empire, then a part of the world." Without recognizing the postwar efforts of the state to produce a national culture, a period that was formative for Frye's own work, his account implies that English Canada bypassed a national formation phase. Consequently, "Canadian writers are, even now [circa 1965], still trying to assimilate a Canadian environment at a time when new techniques of communication, many of which, like television, constitute a verbal market, are annihilating the boundaries of that environment." Frye does not explain the term "environment" but presumably he would include, aside from natural phenomena, the social, economic, political, and technological factors that were drawing Canada into a global network of relationships, in other words, away from the bounded elements of nationalist forms. For Frye, this truncated development helps account for Canadian culture's "fixation on its own past, its penchant for old-fashioned literary techniques, its preoccupation with strangled articulateness" (220).

It is at this point in his argument that Frye enunciates his now-illustrious question, the one that has generated so much speculation about the nature of English Canadian consciousness: "It seems to me," he writes, "that Canadian sensibility has been profoundly disturbed, not so much by our famous problem of identity, important as that is, as by a series of paradoxes which confronts that identity. It is less perplexed by the question 'Who am I?' than by some such riddle as 'Where is here?'"(220). When we, as current readers steeped in the proliferating discourses around globalizing processes, step out of the frame of Frye's endlessly provocative question, we may wonder who can, or would have, the state of consciousness to formulate such a question, and out of what conditions of apprehensiveness. "Where is here," when posed as a question, presumes a subject who is not here but elsewhere, at least in consciousness, and further that such an estrangement causes an anxiety, an anxiety that can perhaps be healed through the question. Further speculation might suggest that the question not only enables the positing of an answer, but is also designed to function as a rhetorical move that preempts the void threatening to dissolve the very possibility of the question—the real anxiety being the hunch that no here is here to be a where. The process of deferral, in any case, seems to motivate the writer to offer as a model for Canadian literature an aesthetic and national formation that compensates for the potentially debilitating split between subject and object in Canadian life, and thus for the threat of the inarticulate—an absence of meaning that, if left untended, would turn into a rational humanist nightmare.

On the surface, Frye's argument makes good and even pragmatic sense. The creation of a working relationship between subject and object—and by implication between literature and place—has been a generative preoccupation of nation-based CanLit studies in providing a thematic and methodological purpose for its cultural and institutional development. What has not been adequately noted, in my view, is that its formation functions as compensation for the otherwise-anxious state of estrangement with its sense of "strangled articulateness." In displacing the anxiety through an aesthetic form, Frye's model of CanLit bears some striking resemblances to Freud's model of civilization in *Civilization and its Discontents*, which functions as a form of compensation for the natural conditions of human suffering. For Freud, each individual organism with its ego drives and libidinal energies seeks to maximize its pleasure and minimize the pain it inevitably suffers because it is alive and mortal. As a humanist and rational formation, civilization works to manage individual egos, which, left on their own, would be in endless battles with other egos. It does so by cordoning off a space in the ego for the superego, a force that is internalized as conscience. Conscience, in turn, ensures that individuals will become social in working together to produce a civilization. While speaking about the regulatory power of conscience, Freud invokes the metaphor of the garrison in a way that prefigures Frye's use of "garrison mentality" (225) to identify colonial settler consciousness in Canada: "Civilization . . . obtains mastery over the individual's dangerous desire for aggression by weakening and disarming and by setting up an agency within him to watch over it, like a garrison in a conquered city" (70–71). Significantly, for Freud civilization progresses through a process akin to colonization: its power derives from its ability to appropriate and transform the materiality of the earth into objects that serve its own human-centred interests, acting in this sense as a rapacious force of technological empowerment. As he comments, "countries have attained a high level of civilization if we find that in them everything which can assist in the exploitation of the earth by man and in his protection against the forces of nature — everything, in short, which is of use to him — is attended to and effectively carried out" (39).

Within the terms of Freud's civilization, art and other creative forms manufacture "illusions" or fantasy sites to make suffering palatable. In such aesthetic forms, we show the "intention of making oneself independent of the external world by seeking satisfaction in internal, psychical processes" (27). By the "displacement of libido" in art forms, so Freud would have us believe,

> the connection with reality . . . is loosened; satisfaction is obtained from illusions, which are recognized as such without the discrepancy between them and reality being allowed to interfere with enjoyment. The region from which these illusions arise is the life of the imagination; at the time when the development of the sense of reality took place, this region was expressly exempted from the demands of reality-testing and was set apart for the purpose of fulfilling wishes which were difficult to carry out. (27)

For Frye, serious literary work begins when writers individuate themselves, detaching themselves from the social world of the "garrison mentality" (analogous to Freud's "reality") to enter the world of literature (analogous to Freud's "illusion"). The "pastoral myth, the vision of a social ideal" (238), which is derived from the forms of literature, embodies the innocence of "childhood" (239), both as a state of pure consciousness and a stage of innocence in the history of civilization. The pastoral myth functions to invent an idealized origin in which the split between subject and object has not occurred. In this pure site, the Canadian writer's wish to assume the condition of indigeneity is fulfilled, and this, Frye says, enables a "kind of rapport with nature which the Indian symbolizes" (239). The pastoral myth, which substitutes for the lack of tradition in a colonial space, also enables a nativization process through which indigenous presence is supplanted, or otherwise appropriated in the interests of Canadian national identity.

Reading Frye's question ("Where is here?") along-side Freud's *Civilization and Its Discontents* is instructive to help us understand the turn in his model of CanLit away from the actual contemporary conditions. Even while Frye believed that his country had already moved beyond the strict boundaries of nationalist forms, he himself desired an aesthetic space for CanLit where the fantasy of the pastoral myth could play itself out. In other words, the turn away from contemporary conditions necessitated the invention of literary origins in the pastoral as an aesthetic formation, one that could compensate for the void of colonial displacement and the imagined threats of a brutal amoral nature that is antithetical to settler consciousness. For Freud, "civiliza-tion" as a form of order constitutes itself through a violent appropriation of what lies outside of its domain, and this begins with the appropriation of nature, including indig-enous presence, to serve its human-centred social ends.

What is striking in reading Frye and Freud together is the alignment of the imagination with the unreal in their work, illusion in Freud and myth in Frye. In both instances, this capacity of consciousness is separated from the more dynamic and conflicted world of social and cultural concerns and situated in an aesthetic sphere that compensates for the dualism of the self and other. Szeman notes that Canadian literature, primarily fiction, exhibits few signs of the nationalist concerns evident in the criticism, but this may signal the effects of the separation of aesthetics from the political sphere, the result of which is the overall devaluation of the imagination as a creative critical force in our lives as citizen consumers. He hints at much of this situation when he asserts that "literature is itself constituted within the circuits of ideological operations of which the belief in the ahistorical autonomy of the literary is itself one of the chief and most powerful examples" (195). In their conception of the imagination, both Frye and Freud remain staunch humanists for whom reason is hierarchically valued over imagination, just as culture-as-civilization is valued over nature, and mind is valued over body.

Although, as Szeman says, Frye does not himself advocate a nation-based literature, his model of an origin in the "pastoral myth" could be incorporated into a nation-based literary criticism that needed a conceptual framework. The belated condition of the nation in Frye's model could, with little difficulty, ground the call for a national culture to bolster a drive for Canadian exceptionalism in the face of a liberal US mass media to the south and the conservative pull of European and British antecedents. Here the "pastoral" as analogous to contact with nature could function temporally as a "pre-colonial" (and thus "pre-modern") ground for the contemporary, and this strategy could enable a nativization process that displaced or otherwise covered over the violence of colonial civilization. What then lies beneath the pastoral is not an ancient well-spring of collective spirits, but the void of spaces — "where is here" — that dark "nature" that Frye says scared the heck out of the settlers who built their garrisons to keep this "wilderness" imagined in their Protestant assumptions at bay.

This reading of Frye's essay as a constituting moment in the history of CanLit studies raises at least three points of importance for thinking through the connectives that bring form, belief, and methodology into a dynamic alignment. First, as simple as this point may be, the strategic use of the pastoral myth shows that CanLit has no necessary existence, as some nationalists would have us believe, but was invented as a form through the methodological split between subject and object. It was this split, posited as a condition of existence, that allowed the products of CanLit to be understood as the creations of the individuation process and not as embedded in the cultural and political trajectories of colonialism. Second, in the production of an identity formation, the analogy between a return to childhood and the turn to becoming native — the basis of the nativization process — rendered invisible the displacement of native cultures and collectives. And third, the teleological imperative of "identity" as an end product established a model of literary formation, and this would include minority formations, such as Asian Canadian, that would focus more on reference and interpretation than on the politics of differential relations that has always underwritten acts of the imagination. It is, in this sense, quite ironic that the current shift in technology towards the personal as the site of mobile bodies has opened up, even necessitated, a rethinking of the ethical implications of creative critical reading and writing practices, practices that sometimes get lost in the rationalist-dominated forms of research and thought that are promulgated and sanctioned in literary studies.

## MEANWHILE, IN THE UNIVERSITY

In their introduction to their essay collection, *Retooling the Humanities: The Culture of Research in Canadian Universities*, Daniel Coleman and Smaro Kamboureli draw attention to the policies of the Social Sciences and Humanities Research Council (SSHRC) as the "barometer" of the "culture of research" governing Canadian universities (2), and rightly so in light of the central role played by SSHRC in vetting and funding the work of academics and graduate students. They conclude that research capitalism has become the dominant model of knowledge production in universities, and in this model, as if to mirror a neoliberal code of conduct, research is valued and validated according to capitalist standards of profit for investment, commercialization, and benefits for consumers. Thus, the public imagined in research capitalism is the "consumer" rather than the "citizen" (10), as the case would be with humanities scholarship that functions to question and critique such normative economic values. The genealogy informing research capitalism, which they trace from the early postwar Massey Commission through the 1980s to the present, exposes the marginalization of critically conscious and progressive humanities research and the complementary formation of institutional policies and attitudes that give priority to projects that service the economic interests of profit, commodity production, and consumerism. They conclude that

> the university has transfigured the resilience it has always displayed into a widespread accommodation of the ideologies and practices of capitalist logic. In so doing it has surrendered its responsibility to generate knowledge that produces critically aware and informed national and global citizens by submitting to the pressure to generate knowledge that meets the needs of the marketplace — a marketplace shaped as much by the demands of the present economic climate as the desire to meet the challenges of the twenty-first century. (31–32)

What we are left to contend with is the corporatization of university spaces, along with a fiercely competitive struggle for research grants, intellectual property rights, and the branding of research. Reinforcing the buyer/seller paradigm, researchers come to be seen more and more as entrepreneurs rather than scholars.

Research capitalism advocates the powerful assumption, in line with a neoliberal agenda, that knowledge is a commodity that is produced, exchanged, and sold in the form of patents and intellectual property rights. This instrumental view of knowledge is, of course, not new, but it has intensified in light of the alliances being forged between university researchers and corporations whose goal is the maximization of profits for its shareholders, not a critical awareness of the perils of commodification. Within this conjunction of knowledge and commodification, humanities scholars, and perhaps even more specifically literary scholars, have to address the belief that researchers, including their students in the classroom, are nothing more than talking heads who are constituted through rationality as the only method of determining what is valued as knowledge and what is not. The ever-present creativity of the living body and the unpredictable resources of the imagination, and the plethora of non-rational tensions and uncertainties that are operative in everyday intellection have to be stabilized and rendered coherent to produce a performatively success-ful discourse for knowledge production. Knowledge and rationality are so consonant in academic culture that other modes, such as intuition, spiritual vision, non-local commu-nication (e.g., ESP or telepathy), and even poetic texts that do not conform to norms of rationality are discounted, and often ridiculed. This is not to deny the power of rationality, but assuming that it is the only form of legitimate knowledge production establishes a boundary that abnormalizes the creative and displaces its central importance in the invention of new forms and the necessary critiques of existing ones.

One of the greatest disservices promulgated in lit-erary studies as a discipline — and this has permeated the modes of assessing performance for graduate studies, pub-lication, promotion, and grants — is the distance assumed between the creative act and the critical contexts brought to visibility in the methodologies we adopt in our teaching and writing practices. Even when we pay lip service to the creative as an embodied mode of consciousness, it is the rational that is sanctified as the sign of legitimate knowl-edge acquisition. Creative texts are assumed to be outside of legitimate knowledge formations. Can we conceive of an institutional future in which a poem or novel that performs the boundaries of representation and an academic essay that talks about the boundaries of representations can be read as equivalent forms of knowledge production in the university? Probably not, at least not in the near future. Are we to conceive of creative texts, then, as the innocent victims of the appropriating claws of institutional mechanisms? Of course not. Texts can never be free from contextualization because their creators are themselves social and somatic beings whose desires are mediated by the same assumptions of their critics. But the unquestioned rational interpretations of textual processes enabled by the various methodological approaches we have devised and continue to devise — whether progressively postcolonial or reactionary postcolonial, hip postmodernism or samo postmodernism, whether critical multiculturalism or management multiculturalism, and so on — often perform their discursive power at the expense of the rich field of indeterminacies that the creative process thrives on, and which produces the somatic fluidities and disequilibriums that we associate with the life energy of the imagination.

Say what? Is it fair to question the honest and hard work of literary scholars who have honed their ratiocinative skills to produce critical essays that present powerfully cogent arguments? Well, perhaps, given that success in the disciplinary space of the university depends on these skills. But my concern is that the largely normalized ascendancy of rationality as the measure of knowledge production in our institutional practices has resulted in the fall of the (excuse my language here) stock value of the imagination, despite the often-begrudging acknowledgement that art production constitutes a form of knowingness. Even then, such acknowledgement arises usually after some form of institutionally sanctioned interpretation has validated its worth. Overall, universities function under the constituting assumption of rationalism that its methodology, based on self-consistency, thesis and proof, and logic, is superior to the affective and sensorial flows of the imagination, affiliated as it is with a somatic consciousness tied to the becomingness of life processes. We see this in the starkly simplistic contestation between *subject* and *object*—comparable to the split in Frye's essay—that still underlies much academic work, even in the face of theoretical work that has demonstrated that this divide serves to structure the value-constructing systems of institutions and their state benefactors. This divide, which resembles a colonial model of knower and known, becomes a big lie without which the fruits of knowledge production could not be picked so easily, and it helps to explain the undermining of autonomy (and therefore personal agency) in current research methodologies. Instead of empowering the personal to assume responsibility for the effects of knowledge production, it gives power over to the regulatory mechanisms of what can broadly be called *disciplinarity*, the belief that rational forms of knowledge form the sole objective of its institutions, and hence the exclusion of other forms of knowing, such as spirituality, myth, belief, ESP, other translocal phenomena, and even poetry. Much of this non-rational material reveals the workings of consciousness as a manifestation of living organisms that are also social beings, ourselves included in our research methods and the thought processes we undergo to arrive at the writing forms we use to represent our work.

Just as the mind is never simply a receptacle but a producer of what comes to appearance in its forms, so too, as Cornelius Castoriadis reminds us, the living organism is never just a passive receptor of external phenomena but is always creating "its sensations," so that "there is a *corporeal imagination*" that is always in play in consciousness. Since the "body is always, in a sense, psychical and the psyche always, in certain regards, somatical" (180), critical thinking, as it unfolds on any given occasion, is bound up with non-visible somatic affects (e.g., of desire, love, hate, disgust, pleasure, fear, anxiety, and so on) that texture the outcome of its more overt intellectual negotiations. Such a range of affects, often at odds with each other, can play a large role in the interpretation or discursive representation of creative texts, perhaps more visibly so in those texts — my own interest in CanLit and Asian Canadian studies — that embody either prescribed or inscribed signs of difference, or so-called deviance from normative regulatory formations. We have called these texts variously in social terms as minority texts, racialized texts, multicultural texts, other texts, and in cultural terms as (fill in the blank identity) Canadian texts. Post-Frye, and in the wake of the identity politics that marked the decades prior to the more powerful ascendancy of neoliberal tenets in the 1990s, such marked texts caused a considerable amount of oppositional and resistant critical work, as well as a considerable amount of defensive critical work, as the model of nation-based CanLit literature underwent the shifting hues of the rainbow — a moving target in the shifting eyes of desire motivating a range of reading practices. If in the dominant language of commodity culture, we have gone *post*, from IP as identity politics to IP as Internet provider, the latter our current source of consumer empowerment, then I believe the time has come to reassess the potency of the reading processes that form both the creative and critical parameters of our work in CanLit studies, and by implication literary studies in general.

## CREATIVE CRITICAL READING PRACTICES

Of all the intellectual activities that are prominent in literary studies, the reading of texts is both taken for granted and is considered to be the most creative of critical acts. For students conditioned to see themselves as receptacles rather than as producers of knowledge, reading becomes largely an unconscious act that gets them through courses. The only time it becomes visible is when a text is no longer decipherable and therefore no longer consumable or otherwise commodified. Literary studies, I think, is very fortunate to have for its sphere of inquiry a methodology that enables an approach to broader dimensions of interpretive processes that involve, if we allow for it, both creative and critical concerns. For what I call creative critical reading I have in mind the kind of reflexive reading practices that complement the multi-faceted contexts that make up the shifting spaces of consciousness in readers who are themselves mobile subjects and, in potential at least, capable of initiating ethical acts that have justice and social equity as modes of desire.

Here, at the risk of faltering in my own terminological deficits, I want to suspend focus on the outcomes of interpretations — those discursive entities that we call critical essays that advance an argument — and draw attention to the methodological possibility offered in the reading process itself. Despite the rigorous training of literary specialists to produce cogent arguments based on a demonstration of contents and sources mastered, the imaginatively saturated immersion in the reading of texts is where, I would predict, we encounter our desires, fears, anxieties, and so on, mirrored in the materiality of the texts, though unfortunately in the instrumental process of constructing a rationally sound argument, much of the non-rational, affective whirlpool of phenomena experienced gets reduced to the plane of logic, commodity, intellectual ownership, and institutional stature.

In active forms of reading, we are allowed to undergo the throes of unknowingness, doubt, excitement, repulsion, attraction, frustration, discovery, revelation, and all comparable states of a consciousness that awaken to the virtual images, narratives, and language that constitute the forms of creative texts. In direct contrast to the more appropriative strategies of reading in disciplines that emphasize the mastering of theme and concept, literary studies begins with the seemingly unproblematic but, as we know, highly unpredictable, contingent, and open-ended act of encountering and negotiating the complicated material and referential elements of texts. While nothing in the arsenal of reading literary signs can prevent appropriative readings based on predetermined assumptions and frameworks, the performance of what I call creative critical reading practices calls for a willingness, not only to be open to images, narratives, language forms, and the experience of alterity, but also to reflect on the overlapping contingencies that govern the assumptions, both personal and social, that are brought into play. The activity of reading then holds the potential of releasing creative (and somatic) energies as well as opening a site for critical (self-)reflection, and therefore a site wherein ethical questions can be posed and explored. As a pedagogical methodology, as well as a primer for writing critical interpretations, creative critical reading practices have the potential to encounter the imagination, both in oneself and in texts, as a projective force that operates in often wily, non-rational, somatic ways in our reading of texts.

In his discussion of ethics, Michel Foucault talks about the self as "not a substance. It is a form, and this form is not primarily or always identical to itself" (290). This loss of the self's armouring, which bpNichol recognized as part of the creative process, opens up the formal dimensions of its precarious embeddedness in somatic and social transferences with far-reaching implications for our relations with others and with the contingencies that compose our imagination of otherness. Daniel Coleman's *In Bed with the Word* draws attention to the "outward-reaching energy" that is inherent in the simple desire to read. "What is important about it is that . . . it flies in the face of solipcism, the myth of autonomy and self-completeness. The desire to read emphasizes a basic generosity toward the Other that is the condition of all language" (14). Without turning a blind eye towards the potential for reading to be used as a means of indoctrination and social engineering, along with Coleman, we need to recognize (even celebrate) reading as a form in which consciousness can enact a more malleable and inclusive range of questions and reflections — about references, for instance, and intent, meaning, framing, positioning, voice, and other literary and extra-literary elements. In such a mode of attention, the reading subject becomes more attuned to fields of differential and asymmetrical relations that constitute the complex of representations that produce the limits of language, thought, and knowledge. How, for instance, might this mode of attention connect with our desire to do justice to CanLit?

In the not-too-distant past, at a time when so-called minority texts were finding their way into course lists, their mere inclusion was read as an ethical and therefore just act. After all, by including minority texts, we were supposedly making space for what had been excluded and we were thereby enabling minority voices to have a place in the institution, even though, as I recall, we tended to shy away from asking how and why they came to be marked or minoritized in the first place. Now that we have, again supposedly, gone beyond this dimension of identity politics, we can see that the institutional incorporation of minority texts as ethical, even when such incorporation made certain minority writers and communities more accessible to readers, remains problematic. I agree with Vikki Bell in *Culture and Performance* that ethical practices are not dependent solely on taking a position for the inclusion of formerly excluded work, or against perceived injustices, or even promoting a cause that might lead to the amelioration of hardships. These can be noble acts that should be encouraged, but whether they constitute ethical acts depends on our modes of questioning the extent of our critical understanding of the contingencies out of which such acts have taken formation. Bell sees ethics "figured neither as a source of politics nor as a political weapon, but as a check on freedom, an inspiration that prompts a continual questioning of one's own positionality, including . . . the conditions of possibility of one's ethical sensibilities" (51). Or to cite from Foucault's *Ethics*: "Freedom is the ontological condition of ethics. But ethics is the considered form that freedom takes when it is informed by reflection" (284). Kamboureli takes this line of thinking further in her provocative critical essay on Yann Martel's *Self*, "The Limits of the Ethical Turn," where she distinguishes between the recent turn to ethics in literary and cultural theory and the necessity, in an "ethical turn," to "remain mindful of the transactions it involves lest they incur violence in lieu of the violence we try to remedy" (945). Much of the difficulty in assessing what constitutes an ethical act has do with the recognition of the conditions and contingencies that produce differential relations from which we benefit or not, according to our differing access to dominant representational schemata. In the forms of literature — in their very textuality — we encounter the potential of the imagination either to open up or to foreclose a reflexive approach to the somatic and social production of cultural values — values that I believe call for constant critique.

The critical reflexivity associated with the ethics of reading practices, as effective as it can be as a methodology for literary studies, is also vulnerable to the discursive forms that translate their fluidity into the regulatory systems of academic norms, norms in which, as I have already noted, the rules of rationality (thesis, argument, evidence, and coherence) become the only measure of legitimacy and authority. There are, however, strong grounds for maintaining the experience of reflexivity, even or especially when drawn into forces of non-rational incommensurability, incoherence, and the absence of proper syntax and grammar. In his account of reading, drawing on the work of Ronald Rolheiser, Coleman goes so far as to compare the reading act to the form of prayer, not prayer as a "series of requests," but prayer as "a specific form of pondering, a patient bearing of tension" (*In Bed With the Word* 109). He develops this point by referring to theologian Rolheiser's notion of prayer as a form in which "one is willing to live in unresolved tension" (qtd. 110). Creative critical reading, then, might be considered a kind of pondering that slows down the interpretive process to the point where readers can imagine the differential relations that are mobile in their consciousness. Such a temporality, in stark contrast to the speeding up of time in the technoscape of commodity culture, allows for a process of reflection in which questions of justice and equity rise to the surface. In this respect, a recent study conducted by specialists of somatic affects is telling. In experiments that measured subjects' response to the pain and suffering of others, the researchers concluded that the speed of information flow in the latest technological outlets, such as cell phones and the Internet, may actually forestall the development of affects such as empathy and compassion. "The rapidity and parallel processing of attention-requiring information, which hallmark the digital age, might reduce the frequency of full experience of such emotions, with potentially negative consequences" (Immordino-Yang 8024).

Against the rapid flow of information in current neoliberal commodity culture, creative critical reading practices, which are the hallmark of literary studies, may be one of the most profound aspects of our work. If, through some technological invention, we could make visible the vast network of energies set into motion when one reader, whose subjectivity has been shaped by an immeasurable complex of somatic and discursive variables, undergoes the language of a text and interacts with other readers who bring to the texts their own complex of variables, we might begin to respect the power of the creative critical imagination, even in instances of misidentification of references, semantic slippages, and all the so-called failures to decode the text through conventional or discipline-specific rules and assumptions. Few disciplines practice reading processes in which the boundaries between self and other become so porous that we necessarily begin to engage in immediate relations with each other. Here pedagogical interventions become a crucial means of preventing collective engagements with texts from falling into solecisms, at which point the "unresolved tension" between self and other would default to dominant power formations. When the tension is maintained, reading practices enter into negotiation with the limits of representations as formations that constitute what comes to be both visible and legible and therefore what becomes invisible and illegible according to normative measures of truth-value.

## A TAKE ON ASIAN CANADIAN

Genealogically, the abstraction Asian Canadian, which strangely enough never referenced anyone in particular, other than those who were abstractly identified or who self-identified under the racialized term Asian, embodies the long history of racialization by the Canadian state. Many who would happily identify themselves as Chinese Canadian or Japanese Canadian or South Asian Canadian would resist referring to themselves as Asian Canadian. As a formation, Asian Canadian came to appearance in the wake of CanLit, during the Cold War era that also shaped Northrop Frye's model of the garrison mentality. Through the production of cultural nationalism, the state sought to shape a more standardized citizenry around coherent beliefs and symbols, but even so, the nation imagined in its policies suffered instability under pressure from external (transnational) and internal (intranational) forces. At the risk of oversimplification, we can trace the shifting parameters of cultural politics through a legacy of concerns that conditioned the arrival and continuing transformation of Asian Canadian:

> ▬ from the cultural homogeneity proposed by the Massey Commission and enacted through agencies such as the Canada Council and the National Film Board and its notion of the nation as coherent;

- to the emergence and problematics of multicultur-alism with its heated debates over the inclusionary and exclusionary boundaries of cultural representa-tions, racialization, and social justice;

- to the ascendancy of the discourse of globalization, which heralded the politics of neoliberalism and the commodification of culture;

- to a highly indeterminate and volatile globaliza-tion in which transnational flows are uncertain and unpredictable, new nationalisms are invented, and old-style or fundamentalist identity politics can have dire consequences.

One of the advantages of studying formations like Asian Canadian, as simultaneously minoritized and emergent, is that the contradictory effects of differential relations between subjects can be more visible than in dominant and therefore normalized formations. Similar to CanLit, to which it has been aligned, Asian Canadian functions in a kind of virtual mode with always-provisional references to socially constituted groups and, as such, has no necessary existence. Despite what some supporters and skeptics might argue, it has no essential reason to be. It could sever its con-nection to Canadian to become Asian, which it might do in time, and its existence would become no more substantial. And, again in time, it might come to signify Canadian alone without the Asian qualifier, and even then, it would remain the floating signifier it has always been. Does this tentative status as a mirage-like form mean that it loses its cultural and aesthetic value as a body of literature and a subject worthy of specialization in the field of literary studies? To the contrary, its very malleability and vulnerability may make it the ideal type for literary studies at a time, such as the present, when we are called to a radical rethinking of critical methodologies that can result in progressive social transformation. Asian and Asian Canadian as terms are both continually produced and created, produced as effects within vast and overlapping social and cultural histories, and created as affects in multiple ways by subjects who choose to situate themselves in its field of references.

For me, a limit frame for this discussion is a recently published posthumous text by Roy K. Kiyooka, one that I was fortunate to edit myself. Kiyooka's *The Artist and the Moose: A Fable of Forget* is striking for the ways in which it enters into negotiation with a nation-based cultural centrism that honed the unidentified narrator's subjectivity but placed him on its almost-invisible margins. In good Canadian fashion, perhaps to accommodate "regional disparities" (17), he is appointed by Prime Minister Jason Decentbaker to head a Royal Commission whose task it is to come up with a twenty-first century multicultural aesthetic. To achieve his mission, the narrator undertakes research on the most iconic Canadian artist of his time, the landscape artist Tom Thomson, who becomes Thomas Aplomb in Kiyooka's text. Aplomb's death in Algonquin Park in July 1917, and particularly the mysterious circumstances surrounding it, had provided the fodder by which cultural nationalists erected a now-creaking national identity. Is it possible that the clues to a twenty-first century aesthetic lie in solving

267 | Doing Justice to CanLit Studies

the unresolved cause of the artist's death? If Aplomb was murdered, and some evidence points that way, who was the guilty person who killed a nascent Canadian icon?

Off the narrator goes to the national archives, acting very much like a diligent academic in pursuit of a hot research project, and there he immerses himself in the archival traces of Aplomb's untimely death while at the same time experiencing the political culture of his nation's capital. The fabulous tale that unfolds, with an exiled-from-his-natural-home ol' Moose as the intrepid narrator's mentor, performs a creative critical reading of the construction of Canadian cultural nationalism, a formation that is constituted through the displacement of its colonial violence. The displacement, and subsequent invention, of a national identity enabled the erasure of the aboriginal communities whose lands had been appropriated. Soon after his death, and in fact because of his death, the aesthetic spaces of Aplomb's art in Algonquin Park, a federally managed site, became the material through which cultural nationalists invented a so-called native tradition that validated the sovereignty of the Canadian state. In perhaps the most prescient moment of the text, Kiyooka's narrator zeroes in on the work of one Judge William Little. In the 1950s, when the reputation of Thomson as national icon was still developing, Judge Little decided to clear up at least one of the mysteries surrounding the artist's body. Contrary to the official story, that the body was moved to the artist's childhood home, did it remain where it was initially interred in Algonquin Park?

While drawing on the judge's narrative in his book, *The Tom Thomson Mystery*, Kiyooka's narrator twists his own narrative to reveal the darker underbelly of colonial history. From the mounds of colonial documents in the archives, he comes to recognize the violence of representation in the official history of the nation, noting that the documents "had been pitilessly mined from the slag heaps of the Laurentian Shield since the advent of Christianity in the New World. Otherwise, his own ruminations kept turning into palimpsests with each new entreaty, whereas the Official Documents kept reiterating (in bold italics) the litany of a hostile Tundra, with every footnote diminishing both 'Moose' and 'Native'" (24). There are shades of the representation of nature as an amoral threatening force in Northrop Frye, who makes a cameo appearance in Kiyooka's text as Friar Northtrope, when the narrator informs his readers: "Ol' Moose balefully agreed with his adversary . . . that the Angles and the Saxons had an unmitigated Garrison Mentality, one that harkened back to the Black Plague and other scourges of the Middle Ages" (85). In any case, back with Judge Little, the narrator recounts that Little and a small band form an expedition to dig up the grave site. They come upon a skeleton that they quickly assume to be the body of the iconic artist. After professional forensic testing, however, they are dismayed to learn that the skeleton is too short and, surprise surprise, also aboriginal. For the narrator, fact transmogrifies into a narrative turn that exposes the limits of representation. Had the white settler/artist Thomas Aplomb, in death, replaced the native, as the advocates of cultural nationalism would have it? Or had Aplomb become native, so that his whiteness had been subsumed as it entered the condition of death in its dislocated condition? Or does the act of digging up the past expose the visibility of a native presence that had been suppressed? The interpretive possibilities multiply according to the shifting positions of readers.

In *The Artist and the Moose*, Kiyooka performs a creative critical reading of a national cultural formation that does not account for the limits of its representation. What is interesting for my discussion here is that Kiyooka began his Tom Thomson project in the mid-to-late 1960s, a period of heightened nationalism and also the period in which Northrop Frye wrote the final words to the nationalist literary project edited by Carl F. Klinck, *Literary History of Canada* (1965). The synchronicity of events, I would suggest, is no accident. But the kind of creative critical intent that is evident in Kiyooka's narrative would have been contrary to the object of desire for cultural nationalists of the time. For literary studies, the model of the pastoral myth was much more conducive to institutionalization and allowed for the development of a referential mode of criticism that could stabilize itself around notions of identity and place, the hallmarks of nation-based CanLit studies. Strangely, or not, depending on our critical lens, the aesthetic and cultural spaces of Kiyooka's *Transcanada Letters*, a companion text to *The Artist and the Moose*, are extensions of those contemporary Canadian conditions identified by Frye, which Frye bypasses in his term "pastoral myth," revealing perhaps his own desire for a more homogenous and conservative literature in Canada. In *Transcanada Letters* Kiyooka recognizes the limits of a nationalist culture that identifies and excludes minorities as well as the generative possibilities of transnational cultural work. Tellingly, the first text in *Transcanada Letters* is not a letter but a report to the Canada Council written from Japan, and it ends with an affirmation of aesthetic forms produced in the conditions of the contemporary, a principle that Northrop Frye may very well have approved:

> *possibilities*
>
> HERE
>
> > (or, Anywhere
> > no larger than Everyman's Vision —
> > > has it ever been more
> > > than this ?
> >
> > ALL THINGS SWIRL
> > making for whats possible
> >
> > > > HERE / NOW (2005, 3)

While Frye reflects on the cultural history of Canadian set-tler culture and methodically constructs a model of literary formations that relies on the European humanist binary so necessary to colonization — civilization over nature — Kiyooka goes trans-Canada, traversing the geographical and cultural extent of the nation as he assembles a multiplicity of voices and subjects who form metonymically the matrix of the body politic in which writers and artists are embedded, and his nation already includes signs of the transnational and global forces that Frye says poses a threat to the autonomy of Canadian literature. In the interplay of methodology and belief, Kiyooka's artist negotiates fragments and contingen-cies, contradiction and revelation, as he moves in and out of the multiple variables that inform the boundaries of his subjectivity to construct a kind of living encyclopedia of Gertrude Stein's "continuous present," which he refers to in the epigraph of *Transcanada Letters*. As weird as it may sound initially, I think it is instructive to imagine the subsequent history of Canadian literary studies had this work achieved the canonic status of Frye, so that "our" beginnings had been more preoccupied with forms of difference in our actually existing conditions rather than with the demarcation of identity boundaries.

The narrator's skepticism in Kiyooka's narrative extends to his research in the national archives, where he discovers that the representations of the present and the past are highly determined by the discourse of dominant institutions. The eventual failure of own quest to unravel the mystery of Thomas Aplomb's death takes on symbolic importance to suggest a productive crisis of knowledge production. Knowledge has limits, and these limits become visible in the experience of finitude. Any pinning down of meaning leads to the appropriation of the creative for pre-determined ends. Representations, as such, are precarious forms that can never be taken at face value.

Unfortunately, literary studies does not have access to a crystal ball to see what might have been or what might yet come to appearance. It remains, nevertheless, for these eyes a speculative possibility to imagine *Transcanada Letters* to be the body found when an intrepid group of scholars went in search of Frye's "Conclusion to a *Literary History of Canada*." Is this kind of transformation, or exchange of critical spirits, possible in this our world of belief in the rational method? If Kamboureli is right, and I believe her, "the constancy of the ethical is infinitely postponed" ("The Limits" 947); because ethics is conditioned by acts in the here and now, it is always possible to invent new possibilities that can alter our understanding of the past. Asian Canadian texts such as *Transcanada Letters* and *The Artist and the Moose*, as well as Wah's *Diamond Grill*, Goto's *The Kappa Child*, Lai's *Salt Fish Girl*, Mathur's *The Short, Happy Life of Harry Kumar*, and, most recently, Wong's *Forage* and her collaborative text with Lai, *Sybil Unrest*, and there are many others, inhabit always-provisional frameworks that take on shifting contours according to the reading practices brought to them. The more effective they are as creative critical forms that make us more conscious of differential relations of power and representation, the more they can make us aware of our responsibilities in generating the desire, not for commodities, but for justice.

## A TENTATIVE CONCLUSION

If, in a post-Frye context, we understand the invention of CanLit to be a strategic move on the part of cultural nationalists in a belated nation, then CanLit has no necessary existence and, similar to other identity formations, such as Asian Canadian, needs to be approached as a provisional and contingent formation and therefore a limit frame that is always open to collective reinvention. As Jacques Derrida reminds us in *Specters of Marx*, "An inheritance is never gathered together, it is never one with itself. Its presumed unity, if there is one, can consist only in the *injunction* to *reaffirm by choosing*" (16). Its future is governed by the agency of its advocates and the forms they produce—and whether actions generate ethical acts or not needs to be measured according to the methodologies and beliefs they adopt and practice. It can no longer be measured simply on the authenticity (or not) of any given identity formation, since any identity formation as such is constituted on exclusionary/inclusionary boundaries. When CanLit is approached as a provisional and contingent formation, the representational frames of its ties to the geographical, legal, cultural, and symbolic elements of Canada manifest a multiplicity of unresolved desires, discourses, and publics. What then comes to be called "the local" is a site of immediacy for differing and deferring subjects whose mobility is always inflected by networks of determinants and indeterminacies, both close to the skin and globally distant in the overlapping conjunctions of moment to moment existence. Research at these limits needs to draw on the resources of the imagination to invent writing forms consonant with those limits. Belief in such a methodological potential is crucial to its enactment in creative critical practices wherein the desire for justice is never far away.

*Notes*

1    In Vancouver, the arrival of Chinese migrant labourers from the Fujian
     province elicited the interventionist activism of a new organization
     called DAARE (Direct Action Against Refugee Exploitation), "formed
     by a group of women in Vancouver to support the rights of the people
     — especially the women — from China seeking refuge in Canada"
     (from a pamphlet). DAARE has been instrumental in speaking back
     to media misrepresentations and in assisting those seeking refugee
     status. Their educational work brought to the public's attention the
     complicit relations between Canada's global capitalist agenda and the
     exploitation of Asian labour — a reinscription of the brutal exploita-
     tion of racialized Chinese railway workers in the nineteenth century.

2    In addition to Penrose's essay, the following resources have been
     helpful in providing a basis for this discussion: Ann Cvetkovich and
     Douglas Kellner, eds., *Articulating the Global and the Local*; Anthony D.
     King, ed., *Culture, Globalization and the World-System*; Fredric Jameson
     and Masao Miyoshi, eds., *The Cultures of Globalization*; and Rob Wilson

and Wimal Dissanayake, eds., *Global / Local*. Along with Penrose, theorists such as Miyoshi and Dirlik also point to the emergent power of the transnational corporation in displacing the concentration of capital within the nation's boundaries and its dispersal across borders in networks that begin to supersede the control of specific nation-states. See, for instance, Dirlik's "The Global in the Local" and Miyoshi's "A Borderless World? From Colonialism to Transnationalism and the Decline of the Nation-State" in *Global / Local*.

3    This is not the occasion to address the specific impact of US control of media representations in Canada as a form of cultural imperialism, except to agree with Fredric Jameson in his "Notes on Globalization" that unequal relations of power underscore the ubiquitous "Americanization" process that is carried out under the auspices of economic trade. As he says, "American mass culture, associated as it is with money and commodities, enjoys a prestige that is perilous for most forms of domestic cultural production" (59) — Canada, for instance — and it is all the more reductive and standardizing as it brings in its folds, to undermine the cultural specificities of local conditions, the figure of the consumer as a kind of cultural patron and the goods s/he consumes as a form of cultural performance.

4    For a critique of the "natural" as constructed, see Stacey Takacs.

5    See Marcia Crosby, as well as work by Roxanne Ng and Daniel Francis. Regarding various mechanisms used by the Canadian state to construct a nation, Jan Penrose points to the use of education to get subjects to identify with the "nation" through constructed narratives of "historical and contemporary events and, perhaps most importantly of all, for standardizing language" (23). The dramatic instance still remains the so-called "Residential Schools" through which First Nations children were deracinated with the intent to re-make them as colonial subjects through the medium of Christian discourses. The state also makes use of national media (print, radio, and television) "for promulgating hegemonic views of what the Canadian nation was or ought to be" (24).

6    See, for instance, Eva Mackey, Veronica Strong-Boag et. al., Daiva Stasiulis and Radha Jhappan, Ninette Kelley and Michael Trebilcock, and Jonathan Kertzer.

7 The critique of multiculturalism is voluminous, and beyond the specific focus of this chapter, but Katharyne Mitchell's essay "In Whose Interest?", focusing on Vancouver, offers a compelling argument for the caution that cultural theorists and activists need to exercise in reading new cultural productions by minoritized artists and writers through the discourse of multiculturalism as developed in Canadian contexts. What is interpreted as progressive or inclusionary, e.g., new texts by Asian Canadian writers, may be seen as such through its complicity with the expansion of transnational Asian capital that requires the language of multiculturalism as a means of covering over, or even mediating, the continuing racialization of Asian Canadians.

8 It is also important to note that "whiteness," as itself a shifting and malleable category, has historically adjusted its exclusionary borders to maintain its normative conditions. Hence "Ukrainians," for instance, as well as East Europeans, initially considered non-white by the largely Anglo-Saxon majority, were eventually incorporated into the sphere of an expanded whiteness, in contrast to "Asians," "Aboriginals," and "Blacks," who have consistently been constituted through variations on their projected otherness.

9 For a fascinating, and meticulous, examination of the effects of legalized racialization on the local conditions of Chinese Canadian subjects in Saskatchewan in the early part of this century, see Constance Backhouse's legal "narrative" (her term) on two trials set in Moose Jaw, Saskatchewan in May 1912. Two "Chinese" men, Quong Wing and Quong Sing, had been charged with a recently passed provincial statute — the "first of its kind in Canada" (315) — that made it an offence for "Chinese" to hire "white women" in their businesses.

10 For further discussion of this early history, see Patricia Roy, Kay Anderson, and Ken Adachi.

11 See, for instance, the complicated debates that have formed around the term in Anne McClintock et. al., eds.; Iain Chambers and Lidia Curti, eds.; and Patrick Williams and Laura Chrisman, eds.; its Canadian variations can be found in *Past the Last Post*, edited by Ian Adam and Helen Tiffin; and the special issues *Testing the Limits*, edited by Diana Brydon and *Postcolonialism and Its Discontents*, edited by Pamela McCallum, Stephen Slemon, and Aruna Srivastava.

## TURNING IN, TURNING OUT
### THE SHIFTING FORMATIONS OF JAPANESE CANADIAN FROM UPROOTING TO REDRESS

*1*   The series, published with the support of the federal government, was called "Generations: A History of Canada's People." The reference to "Supply and Services Canada" is found not in the publication, but in Multiculturalism and Citizenship Canada 1993, *Resource Guide of Publications Supported by Multiculturalism Programs, 1973–1992* (26).

*2*   See Kirsten Emiko McAllister's essay, which examines the critical implications of the processes through which Japanese Canadians narrated themselves into the nation. Thanks to Kirsten for sharing with me an early draft of her essay.

*3*   From the language on the identification cards of my grandparents, Tokusaburo and Yoshi Ooto, who were registered on August 7, 1941.

## CAN ASIAN ADIAN?
### READING SOME SIGNS OF ASIAN CANADIAN

*1*   For discussions of the rapidly shifting demographics of the so-called Asian presence and the resurgence of anti-Asian racism in Canada, see the collection of essays in *The Silent Debate*, the proceedings of a conference held in Vancouver in 1997. "In 1994," as Aprodicio A. Laquian and Eleanor A. Laquian point out in their introduction, "a total of 142,997 Asians were admitted to Canada, making up 63.8 per cent of the total number of immigrants" (3).

## "INSIDE THE BLACK EGG"
### CULTURAL PRACTICE, CITIZENSHIP, AND BELONGING IN A GLOBALIZING CANADIAN NATION

*1*   The integral relationship between property and the discourse of rights helps to explain the implications of the issue of cultural appro- priation that raged in Canadian cultural circles in the late 1980s and early 1990s. The controversy requires a separate essay, but here it's useful to remind ourselves that the question of ownership over the products of the imagination remains an ethical dilemma for cultural creators.

*2*   This subtitle is a variation on a very useful essay on nation formation by Katherine Verdery, "Whither 'Nation' and 'Nationalism'?".

## A POETICS OF THE HYPHEN
### FRED WAH, ASIAN CANADIAN, AND CRITICAL METHODOLOGY

1   Tomlinson references Roland Robertson's use of this term to insist that "the local and the global . . . do not exist as cultural polarities but as mutually 'interpenetrating' principles." Robertson, he says, appropriated the term "from (originally Japanese) business discourse where essentially it refers to a 'micro-marketing' strategy — 'the tailoring and advertising of goods and services on a global or near-global basis to increasingly differentiated local and particular markets'" (195–96). See Robertson, "Globalization: Time-space and Homogeneity-heterogeneity," *Global Modernities,* eds. Mike Featherstone, Scott Lash, and Roland Robertson (Thousand Oaks, CA: Sage, 1995), 23–44.

## ARE YOU RESTLESS TOO? NOT TO WORRY, SO IS RITA WONG
### TOWARDS A POETICS OF THE APPREHENSIVE

1   In "Why Is France Burning?" Doug Ireland explains the volatile implications of the word *karcher*: "'Karcher' is the well-known brand name of a system of cleaning surfaces by super-high-pressure sand-blasting or water-blasting that very violently peels away the outer skin of encrusted dirt — like pigeon-shit — even at the risk of damaging what's underneath. To apply this term to young human beings and proffer it as a strategy is a verbally fascist insult and, as a policy proposed by an Interior Minister, is about as close as one can get to hollering 'ethnic cleansing' without actually saying so. It implies raw police power and force used very aggressively, with little regard for human rights."

2   My reading of Rita Wong's poems here is based on her chapbook, *Nervous Organism*, published in a limited edition in 2003. The poems are included in her book, *Forage*, which received the Dorothy Livesay Poetry Award for 2003. The page references are to *Forage*. In my discussion of her poems from this book, I indicate the page number with the title of the poem but not with the individual lines cited. Thanks to Rita Wong for sharing with me her unpublished essays, "Consensual Practices" and "Re Sounding Dissent in a Time-and-Space of Imperial Delirium."

3    Wong acknowledges the source of the title in a sentence from
     Northrop Frye's *Anatomy of Criticism*. The sentence, which is hand-
     written as a frame around the poem, reads: "Some philosophers
     who assume that all meaning is descriptive meaning tell us that, as
     a poem does not describe things rationally, it must be a description
     of emotion. According to this, the literal core of poetry would be a
     *cri de Coeur*, to use the elegant expression, the direct statement of a
     nervous organism confronted with something that seems to demand
     an emotional response, like a dog howling at the moon" (qtd. in
     *Forage* 20).

4    In Wong's *Forage,* only the first of the four indented lines of "domes-
     tic operations" is in italics. Here I am following the form used in
     her chapbook *Nervous Organism* where all four lines, although not
     indented, are in italics. In email correspondence, Wong acknowledged
     that all four lines should have been in italics in *Forage.*

5    See François Debrix's critical reading of Robert D. Kaplan's *Warrior
     Politics: Why Leadership Demands a Pagan Ethos* (New York: Random
     House, 2002). Debrix argues that this work transforms the abjection
     that set in post-9/11 into an aggressive discourse of "war and terror"
     that advocates "a return to the warrior way of ruling one's state and
     dominating others" (1160), thus portraying war as a "glorious politi-
     cal activity" (1162). Debrix reads two other books in the same light:
     Michael Ledeen's *The War Against the Terror Masters: What It Happened,
     Where We Are Now, How We'll Win* (New York: St Martin's Griffin,
     2003), and Victor David Hanson's *An Autumn of War: What America
     Learned from September 11 and the War on Terrorism* (New York: Anchor
     Books, 2002).

6    This discourse established a social milieu in which, as Judith Butler
     argues in "Explanation and Exoneration, or What We Can Hear,"
     critiques of US militarism were read as "complicitous with terrorism"
     (177) or otherwise censored by the mainstream media. As she writes,
     "The cry that 'there is no excuse for September 11' has become a means
     by which to stifle any serious public discussion of how US foreign
     policy has helped to create a world in which such acts of terror are
     possible" (178).

1    Irene Tsuyuki's experience is noted in Roy Miki and Cassandra
     Kobayashi's, *Justice in Our Time* (49), and told in her own words in
     Irene Tsuyuki, "The Second Uprooting: Exiled to Japan."

2    In Joy Kogawa's *Obasan*, Naomi's brother Stephen comes to feel shame
     for being Japanese partly through internalizing the media representa-
     tion of Japanese soldiers. In writing to her sister, Naomi and Stephen's
     mother, in Japan, Aunt Emily comments that "Stephen spends his
     time reading war comics that he gets from the neighbourhood boys.
     All the Japs have mustard-coloured faces and buck teeth" (101).

3    The redress settlement of September 22, 1988, which included funding
     assistance for creative projects, was the impetus for a sharp increase
     in Japanese Canadian cultural production. I use the term post-redress
     to acknowledge the settlement as a turning point that allowed for the
     concept of redress to be disseminated beyond its Japanese Canadian
     boundaries.

4    As early as 1869, Yasukuni Shrine, the highly regarded shrine located
     in Tokyo near the Imperial Palace, was deemed to be the national site
     to honour those who died in warfare for the emperor. At the outset
     of the Meiji era, government leaders were intent on creating a strong
     imperialistic nation-state held together by a Shinto belief system.
     The belief in sacrificial death for the emperor made loyalty to the
     Japanese empire sacrosanct, and Yasukuni Shrine ensured that those
     who died for the emperor would be honoured as gods by the general
     populace. More recently, Yasukuni Shrine provoked international
     outrage, especially from Korea and China, as different Japanese prime
     ministers attended ceremonial commemorations for the war dead. For
     critics of Japan's wartime record of atrocities, such visits confirmed
     that Japanese leaders were honouring soldiers whose actions should be
     condemned. These controversies and other aspects of Yasukuni Shrine
     have generated numerous critical commentaries (see Harry Haroo-
     tunian, "Memory, Mourning, and National Morality"). Other than
     those cited in this article, several other articles helped me understand
     the current politics of memory around the shrine. See Jeff Kingston,
     "Awkward Talisman: War Memory, Reconciliation and Yasukuni";

Brian Masshardt, "Mobilizing from the Margins: Domestic Citizen Politics and Yasukuni Shrine"; Masaki Matsubara, "Cultural Memory, Ventriloquism, and Performance"; Michiko Maekawa, "The Politics and Culture of Contemporary Religion in Japan"; John Nelson, "Social Memory as Ritual Practice"; and Daiki Shibuichi, "The Yasukuni Shrine Dispute and the Politics of Identity in Japan."

5   Through an analysis of documents and diaries written by members of the Special Attack Forces, Emiko Ohnuki-Tierney shows that the university students who were coerced into carrying out suicidal missions were often well-read intellectuals. Rather than passively accepting their fate, they wrestled with their relationship to the military leaders' propaganda. In many instances, they consciously rejected the belief that they were sacrificing themselves for the emperor, and instead came to believe that they were fighting to protect the lives of their families and friends.

6   The will not to remember may be the effect of the wartime condition termed "the *kyodatsu* condition, a sense of 'exhaustion and despair'" (Dower 87–89), which descended on Japanese social life in the immediate postwar years because of the extreme poverty, deprivation, and hopelessness. According to Dower, this condition helps explain why "a pervasive victim consciousness took root, leading many Japanese to perceive themselves as the greatest sufferers from the recent war. The misery on hand was far more immediate and palpable than accounts of the devastation that the imperial forces had wreaked on strangers in distant lands" (119).

7   For a discussion of the "powerful void at the center of the modern Japanese body politic," see Yasushi Uchiyamada, "The Face of the Japanese Body Politic." Uchiyamada examines the power of the state's representation of the war dead as evident in Prime Minister Junichiro Koizumi's visits to Yasukuni Shrine, arguing that the ritual commemoration of the war dead "transforms the fallen soldiers into the victims of the war, into the martyrs of the nation, and into the cause of Japan's postwar economic miracle" (283).

8   For an excellent introduction to some of the people who have been active in minority struggles in Japan, see David Suzuki and Keibo Oiwa, *The Japan We Never Knew*.

1   See, for instance, Robert Lecker's "'A Quest for the Peaceable Kingdom': The Narrative in Northrop Frye's Conclusion to the *Literary History of Canada*'" and the essays collected in *Where Is Here Now?*, a special millennium issue of *Essays on Canadian Writing* (eds. Lecker and Kevin Flynn).

2   Here it is difficult not to wonder whether Szeman would have reached the same conclusion had he chosen to focus on poetry, and especially the Canadian long poem, where questions of place, localism, regionalism, and centralism have been heavily debated in what can be read as nation-bounded frameworks. I am thinking of the long-poem poets such as Margaret Atwood, Dennis Lee, Eli Mandel, Robert Kroetsch, bpNichol, George Bowering, Daphne Marlatt, and Fred Wah, and there are many others.

# Works Cited

Adachi, Ken. *The Enemy That Never Was: A History of the Japanese Canadians.* Toronto: McClelland and Stewart, 1976.

Adam, Ian, and Helen Tiffin, eds. *Past the Last Post: Theorizing Post-Colonialism and Post-Modernism.* New York: Harvester Wheatsheaf, 1991.

Ahmed, Sara. *Strange Encounters: Embodied Others in Post-Coloniality.* London: Routledge, 2000.

Alberts, Sheldon. "Washington ads aim to show Canada is pulling its weight." *Vancouver Sun,* March 30, 2006.

Anderson, Kay. *Vancouver's Chinatown: Racial Discourse in Canada, 1875–1980.* Montreal: McGill-Queen's UP, 1991.

Axtmann, Roland. "Collective Identity and the Democratic Nation-State in the Age of Globalization." *Articulating the Global and the Local: Globalization and Cultural Studies.* Eds. Ann Cvetkovich and Douglas Kellner. Boulder, Colorado: Westview, 1997. 33–54.

Backhouse, Constance. "The White Women's Labor Laws: Anti-Chinese Racism in Early Twentieth-Century Canada." *Law and History Review* 14.2 (Fall 1996): 315–368.

Bannerji, Himani. *The Dark Side of the Nation: Essays on Multiculturalism, Nationalism and Gender.* Toronto: Canadian Scholars' P, 2000.

Beauregard, Guy. "Asian Canadian Studies: Unfinished Projects." *Asian Canadian Studies*. Spec. issue of *Canadian Literature* 199 (Winter 2008): 6–27.

Bell, Vikki. *Culture and Performance: The Challenge of Ethics, Politics and Feminist Theory*. Oxford: Berg, 2007.

Bhabha, Homi K. *The Location of Culture*. London and New York: Routledge, 1994.

Bleiker, Roland. *Popular Dissent, Human Agency and Global Politics.* Cambridge, UK: Cambridge UP, 2000.

Bourdieu, Pierre. *Language and Symbolic Power*. Ed. John B. Thompson. Trans. Gino Raymond and Matthew Adamson. Cambridge: Harvard UP, 1991.

Brown, Wendy. *States of Injury: Power and Freedom in Late Modernity*. Princeton: Princeton UP, 1995.

Brydon, Diana, ed. *Testing the Limits: Postcolonial Theories and Canadian Literature*. Spec. issue of *Essays on Canadian Writing* 56 (Fall 1995).

Butler, Judith. *Excitable Speech: A Politics of the Performative*. New York: Routlege, 1997.

———. "Explanation and Exoneration, or What We Can Hear." *Social Text* 20.3 (2002): 177–188.

———. *Precarious Life: The Powers of Mourning and Violence*. London and New York: Verso, 2004.

———. *The Psychic Life of Power: Theories in Subjection*. Stanford: Stanford UP, 1997.

Canada: Special Committee on Visible Minorities in Canadian Society. *Equality Now!: Report of the Special Committee on Visible Minorities in Canadian Society*. Ottawa: Queen's Printer, 1984.

———. Department of Canadian Heritage. "Frequently Asked Questions: The International Cultural Diversity Agenda and a New International Instrument on Cultural Diversity." February 21 2003 <www.pch.gc.ca/progs/ai-ia/ridp-irpd/faq/index_e.cfm> (June 3 2003).

Canclini, Néstor García. "The State of War and the State of Hybridization." *Without Guarantees: In Honour of Stuart Hall*. Eds. Paul Gilroy, Lawrence Grossberg, and Angela McRobbie. London: Verso, 2000. 38–52.

Castles, Stephen and Alastair Davidson. *Citizenship and Migration: Globalization and the Politics of Belonging*. New York: Routledge, 2000.

Castoriadis, Cornelius. *World in Fragments: Writings on Politics, Society, Psychoanalysis and the Imagination*. Ed. and Trans. David Ames Curtis. Stanford: Stanford U P, 1997.

Chambers, Iain, and Lidia Curti, eds. *The Post-Colonial Question: Common Skies, Divided Horizons*. London: Routledge, 1996.

Chao, Steve. "The Backlash Against Chinese Migrants: One Reporter's Perspective." *Rice Paper* 5.4 (2000): 20–21.

Chong, Denise. *The Concubine's Children*. Toronto: Penguin, 1994.

Chow, Rey. "The Age of the World Target: Atom Bombs, Alterity, Area Studies." *The Age of the World Target: Self-Referentiality in War, Theory, and Comparative Work*. Durham: Duke U P, 2006. 25–43.

—————. "The Secrets of Ethnic Abjection." *The Protestant Ethnic and the Spirit of Capitalism*. New York: Columbia U P, 2002. 128–152.

Chuh, Kandice. *Imagine Otherwise: On Asian American Critique*. Durham: Duke U P, 2003.

Coleman, Daniel, and Smaro Kamboureli. "Introduction: Canadian Research Capitalism: A Genealogy of Critical Moments." *Retooling the Humanities: The Culture of Research in Canadian Universities*. Eds. Daniel Coleman and Smaro Kamboureli. Edmonton: U of Alberta P, 2011. 1–39.

Coleman, Daniel. "From Canadian Trance to Transcanada: White Civility to Wry Civility in the CanLit Project." *Trans.Can.Lit: Resituating the Study of Canadian Literature*. Eds. Smaro Kamboureli and Roy Miki. Waterloo: Wilfrid Laurier U P, 2007. 25–43.

—————. *In Bed with the Word: Reading, Spirituality, and Cultural Politics*. Edmonton: U of Alberta P, 2009.

Connolly, William E. *Neuropolitics: Thinking, Culture, Speed*. Minneapolis: U of Minnesota P, 2002.

Cook, Haruko Taya and Theodore F. Cook. "A Lost War in Living Memory: Japan's Second World War." *European Review* 11.4 (2003): 573–593.

Crosby, Marcia. "Construction of the Imaginary Indian." *Vancouver Anthology: The Institutional Politics of Art*. Ed. Stan Douglas. Vancouver: Talonbooks, 1991. 267–90.

Day, Richard J.F. *Multiculturalism and the History of Canadian Diversity*. Toronto: U of Toronto P, 2000.

de Certeau, Michel. *The Practice of Everyday Life*. Trans. Steven Rendall. Berkeley: U of California P, 1988.

Debrix, François. "Discourses of War, Geographies of Abjection: Reading Contemporary American Ideologies of Terror." *Third World Quarterly* 26.7 (2005): 1157–1172.

Derrida, Jacques. *Specters of Marx. The State of the Debt, the Work of Mourning, and the New International.* Trans. Peggy Kamuf. New York: Routledge, 1994.

Direct Action Against Refugee Exploitation. *Movement Across Borders: Chinese Women Migrants in Canada.* Vancouver: DAARE, 2001.

Dirlik, Arif. "The Global in the Local." *Global/Local: Cultural Production and the Transnational Imaginary.* Eds. Rob Wilson and Wimal Dissanayake. Durham: Duke UP, 1996. 21–45.

Dower, John K. *Embracing Defeat: Japan in the Wake of World War II.* New York: W.W. Norton, 1999.

DuBois, W.E.B. *The Souls of Black Folk.* New York: Dover, 1994.

Earhart, David C. "All Ready to Die: Kamikazefication and Japan's Wartime Ideology." *Critical Asian Studies* 37.4 (2005): 569–596.

Fassin, Didier. "Riots in France and Silent Anthropologists." *Anthropology Today* 22.1 (February 2006): 1–3.

Fleras, Augie, and Jean Leonard Elliott. *The Challenge of Diversity: Multiculturalism in Canada.* Scarborough, ON: Nelson, 1992.

Foucault, Michel. *Ethics: Subjectivity and Truth.* Ed. Paul Rabinow. New York: New Press, 1994.

Francis, Daniel. *The Imaginary Indian: The Image of the Indian in Canadian Culture.* Vancouver: Arsenal Pulp, 1992.

Freud, Sigmund. *Civilization and Its Discontents.* Ed. and Trans. James Strachey. New York: W.W. Norton, 1961.

Frye, Northrop. "Conclusion to a *Literary History of Canada.*" *Bush Garden: Essays on the Canadian Imagination.* Toronto: Anansi, 1971. 213–251.

Gagnon, Monika Kin, and Scott Toguri McFarlane. "The Capacity of Cultural Difference." Minister's Forum on Diversity and Culture, Ottawa, April 22–23, 2003.

Gilbert, Jeremy. "Against the Commodification of Everything." *Cultural Studies* 22.5 (September 2008): 551–566.

Godard, Barbara. "Notes from the Cultural Field: Canadian Literature from Identity to Hybridity." *Essays on Canadian Literature* 72 (Winter 2000): 209–47.

Goellnicht, Donald G. "A Long Labour: The Protracted Birth of Asian Canadian Literature." *Essays on Canadian Writing* 72 (Winter 2000): 1–41.

Goellnicht, Donald G., and Eleanor Ty, eds. *Asian North American Identities: Beyond the Hyphen.* Bloomington and Indianapolis: Indiana U P, 2004.

Goto, Hiromi. *Chorus of Mushrooms.* Edmonton: NeWest, 1994.

———. *The Kappa Child.* Calgary: Red Deer, 2001.

———. "Translating the Self: Moving Between Cultures." *West Coast Line* 30.2, No. 20 (Fall 1996): 111–113.

Grossberg, Lawrence. "On Postmodernism and Articulation: An Interview with Stuart Hall." *Stuart Hall: Critical Dialogues in Cultural Studies.* Eds. David Morley and Kuan-Hsing Chen. New York: Routledge, 1996. 131–150.

Hall, Stuart. "Cultural Identity and Diaspora." *Colonial Discourse and Post-Colonial Theory: A Reader.* Eds. Patrick Williams and Laura Chrisman. New York: Columbia U P, 1994. 392–403.

———. "The Local and the Global: Globalization and Ethnicity." *Dangerous Liaisons: Gender, Nation, and Postcolonial Perspectives.* Eds. Anne McClintock, Aamir Mufti, and Ella Shohat. Minneapolis: U of Minnesota P, 1997. 173–187.

———. "When Was 'The Post-Colonial'?: Thinking at the Limit." *The Post-Colonial Question: Common Skies, Divided Horizons.* Eds. Iain Chambers and Lidia Curti. London and New York: Routledge, 1996. 242–260.

Harootunian, Harry. "Memory, Mourning, and National Morality: Yasukuni Shrine and the Reunion of State and Religion in Postwar Japan." *Nation and Religion: Perspectives on Europe and Asia.* Eds. Peter Van Der Veer and Hartmut Lehmann. Princeton: Princeton U P, 1999. 144–160.

Harvey, David. *The New Imperialism.* New York: Oxford U P, 2005.

Hein, Laura. "War Compensation: Claims Against the Japanese Government and Japanese Corporations for War Crimes." *Politics and the Past: On Repairing Historical Injustices.* Eds. John Torpey. Laham, M D: Rowman and Littlefield, 2003, 127–147.

Henderson, Jennifer, and Pauline Wakeham, eds. "Introduction." *Reconciling Canada: Critical Perspectives on the Culture of Redress.* 1–30. In process.

Ibrahim, Yasmin. "The Technological Gaze: Event Construction and the Mobile Body." *M/C Journal* 10.1 (2007). May 10, 2007 <http://journal.media-culture.org.au/0703/03-ibrahim.php>.

Immordino-Yang, Mary Helen et. al. "Neural Correlates of Admiration and Compassion." *Proceedings of the National Academy of Science* 106.19 (May 12, 2009): 8021–8026.

Ireland, Doug. "Why Is France Burning?" *Direland*, November 6, 2005 <http://direland.typepad.com/ direland/2005/11/why_is_france_b.html>.

Jameson, Fredric. "Notes on Globalization as a Philosophical Issue." *The Cultures of Globalization*. Eds. Fredric Jameson and Masao Miyoshi. Durham: Duke UP, 1998. 54–77.

Japanese Canadian Centennial Project. *A Dream of Riches: Japanese Canadians, 1877–1977*. Vancouver: Japanese Canadian Centennial Project, 1978.

Kam, Winston C. "Inside the Black Egg." *West Coast Line* 30.1, No. 19 (Spring 1996): 90–4.

Kamboureli, Smaro. "Faking It: Fred Wah and the Postcolonial Imaginary." *Etudes Canadiennes/Canadian Studies* (France) 54 (2003): 115–132.

———. "The Limits of the Ethical Turn: Troping Towards the Other, Yann Martel, and *Self*." *University of Toronto Quarterly* 76.3 (2007): 937–961.

———. *Scandalous Bodies: Diasporic Literature in English Canada*. Toronto: Oxford UP, 2000.

Keaten, Jamey. "Anger Simmers Among Youth in Paris Projects." *Vancouver Sun*. November 5, 2005.

Kelley, Ninette, and Michael Trebilcock. *The Making of the Mosaic: A History of Canadian Immigration Policy*. Toronto: U of Toronto P, 1998.

Kertzer, Jonathan. *Worrying the Nation: Imagining a National Literature in English Canada*. Toronto: U of Toronto P , 1998.

King, Thomas, ed. *All My Relations: An Anthology of Contemporary Native Fiction*. Toronto: McClelland and Stewart, 1990.

Kingston, Jeff. "Awkward Talisman: War Memory, Reconciliation and Yasukuni." *East Asia* 24 (2007): 295–318.

Kitagawa, Muriel. *This Is My Own: Letters to Wes and Other Writings on Japanese Canadians, 1941–1948*. Ed. Roy Miki. Vancouver: Talonbooks, 1985.

Kiyooka, Roy K. *StoneDGloves*. Toronto: Coach House, 1970; repr. 1983.

———. *Transcanada Letters*. Vancouver: Talonbooks, 1975.

———. *Transcanada Letters*. Ed. Smaro Kamboureli. Edmonton: NeWest, 2005.

———. "Dear Lucy Fumi: c/o Japanese Canadian Redress Secretariat." *West Coast Line* 24.3, No. 3 (Winter 1990): 125–6.

———. "We Asian North Americanos." *West Coast Line* 24.3 (Winter 1990): 116–18.

———. *Pacific Rim Letters*. Ed. Smaro Kamboureli. Edmonton: NeWest, 2005.

———. *Pacific Windows: The Collected Poems of Roy K. Kiyooka*. Ed. Roy Miki. Vancouver: Talonbooks, 1997.

———. *The Artist and the Moose: A Fable of Forget*. Ed. Roy Miki. Vancouver: LINEbooks, 2009.

Kogawa, Joy. *Obasan*. Toronto: Penguin, 1981.

Kymlicka, Will. *Multicultural Citizenship: A Liberal Theory of Minority Rights*. Oxford, UK: Clarendon, 1995.

Lai, Larissa. *When Fox Is a Thousand*. Vancouver: Press Gang, 1995.

———. "Corrupted Lineage: Narrative in the Gaps of History." *In-Equations: can-asia pacific*. Eds. Glen Lowry and Sook C. Kong. Spec. issue of *West Coast Line* 34.3, No. 33 (Winter 2001): 40–53.

———. *Salt Fish Girl*. Toronto: Thomas Allen, 2002.

———. "Fish Talk." Unpublished paper.

Lai, Larissa and Rita Wong. *Sybil Unrest*. Burnaby, BC: LINEbooks, 2008.

Laidi, Zaki. *A World Without Meaning: The Crisis of Meaning in International Politics*. Trans. June Burnham and Jenny Coulon. London and New York: Routledge, 1998.

Laquian, Eleanor, and Aprodicio Laquain, Terry McGee, eds. *The Silent Debate: Asian Immigration and Racism in Canada*. Vancouver: Institute of Asian Research, 1998.

Lecker, Robert. "'A Quest for a Peaceable Kingdom': The Narrative in Northrop Frye's "Conclusion" to the *Literary History of Canada*." *Making It Real: The Canonization of English-Canadian Literature*. Toronto: Anansi, 1995.

Lecker, Robert and Kevin Flynn, eds. *Where Is Here Now?* Spec. Issue, *Essays in Canadian Writing*, 71 (Fall 2000).

Lee, Chris. "Enacting the Asian Canadian." *Asian Canadian Studies*. *Canadian Literature* 199 (Winter 2008): 28–44.

Lee, SKY. *Disappearing Moon Cafe*. Vancouver: Douglas and McIntyre, 1990.

Li, Peter S. *Destination Canada: Immigration Debates and Issues*. Don Mills, ON: Oxford UP, 2003.

Little, William T. *The Tom Thomson Mystery*. Toronto: McGraw-Hill, 1970.

Lloyd, David. "Ethnic Cultures, Minority Discourses and the State." *Colonial Discourse / Postcolonial Theory*. Eds. Francis Barker, Peter Hulme, and Margaret Iversen. Manchester: Manchester UP, 1994. 221–38.

Mackey, Eva. *The House of Difference: Cultural Politics and National Identity in Canada*. Toronto: U of Toronto P, 2002.

Macklem, Patrick. *Indigenous Difference and the Constitution of Canada*. Toronto: U of Toronto P, 2001.

Maekawa, Michiko. "The Politics and Culture of Contemporary Religion in Japan." *Nanzan Bulletin* 26 (2002): 44–59.

Masshardt, Brian. "Mobilizing from the Margins: Domestic Citizen Politics and Yasukuni Shrine." *East Asia* 24 (2007): 319–335.

Massumi, Brian. "Fear (The Spectrum Said)." *Positions: East Asia Cultures Critique* 13.1 (2005): 31–48.

————. *Parable of the Virtual: Movement, Affect, Sensation*. Durham: Duke UP, 2002.

Mathur, Ashok. *Once Upon An Elephant*. Vancouver: Arsenal Pulp, 1998.

————. *The Short, Happy Life of Harry Kumar*. Vancouver: Arsenal Pulp, 2001.

Matsubara, Masaki. "Cultural Memory, Ventrioquism, and Performance: Reflections on Yasukuni Shrine." *Acta Orientalia Vilnensia* 7.1–2 (2006): 27–43.

McAllister, Kirsten Emiko. "Narrating Japanese Canadians In and Out of the Canadian Nation: A Critique of Realist Forms of Representation." *Canadian Journal of Communication* 24 (1999): 79–103.

McCallum, Pamela, Stephen Slemon, and Aruna Srivastava, eds. *Postcolonialism and Its Discontents*. Spec. issue of *Ariel* 26.1 (January 1995).

McClintock, Anne. "The Angel of Progress": Pitfalls of the Term 'Post-colonialism'." *Colonial Discourse and Post-Colonial Theory: A Reader*. Eds. Patrick Williams and Laura Chrisman. New York: Columbia UP, 1994. 291–304.

McClintock, Anne, Aamir Mufti, and Ella Shohat, eds. *Dangerous Liaisons: Gender, Nation, and Postcolonial Perspectives.* Minneapolis: U of Minnesota P, 1997.

McFarlane, Scott. "The Haunt of Race: Canada's Multiculturalism Act, the Politics of Incorporation, and Writing Thru Race." *Fuse* 18.3 (Spring 1995): 18–31.

McGonegal, Julie. "Hyphenating the Hybrid 'I': (Re)Visions of Racial Mixedness in Fred Wah's *Diamond Grill.*" *Essays on Canadian Writing* 75 (Winter 2002): 177–95.

Miki, Roy. "Roy Kiyooka: An Interview." *Inalienable Rice: A Chinese and Japanese Canadian Anthology.* Vancouver: Powell Street Revue and The Chinese Canadian Writers Workshop, 1979. 58–64.

———. *Broken Entries: Race Subjectivity Writing.* Toronto: Mercury, 1998.

Miki, Roy, and Cassandra Kobayashi. *Justice in Our Time: The Japanese Canadian Redress Settlement.* Vancouver and Winnipeg: Talonbooks and National Association of Japanese Canadians, 1991.

Mitchell, Katharyne. "In Whose Interest? Transnational Capital and the Production of Multiculturalism in Canada." *Global/Local.* Eds. Rob Wilson and Wimal Dissanayake. Durham: Duke UP, 1996. 219–251.

Miyoshi, Masao. "A Borderless World? From Colonialism to Transnationalism and the Decline of the Nation-State." *Global/Local: Cultural Production and the Transnational Imaginary.* Eds. Rob Wilson and Wimal Dissanayake. Durham and London: Duke UP, 1996. 78–106.

———. "Sites of Resistance in the Global Economy." *boundary 2* 22.1 (1995): 61–84.

Morris, Robyn. "'Sites of Articulation': An Interview with Larissa Lai." *West Coast Line* 38.2, No. 44 (2004): 21–30.

Multiculturalism and Citizenship Canada. *Resource Guide of Publications Supported by Multiculturalism Programs, 1972–1992.* Ottawa: Minister of Supplies and Services Canada, 1993.

National Association of Japanese Canadians. *Democracy Betrayed: The Case for Redress.* Winnipeg: National Association of Japanese Canadians, 1984.

Nelson, John. "Social Memory as Ritual Practice: Commemorating Spirits of the Military Dead at Yasukuni Shinto Shrine." *The Journal of Asian Studies* 62.2 (May 2003): 443–467.

Ng, Roxanne. "Racism, Sexism, and Nation Building in Canada." *Race, Identity and Representation in Education.* Eds. Cameron McCarthy and Warren Chrichlow. New York: Routledge, 1993. 50–59.

Nichol, bp. " 'Syntax Equals the Body Structure': bpNichol, in Conversation, with Daphne Marlatt and George Bowering." *Meanwhile: The Critical Writings of bpNichol.* Ed. Roy Miki. Vancouver: Talonbooks, 2002. 273–297.

*Obaachan's Garden.* Dir. Linda Ohama. National Film Board, 2001.

Ohnuki-Tierney, Emiko. *Kamikaze, Cherry Blossoms; and Nationalisms: The Militarization of Aesthetics in Japanese History.* Chicago: U of Chicago P, 2002.

Ong, Aihwa. "Cultural Citizenship as Subject Making: Immigrants Negotiate Racial and Cultural Boundaries in the United States." *Race, Identity, and Citizenship: A Reader.* Eds. Rodolfo D. Torres, Louis F. Mirón, and Jonathan Xavier Inda. Malden, MA: Blackwell, 1999. 262–93.

Parks, Bradley C., and J. Timmons Roberts. "Globalization, Vulnerability to Climate Change, and Perceived Injustice." *Society and Natural Resources* 19 (2006): 337–355.

Pennee, Donna Palmateer. "Literary Citizenship: Culture (Un)Bounded, Culture (Re)Distributed." *Home-Work: Postcolonialism, Pedagogy, and Canadian Literature.* Ed. Cynthia Sugars. Ottawa: U of Ottawa P, 2004. 75–85.

Penrose, Jan. "Construction, De(con)struction, and Reconstruction: The Impact of Globalization and Fragmentation on the Canadian Nation-State." *International Journal of Canadian Studies* 16 (1997): 15–49.

Pinder, Leslie Hall. "To the Fourth Wall." *Vancouver Forum: Old Powers, New Forces.* Ed. Max Wyman. Vancouver: Douglas and McIntyre, 1992. 19–51.

Project for the New American Century. "Statement of Principles." <http://www.newamericancentury.org/statementofprinciples.htm>.

Pugliese, David. "Afghanistan Costs Hit $2B." *Vancouver Sun.* March 3, 2006.

*The Return.* Dir. Fumiko Kiyooka. You've Been Dreaming Pictures, 1998.

Roy, Arundhati. *Power Politics.* Second Edition. Cambridge, MA: South End, 2001.

Roy, Patricia. *A White Man's Province: British Columbia Politicians and Chinese and Japanese Immigrants, 1858–1914.* Vancouver: U of British Columbia P, 1989.

Sakamoto, Kerri. *The Electrical Field.* Toronto: Vintage, 1998.

———. "Surviving History: Kerri Sakamoto interviewed by Pilar Cuder-Domínguez." *Journal of Commonwealth Literature* 41.3 (2006): 137–143.

———. *One Hundred Million Hearts.* Toronto: Vintage Canada, 2004.

Schacter, Daniel L. *Searching for Memory: The Brain, the Mind, and the Past.* New York: Basic Books, 1996.

Scott, F.R. "Laurentian Shield." *The Collected Poems of F.R. Scott.* Toronto: McClelland and Stewart, 1981. 58.

Seaton, Philip. "Reporting the 2001 Textbook and Yasukuni Shrine Controversies: Japanese War Memory and Commemoration in the British Media." *Japan Forum* 17.3 (2005): 287–309.

Serres, Michel. *The Natural Contract.* Trans. Elizabeth MacArthur and William Paulson. Ann Arbor: U of Michigan P, 1995.

Shibuichi, Daiki. "The Yasukuni Shrine Dispute and the Politics of Identity in Japan: Why All the Fuss?" *Asian Survey* 45.2 (2005): 197–215.

Shiva, Vandana. *Tomorrow's Biodiversity.* New York: Thames and Hudson, 2000.

Simmons, Alan B. "Globalization and Backlash Racism in the 1990s: The Case of Asian Immigration to Canada." *The Silent Debate: Asian Immigration and Racism in Canada.* Eds. Eleanor Laquian, Aprodicio Laquain, and Terry McGee. Vancouver: Institute of Asian Research, 1998. 29–50.

Stasiulis, Daiva, and Radha Jhappan. "The Fractious Politics of a Settler Society: Canada." *Unsettling Settler Societies: Articulations of Gender, Race, Ethnicity and Class.* Eds. Daiva Stasiulis and Nira Yuval-Davis. London: Sage, 1995. 95–131.

Strong-Boag, Veronica, Sherrill Grace, Avigail Eisenberg, and Joan Anderson, eds. *Painting the Maple: Essays on Race, Gender, and the Construction of Canada.* Vancouver: UBC P, 1998.

Sunahara, Ann Gomer. *The Politics of Racism: The Uprooting of Japanese Canadians During the Second World War.* Toronto: James Lorimer, 1981.

Suzuki, David, and Keibo Oiwa. *The Japan We Never Knew: A Journey of Discovery.* Toronto: Stoddart, 1996.

Szeman, Imre. "The Persistence of the Nation: Literature and Criticism in Canada." *Zones of Instability: Literature, Postcolonialism and the Nation.* Baltimore: Johns Hopkins UP, 2003. 152–198.

Takacs, Stacy. "Alien-Nation: Immigration, National Identity and Transnationalism." *Cultural Studies* 13.4 (October 1999): 591–620.

Takata, Toyo. *Nikkei Legacy: The Story of Japanese Canadians from Settlement to Today.* Toronto: NC, 1983.

Thien, Madeleine. *Certainty.* McClelland and Stewart, 2006.

Tomlinson, John. *Globalization and Culture.* Chicago: U of Chicago P, 1999.

Tsuyuki, Irene. "The Second Uprooting: Exiled to Japan." *Homecoming '92: Where the Heart Is.* Ed. Randy Enomoto. Vancouver: NRC, 1993. 40–41.

Uchiyamada, Yasushi. "The Face of the Japanese Body Politic." *PoLAR: Political and Legal Anthropology Review* 28.4 (Autumn 2005): 282–306.

Urquhart, Conal. "US Scientists 'Close' to Identifying Genuis Genes." Vancouver *Sun*, August 10, 2000.

Verdery, Katherine. "Whither 'Nation' and 'Nationalism'?" *Mapping the Nation.* Ed. Gopal Balakrishnan. London: Verso, 1996. 226–234.

Wah, Fred. *Diamond Grill.* Edmonton: NeWest, 1996.

———. *Faking It: Poetics and Hybridity, Critical Writing 1984–1999.* Edmonton: NeWest, 2000.

Ward, Peter W. *White Canada Forever: Popular Attitudes and Public Policy Toward Orientals in British Columbia.* Montreal: McGill-Queen's UP, 1990.

*White Light/Black Rain: The Destruction of Hiroshima and Nagasaki.* Dir. Steven Okazaki. HBO Home Video, 2007.

Whitman, Walt. *Leaves of Grass: The First (1855) Edition.* Ed. Malcolm Cowley. New York: Viking, 1959.

Williams, Patrick and Laura Chrisman, eds. *Colonial Discourse and Post-Colonial Theory: A Reader.* New York: Columbia UP, 1994.

Wilson, Rob, and Wimal Dissanayake, eds. *Global/Local: Cultural Production and the Transnational Imaginary.* Durham: Duke UP, 1996.

Wong, Rita. "Consensual Practices: Thinking Through the Intimate Relations Between Poetry, Pedagogy and Political Engagement." Unpublished essay.

———. *Forage.* Gibson's Landing, BC: Nightwood, 2007.

———. *Monkey Puzzle.* Vancouver: Press Gang, 1998.

———. *Nervous Organism.* Burnaby: SFU, 2003.

———. "Re Sounding Dissent in a Time-and-Space of Imperial Delirium." Unpublished essay.

Wong, Sau-Ling C. "Denationalization Reconsidered: Asian American
      Cultural Criticism at a Theoretical Crossroads." *Amerasia* 21.1-2
      (1995): 1–27.
Woodsworth, J. S. *Strangers Within Our Gates: Or, Coming Canadians.*
      Toronto: F.C. Stephenson, 1909.
Yoneyama, Lisa. *Hiroshima Traces: Time, Space, and the Dialectics of Memory.*
      Berkeley: U of California P, 1999.
Zizek, Slavoj. *The Sublime Object of Ideology.* London: Verso, 1989.

# Index

# B

B&B Commission. *See* Royal
Commission on Bilingualism
and Biculturalism
Backhouse, Constance, 277n9
Bannerji, Himani, 128
Beauregard, Guy, xi
Bell, Vikki, 261–2
Berlin Wall, 37, 86
Bhabha, Homi, 11, 61
biotechnology, 41–2
biotext, 107. *See also* Wah, Fred
Bleiker, Roland, 67
body, 181–4, 194, 203, 236–8. *See
also* racialization
Bourdieu, Pierre, 149
British North America Act, 45, 123
Brown, Wendy, 14–15
Brydon, Diana, 277n11
Butler, Judith: *Excitable Speech*,
82, 92; "Explanation and
Exoneration," 280–81n7;
*Precarious Life*, 200–01; *Psychic
Life of Power*, 51, 204

# C

Canada: Anglo-centrism of, 4–5,
45–6; assimilation and, 4, 80;
bilingualism, 6, 131; coat of
arms, 5; constitution of, 84;
contradictions of state, 84;
ethnocentrism of, 53; flags,
6; foreign relations and,
121–22; immigration, 4, 47, 133;
minorities in, 3, 7–8, 11, 44;
multicultural policy of, 12, 87,

131–2, 136; national anthems, 5;
and War on Terror, 191–2, 197–8
Canada Council, 3, 265
Canadian Charter of Rights and
Freedoms, 84
Canadian literature, 2, 3, 55, 115,
243–52, 273–4
*Canadian Literature* (journal), xi
Canadian Multiculturalism Act, 98
CanLit. *See* Canadian literature
capitalism: Canada and, 46, 86;
global, 32, 39, 40, 58; research,
252–4; underside of, 32
Castles, Stephen, 122
Castoriadis, Cornelius, 257
Chambers, Iain, 277n11
Chao, Steve, 31–4
Chinese Canadian (term), 100–102
Chinese Canadians, 4, 11, 33,
49, 100, 104. *See also* Asian
Canadians
Chinese Exclusion Act. *See* Chinese
Immigration Act (Canada)
Chinese Immigration Act (Canada),
48, 104, 109
Chong, Denise, 100–106
Chow, Rey, 161, 224–5
Chrisman, Laura, 277n11
Chuh, Kandice, 233
citizen (term), 124–5
citizen as consumer, 134, 252
citizenship, 131, 134–5
Citizenship Act (Canada), 3
Cold War, 8, 36–7, 86
Coleman, Daniel, 4, 252–3, 260–61,
263
colonialism, 19, 43, 45, 122–5

minority (term), 125–6, 128, 133
minority texts, 257–8, 261–2
Mitchell, Katharyne, 277n7
Miyoshi, Masao, 32, 275n2
Morris, Robyn, 167
Multicultural Directorate, 68–9
multiculturalism, 12, 87,
    130–36. *See also* Canadian
    Multiculturalism Act

**N**

Nagano, Manzo, 69
nation: formation, 1–2, 130;
    instability of, 1, 9, 40–41;
    rearticulation of, 34, 43, 52
National Association of Japanese
    Canadians (NAJC), 68–9, 83,
    84–5, 211
National Film Board (Canada), 265
National Japanese Canadian
    Citizens' Association (NJCCA).
    *See* National Association of
    Japanese Canadians (NAJC)
Nelson, John, 282n4
neoliberalism, 86, 134
Ng, Roxanne, 276n5
Nichol, bp, 235–6
Nike, 32
9/11, 187–9, 196
*nisei*, 12, 21, 70–71, 74–5, 76
Nisei Mass Evacuation Group, 76
North American Free Trade
    Agreement (NAFTA), 40, 86

**O**

"O Canada," 5
Ohama, Linda, 88–9
Ohnuki-Tierney, Emiko, 218, 282n5
Oiwa, Keibo, 283n8
Okazaki, Steven, 216
Ong, Aihwa, 138
orientalization. *See* Asianization
Osaka World Fair. *See* Expo '70

**P**

Parks, Bradley C., 178–9
pastoral myth (Frye), 244, 248–51
pedagogy, 150–51, 170
Pennee, Donna Palmateer, 12
Penrose, Jan, 40, 45–6, 276n5
Pinder, Leslie Hall, 172–3
post (prefix), 35–6, 42, 51, 57
postcolonialism, 28, 58–9
postmodernism, 24, 56, 255
Pratt, Louise, 163–4
Project for the New American
    Century, 196–7
Provincial Elections Act (BC), 49, 86

**R**

racialization, 17, 28, 34, 70, 98; in
    Canada, 72–4, 104, 106, 265;
    language of, 48, 74, 75, 79, 94
racism: in Canada, 13, 46–7,
    79–80, 98, 278n1[2]; in France,
    179–80; redress and, 70, 83,
    230; Fred Wah and, 111. *See also*
    *under* Asian Canadian (term),
    Japanese Canadians

reading practices, 113–5, 258–65

redress: movement, 82–3, 215; settlement, 84–7, 89, 208, 281n3. *See also under* racism

Redress Advisory Committee, 211–2

repatriation, 210–11

representation, 39, 52; Asian Canadians and, 8, 54, 113, 153; Canada and, 123, 134, 139–40, 269, 272; Denise Chong and, 100–101, 114; Japan and, 224, 228; Japanese Canadians and, 85, 212; Roy K. Kiyooka and, 22, 269, 272; limits of, 100, 165, 195, 272; minority subjects and, 96, 135; Kerri Sakamoto and, 212; of texts, 257, 261; Fred Wah and, 160, 165; Rita Wong and, 190, 195

Residential Schools, 276n5

*Rice Paper*, 31

Rifken, Jeremy, 41

Roberts, J. Timmons, 178–9

Robertson, Roland, 279n1[1]

Roy, Arundhati, 191

Roy, Patricia, 277n10

Royal American Show, 66

Royal Commission on Bilingualism and Biculturalism, 6, 131

S

Sakamoto, Kerri, 56, 209, 212–33

*sansei*, 71, 81, 210

Sarkozy, Nicolas, 180

Schacter, Daniel, 66

Scott, F.R., 124

Seaton, Philip, 228–9

Second World War, 70, 207–33

Serres, Michel, 177

Shibuichi, Daiki, 282n4

*shin-issei*, 71

Shiva, Vandana, 186, 193–4

Shoyama, Tom, 70

*Single Stick Duel* (Goya), 177

Slemon, Stephen, 277n11

snakeheads, 33

social justice, 83–7

Social Sciences and Humanities Research Council (SSHRC), 252

South Asians, 49. *See also* Asian Canadians

Srivastava, Aruna, 277n11

Stasiulis, Daiva, 276n6

Stein, Gertrude, 272

Strong-Boag, Veronica, 276n6

subject, 3, 117–8; and abjection, 73; and articulation, 43, 55, 99; and Asian Canadians, 154, 208; and Judith Butler, 51, 204; and capitalism, 38; and Denise Chong, 101, 104–5; as consumer, 237–41; formation, xii, 20, 87, 101, 105, 110, 204, 208; and Northrop Frye, 244–8, 251, 256; and globalization, 34, 59–60, 237; and Hiromi Goto, 96; and Japanese Canadians, 46, 75–7, 82, 86, 87, 229; and Roy K. Kiyooka, 13–4, 20–21, 24, 271–2; and minority subjects, 56, 96, 106, 113, 125–7, 135, 169; and Kerri Sakamoto,